UNLV ENGLISH 102:
Rhetoric, Research, and Writing

UNIVERSITY OF NEVADA, LAS VEGAS

This volume has been customized by the school for which it was published to give you the best educational value. Chapters and pages may have been altered, added, deleted, or rearranged. Pagination and chapter numbers may be non-sequential. This volume is meant solely for use at this school.

NORTON
CUSTOM

Copyright © 2018 by W. W. Norton & Company, Inc.

Materials may be included from the following:

Everyone's an Author 2e (Andrea Lunsford et al.)
Copyright © 2017, 2013 by W. W. Norton & Company, Inc.
The Norton Field Guide to Writing 4e (Richard Bullock)
Copyright © 2016, 2013, 2010, 2009, 2007, 2006 by W. W. Norton & Company, Inc.
They Say/I Say with Readings, 4e (Gerald Graff, Cathy Birkenstein, and Russel Durst)
Copyright © 2018, 2017, 2015, 2014, 2012, 2010, 2009, 2006 by W. W. Norton & Company, Inc.
The Norton Custom Library (Elizabeth Rodriguez Kessler et. al.)
Copyright © 2018 by W. W. Norton & Company, Inc.

All rights reserved
Printed in Canada

First Edition
Editor: Marilyn Moller
Custom editor: Katie Hannah
Custom assistant editor: Laura Dragonette
Editorial assistants: Erica Wnek, Tenyia Lee
Managing editor: Marian Johnson
Developmental editor: John Elliott
Project editor: Rebecca Homiski
Custom project editor: Hannah Bachman
Marketing manager: Lib Triplett
Emedia editor: Cliff Landesman
Photo editor: Trish Marx
Production manager: Jane Searle
Custom production manager: Stephen Sajdak
Design director: Rubina Yeh
Designer: Jo Anne Metsch
Composition and layout: Carole Desnoes
Manufacturing: Transcontinental

Copyright covers material written expressly for this volume by the editors, as well as the compilation of material for this volume. It does not cover the individual selections herein that first appeared elsewhere. Permission to reprint these selections has been obtained by W. W. Norton & Company, for this edition only. Further reproduction by any means, electronic or mechanical, including photocopying and recording, or by any information storage or retrieval system, must be arranged with the individual copyright holders noted.

ISBN 978-0-393-67159-9

W. W. Norton & Company, Inc., 500 Fifth Avenue, New York, NY 10110
www.wwnorton.com

W. W. Norton & Company, Ltd., 15 Carlisle Street, London WID 3BS
3 4 5 6 7 8 9 0

CONTENTS

1 Writing in Academic Contexts 1

2 Reading in Academic Contexts 7

3 The Rhetorical Situation 27

4 Starting Your Research 41

5 Evaluating Sources 51

6 Synthesizing Ideas 61

7 Quoting, Paraphrasing, Summarizing 69

8 Giving Credit, Avoiding Plagiarism 85

9 Annotated Bibliographies 93

10 Arguing 113

11 Arguing a Position 131

12 Beginning and Ending 157

13 Guiding Your Reader 169

14 Assessing Your Own Writing 175

15 Getting Response and Revising 181

16 Editing and Proofreading 187

17 MLA Style 193

18 APA Style 253

Readings 298

JUANA MORA, *Acculturation is Bad for Our Health: Less Fast Food, More Nopalitos* 299

OLGA KHAZAN, *Why Don't Convenience Stores Sell Better Food?* 307

SARA GOLDRICK-RABB, KATHARINE BROTON, AND EMILY BRUNJES COLOR, *Expanding the National School Lunch Program to Higher Education* 314

RACHEL CARSON, *The Obligation to Endure* 330

CAROLE CADWALLADR, *Google, Democracy, and the Truth About Internet Search* 338

ANDREA LUNSFORD, *Our Semi-Literate Youth* 354

MICHAELA CULLINGTON, *Does Texting Affect Writing?* 360

STEPHANIE OWEN AND ISABEL SAWHILL, *Should Everyone Go to College?* 370

MICHELLE ALEXANDER, *The New Jim Crow* 385

GABRIELA MORO, *Minority Student Clubs: Segregation or Integration?* 404

JOHN MCWHORTER, *Why Redskins is a Bad Word* 412

DIANE GUERRERO, *My Parents Were Deported* 416

Credits 419

ONE

Writing in Academic Contexts

WRITE AN ESSAY arguing whether genes or environment do more to determine people's intelligence. Research and write a report on the environmental effects of electricity-generating windmills. Work with a team to write a proposal and create a multimedia presentation for a sales campaign. Whatever you're studying, you're surely going to be doing a lot of writing, in classes from various disciplines—the above assignments, for example, are from psychology, environmental science, and marketing. Academic writing can serve a number of different purposes—to argue for what you think about a topic and why, to report on what's known about an issue, to propose a solution for some problem, and so on. Whatever your topics or purposes, all academic writing follows certain conventions, ones you'll need to master in order to join the conversations going on across campus. This chapter describes what's expected of academic writing—and of academic writers.

What's Expected of Academic Writing

Evidence that you've considered the subject thoughtfully. Whether you're composing a report, an argument, or some other kind of writing, you need to demonstrate that you've thought seriously about the topic and done any necessary research. You can use various ways to show that you've considered the subject carefully, from citing authoritative sources to incorporating information you learned in class to pointing out connections among ideas.

An indication of why your topic matters. You need to help your readers understand why your topic is worth exploring and why your writing is worth reading. Even if you are writing in response to an assigned topic, you can better make your point and achieve your purpose by showing your readers why your topic is important and why they should care about it. For example, in "Throwing Like a Girl," James Fallows explains why his topic, the differences between the ways men and women throw a baseball, is worth writing about:

> The phrase "throwing like a girl" has become an embattled and offensive one. Feminists smart at its implication that to do something "like a girl" is to do it the wrong way. Recently, on the heels of the O. J. Simpson case, a book appeared in which the phrase was used to help explain why male athletes, especially football players, were involved in so many assaults against women. Having been trained (like most American boys) to dread the accusation of doing anything "like a girl," athletes were said to grow into the assumption that women were valueless, and natural prey.

By explaining that the topic matters because it reflects attitudes about gender that have potentially serious consequences, he gives readers reason to read on about the mechanics of "throwing like a girl."

A response to what others have said. Whatever your topic, it's unlikely that you'll be the first one to write about it. And if, as this chapter assumes, all academic writing is part of a larger conversation, you are in a way adding your own voice to that conversation. One good way of doing that is to present your ideas as a response to what others have said about your topic—to begin by quoting, paraphrasing, or summarizing what others have said and then to agree, disagree, or both.

For example, in an essay arguing that organ sales will save lives, Joanna MacKay says, "Some agree with Pope John Paul II that the selling of organs is morally wrong and violates 'the dignity of the human person.'" But she then responds—and disagrees, arguing that "the morals we hold are not absolute truths" and that "peasants of third world countries" might not agree with the pope.

A clear, appropriately qualified thesis. When you write in an academic context, you're expected to state your main point explicitly, often in a thesis statement. MIT student Joanna MacKay states her thesis clearly in her essay "Organ Sales Will Save Lives": "Governments should not ban the sale of human organs; they should regulate it." Often you'll need to qualify your thesis statement to acknowledge that the subject is complicated and there may be more than one way of seeing it or exceptions to the generalization you're making about it. Here, for example, is a qualified thesis, from an essay evaluating the movie *Juno* by Ali Heinkamp, a student at Wright State University: "Although the situations *Juno's* characters find themselves in and their dialogue may be criticized as unrealistic, the film, written by Diablo Cody and directed by Jason Reitman, successfully portrays the emotions of a teen being shoved into maturity way too fast." Heinkamp makes a claim that *Juno* achieves its main goal, while acknowledging at the beginning of the sentence that the film may be flawed.

Good reasons supported by evidence. You need to provide good reasons for your thesis and evidence to support those reasons. For example, Joanna MacKay offers several reasons why sales of human kidneys should be legalized: there is a surplus of kidneys, the risk to the donor is not great, and legalization would allow the trade in kidneys to be regulated. Evidence to support your reasons sometimes comes from your own experience but more often from published research and scholarship, research you do yourself or firsthand accounts by others.

Compared with other kinds of writing, academic writing is generally expected to be more objective and less emotional. You may find *Romeo and Juliet* deeply moving or cry when you watch *Titanic*—but when you write about the play or the film for a class, you must do so using evidence from the text to support your thesis. You may find someone's ideas deeply offensive, but you should respond to them with reason rather than with emotional appeals or personal attacks.

Acknowledgment of multiple perspectives. Debates and arguments in popular media are often framed in "pro/con" terms, as if there were only two sides to any given issue. Once you begin seriously studying a topic, though, you're likely to find that there are several sides and that each of them deserves serious consideration. In your academic writing, you need to represent fairly the range of perspectives on your topic—to explore three, four, or more positions on it as you research and write. In her report, "Does Texting Affect Writing," Marywood University student Michaela Cullington, for example, examines texting from several points of view: teachers' impressions of the influence of texting on student writing, the results of several research studies, and her own survey research.

A confident, authoritative stance. If one goal of academic writing is to contribute to a larger conversation, your tone should convey confidence and establish your authority to write about your subject. Ways to achieve such a tone include using active verbs ("X claims" rather than "it seems"), avoiding such phrases as "in my opinion" and "I think," and writing in a straightforward, direct style. Your writing should send the message that you've done the research, analysis, and thinking and know what you're talking about. For example, here is the final paragraph of Michaela Cullington's essay on texting and writing:

> On the basis of my own research, expert research, and personal observations, I can confidently state that texting is not interfering with students' use of standard written English and has no effect on their writing abilities in general. It is interesting to look at the dynamics of the arguments over these issues. Teachers and parents who claim that they are seeing a decline in the writing abilities of their students and children mainly support the negative-impact argument. Other teachers and researchers suggest that texting provides a way for teens to practice writing in a casual setting and thus helps prepare them to write formally. Experts and students themselves, however, report that they see no effect, positive or negative. Anecdotal experiences should not overshadow the actual evidence.

Cullington's use of simple, declarative sentences ("Other teachers and researchers suggest . . ."; "Anecdotal experiences should not overshadow . . .") and her straightforward summary of the arguments surrounding texting, along with her strong, unequivocal ending ("texting is not interfering with students' use of standard written English"), lend her writing a confident tone. Her stance sends the message that she's done the research and knows what she's talking about.

Carefully documented sources. Clearly acknowledging sources and documenting them carefully and correctly is a basic requirement of academic writing. When you use the words or ideas of others—including visuals, video, or audio—those sources must be documented in the text and in a works cited or references list at the end. (If you're writing something that will appear online, you may also refer readers to your sources by using hyperlinks in the text; ask your instructor if you need to include a list of references or works cited as well.)

Careful attention to correctness. Whether you're writing something formal or informal, in an essay or an email, you should always write in complete sentences, use appropriate capitalization and punctuation, and check that your spelling is correct. In general, academic writing is no place for colloquial language, slang, or texting abbreviations. If you're quoting someone, you can reproduce that person's writing or speech exactly, but in your own writing you try hard to be correct—and always proofread carefully.

What's Expected of College Writers: The WPA Outcomes

Writing is not a multiple-choice test; it doesn't have right and wrong answers that are easily graded. Instead, your readers, whether they're teachers or anyone else, are likely to read your writing with various things in mind: does it make sense, does it meet the demands of the assignment, is the grammar correct, to name just a few of the things readers may look for. Different readers may notice different things, so sometimes it may seem to you that their response—and your grade—is unpredictable. It should be good to know, then, that writing teachers across the nation have come to some agreement on certain "outcomes," what college students should know and be able to do by the time you finish a first-year writing course. These outcomes have been defined by the National Council of Writing Program Administrators (WPA). Here's a brief summary of these outcomes.

Knowledge of Rhetoric

- Understand the rhetorical situation of texts that you read and write.

- Read and write texts in a number of different genres and understand how your purpose may influence your writing.

- Adjust your voice, tone, level of formality, design, and medium as is necessary and appropriate.

- Choose the media that will best suit your audience, purpose, and the rest of your rhetorical situation.

Critical Thinking, Reading, and Composing

- Read and write to inquire, learn, think critically, and communicate.
- Read for content, argumentative strategies, and rhetorical effectiveness.
- Find and evaluate popular and scholarly sources.
- Use sources in various ways to support your ideas.

Processes

- Use writing processes to compose texts and explore ideas in various media.
- Collaborate with others on your own writing and on group tasks.
- Reflect on your own writing processes.

Knowledge of Conventions

- Use correct grammar, punctuation, and spelling.
- Understand and use genre conventions and formats in your writing.
- Understand intellectual property and document sources appropriately.

TWO

Reading in Academic Contexts

WE READ NEWSPAPERS to know about the events of the day. We read textbooks to learn about history, chemistry, and other academic topics—and other academic sources to do research and develop arguments. We read tweets and blogs to follow (and participate in) conversations about issues that interest us. And as writers, we read our own writing to make sure it says what we mean it to say and proofread our final drafts to make sure they say it correctly. In other words, we read many kinds of texts for many different purposes. This chapter offers a number of strategies for various kinds of reading you do in academic contexts.

Taking Stock of Your Reading

One way to become a better reader is to understand your reading process; if you know what you do when you read, you're in a position to decide what you need to change or improve. Consider the answers to the following questions:

- What do you read for pleasure? for work? for school? Consider all the sorts of reading you do: books, magazines, and newspapers, websites, *Facebook*, texts, blogs, product instructions.

- When you're facing a reading assignment, what do you do? Do you do certain things to get comfortable? Do you play music or seek quiet? Do you plan your reading time or set reading goals for yourself? Do you flip through or skim the text before settling down to read it, or do you start at the beginning and work through it?

- When you begin to read something for an assignment, do you make sure you understand the purpose of the assignment—why you must read this text? Do you ever ask your instructor (or whoever else assigned the reading) what its purpose is?

- How do you motivate yourself to read material you don't have any interest in? How do you deal with boredom while reading?

- Does your mind wander? If you realize that you haven't been paying attention and don't know what you just read, what do you do?

- Do you ever highlight, underline, or annotate text as you read? Do you take notes? If so, what do you mark or write down? Why?

- When you read text you don't understand, what do you do?

- As you anticipate and read an assigned text, what attitudes or feelings do you typically have? If they differ from reading to reading, why do they?

- What do you do when you've finished reading an assigned text? Write out notes? Think about what you've just read? Move on to the next task? Something else?

- How well do your reading processes work for you, both in school and otherwise? What would you like to change? What can you do to change?

The rest of this chapter offers advice and strategies that you may find helpful as you work to improve your reading skills.

READING STRATEGICALLY

Academic reading is challenging because it makes several demands on you at once. Textbooks present new vocabulary and new concepts, and picking out the main ideas can be difficult. Scholarly articles present content and arguments you need to understand, but they often assume that readers already know key concepts and vocabulary and so don't generally provide background information. As you read more texts in an academic field and begin to participate in its conversations, the reading will become easier, but in the meantime you can develop strategies that will help you to read effectively.

Thinking about What You Want to Learn

To learn anything, we need to place new information into the context of what we already know. For example, to understand photosynthesis, we need to already know something about plants, energy, and air, among other things. To learn a new language, we draw on similarities and differences between it and any other languages we know. A method of bringing to conscious attention our current knowledge on a topic and of helping us articulate our purposes for reading is a list-making process called KWL+. To use it, create a table with three columns:

K: What I Know	W: What I Want to Know	L: What I Learned

Before you begin reading a text, list in the "K" column what you already know about the topic. Brainstorm ideas, and list terms or phrases that come to mind. Then group them into categories. Also before reading, or after reading the first few paragraphs, list in the "W" column questions you have that you expect, want, or hope to be answered as you read. Number or reorder the questions by their importance to you.

Then, as you read the text or afterward, list in the "L" column what you learned from the text. Compare your "L" list with your "W" list to see what you still want or need to know (the "+")—and what you learned that you didn't expect.

Previewing the Text

It's usually a good idea to start by skimming a text—read the title and subtitle, any headings, the first and last paragraphs, the first sentences of all the other paragraphs. Study any illustrations and other visuals. Your goal is to get a sense of where the text is heading. At this point, don't stop to look up unfamiliar words; just mark them in some way to look up later.

Adjusting Your Reading Speed to Different Texts

Different texts require different kinds of effort. Some that are simple and straightforward can be skimmed fairly quickly. With academic texts, though, you usually need to read more slowly and carefully, matching the pace of your reading to the difficulty of the text. You'll likely need to skim the text for an overview of the basic ideas and then go back to read it closely. And then you may need to read it yet again. (But do try always to read quickly enough to focus on the meanings of sentences and paragraphs, not just individual words.) With visual texts, too, you'll often need to look at them several times, moving from gaining an overall impression to closely examining the structure, layout, and other visual features—and exploring how those features relate to any accompanying verbal text.

Looking for Organizational Cues

As you read, look for cues that signal the way the text's ideas are organized and how each part relates to the ones around it:

The introductory paragraph and thesis often offer a preview of the topics to be discussed and the order in which they will be addressed. Here, for example, is a typical thesis statement for a report: *Types of prisons in the United States include minimum and medium security, close security, maximum security, and supermax.* The report that follows should explain each type of prison in the order stated in the thesis.

Transitions help guide readers in following the direction of the writer's thinking from idea to idea. For example, "however" indicates an idea that contradicts or limits what has just been said, while "furthermore" indicates one that adds to or supports it.

Headings identify a text's major and minor sections, by means of both the headings' content and their design.

Thinking about Your Initial Response

Some readers find it helps to make brief notes about their first response to a text, noting their reaction and thinking a little about why they reacted as they did.

What are your initial reactions? Describe both your intellectual reaction and any emotional reaction, and identify places in the text that caused you to react as you did. An intellectual reaction might consist of an evaluation

("I disagree with this position because . . ."), a connection ("This idea reminds me of . . ."), or an elaboration ("Another example of this point is . . ."). An emotional reaction could include approval or disapproval ("YES! This is exactly right!" "NO! This is so wrong!"), an expression of feeling ("This passage makes me so sad"), or one of appreciation ("This is said so beautifully"). If you had no particular reaction, note that, too.

What accounts for your reactions? Are they rooted in personal experiences? aspects of your personality? positions you hold on an issue? As much as possible, you want to keep your opinions from interfering with your understanding of what you're reading, so it's important to try to identify those opinions up front.

Dealing with Difficult Texts

Let's face it: some texts are difficult. You may have no interest in the subject matter, or lack background knowledge or vocabulary necessary for understanding the text, or simply not have a clear sense of why you have to read the text at all. Whatever the reason, reading such texts can be a challenge. Here are some tips for dealing with them:

Look for something familiar. Texts often seem difficult or boring because we don't know enough about the topic or about the larger conversation surrounding it to read them effectively. By skimming the headings, the abstract or introduction, and the conclusion, you may find something that relates to something you already know or are at least interested in—and being aware of that prior knowledge can help you see how this new material relates to it.

Look for "landmarks." Reading a challenging academic text the first time through can be like driving to an unfamiliar destination on roads you've never traveled: you don't know where you're headed, you don't recognize anything along the way, and you're not sure how long getting there will take. As you drive the route again, though, you see landmarks along the way that help you know where you're going. The same goes for reading a difficult text: sometimes you need to get through it once just to get some idea of what it's about. On the second reading, now that you have "driven the route," look for the ways that the parts of the text relate to one another, to other texts or course information, or to other knowledge you have.

Monitor your understanding. You may have had the experience of reading a text and suddenly realizing that you have no idea what you just read. Being able to monitor your reading—to sense when you aren't understanding the text and need to reread, focus your attention, look up unfamiliar terms, take some notes, or take a break—can make you a more efficient and better reader. Keep these questions in mind as you read: What is my purpose for reading this text? Am I understanding it? Does it make sense? Should I slow down, reread, annotate? skim ahead and then come back? pause to reflect?

Be persistent. Research shows that many students respond to difficult texts by assuming they're "too dumb to get it"—and quit reading. Successful students, on the other hand, report that if they keep at a text, they will come to understand it. Some of them even see difficult texts as challenges: "I'm going to keep working on this until I make sense of it." Remember that reading is an active process, and the more you work at it the more successful you will be.

Annotating

Many readers find it helps to annotate as they read: highlighting keywords, phrases, sentences; connecting ideas with lines or symbols; writing comments or questions in the margin or on sticky notes; circling new words so you can look up the definitions later; noting anything that seems noteworthy or questionable. Annotating forces you to read for more than just the surface meaning. Especially when you are going to be writing about or responding to a text, annotating creates a record of things you may want to refer to.

Annotate as if you're having a conversation with the author, someone you take seriously but whose words you do not accept without question. Put your part of the conversation in the margin, asking questions, talking back: "What's this mean?" "So what?" "Says who?" "Where's evidence?" "Yes!" "Whoa!" or even ☺ or ☹ or texting shorthand like LOL or INTRSTN. If you're reading a text online, you may be able to copy it and annotate it electronically. If so, make your annotations a different color from the text itself.

What you annotate depends upon your purpose, or what you're most interested in. If you're analyzing a text that makes an explicit argument, you would probably underline the thesis statement, and then the reasons and evidence that support that statement. It might help to restate those ideas in your own words in the margins—in order to understand them, you need to put them in your own words! If you are trying to identify patterns, you might highlight each pattern in a different color or mark it with a sticky note and write any questions or notes about it in that color. You might annotate a visual text by circling and identifying important parts of the image.

There are some texts that you cannot annotate, of course—library books, some materials you read on the web, and so on. Then you will need to use sticky notes or make notes elsewhere, and you might find it useful to keep a reading log for this purpose.

A Sample Annotated Text

HERE IS *an excerpt from* Justice: What's the Right Thing to Do?, *a book by Harvard professor Michael J. Sandel, annotated by a writer who was doing research for a report on the awarding of military medals:*

What Wounds Deserve the Purple Heart?

On some issues, questions of virtue and honor are too obvious to deny. Consider the recent debate over who should qualify for the Purple Heart. Since 1932, the U.S. military has awarded the medal to soldiers wounded or killed in battle by enemy action. In addition to the honor, the medal entitles recipients to special privileges in veterans' hospitals.

Purple Heart given for wounding or death in battle.

Since the beginning of the current wars in Iraq and Afghanistan, growing numbers of veterans have been diagnosed with post-traumatic stress disorder and treated for the condition. Symptoms include recurring nightmares, severe depression, and suicide. At least three hundred thousand veterans reportedly suffer from traumatic stress or major depression. Advocates for these veterans have proposed that they, too, should qualify for the Purple Heart. Since psychological injuries can be at least as debilitating as physical ones, they argue, soldiers who suffer these wounds should receive the medal.

PTSD increasingly common among veterans.

Argument: Vets with PTSD should be eligible for PH because psych. injuries are as serious as physical.

After a Pentagon advisory group studied the question, the Pentagon announced, in 2009, that the Purple Heart would be

2009: Military says no: PTSD injuries "not intentionally caused by enemy" and are hard to diagnose.

reserved for soldiers with physical injuries. Veterans suffering from mental disorders and psychological trauma would not be eligible, even though they qualify for government-supported medical treatment and disability payments. The Pentagon offered two reasons for its decision: traumatic stress disorders are not intentionally caused by enemy action, and they are difficult to diagnose objectively.

Did the Pentagon make the right decision? Taken by themselves, its reasons are unconvincing. In the Iraq War, one of the most common injuries recognized with the Purple Heart has been a punctured eardrum, caused by explosions at close range. But unlike bullets and bombs, such explosions are not a deliberate enemy tactic intended to injure or kill; they are (like traumatic stress) a damaging side effect of battlefield action. And while traumatic disorders may be more difficult to diagnose than a broken limb, the injury they inflict can be more severe and long-lasting.

As the wider debate about the Purple Heart revealed, the real issue is about the meaning of the medal and the virtues it honors. What, then, are the relevant virtues? Unlike other military medals, the Purple Heart honors sacrifice, not bravery. It requires no heroic act, only an injury inflicted by the enemy. The question is what kind of injury should count.

A veteran's group called the Military Order of the Purple Heart opposed awarding the medal for psychological injuries, claiming that doing so would "debase" the honor. A spokesman for the group stated that "shedding blood" should be an essential qualification. He didn't explain why bloodless injuries shouldn't count. But Tyler E. Boudreau, a former Marine captain who favors including psychological injuries, offers a compelling analysis of the dispute. He attributes the opposition to a deep-seated attitude in the military that views post-traumatic stress as a kind of weakness. "The same culture that demands tough-mindedness also encourages skepticism toward the suggestion that the violence of war can hurt the healthiest of minds . . . Sadly, as long as our military culture bears at least a quiet contempt for the psychological wounds of war, it is unlikely those veterans will ever see a Purple Heart."

So the debate over the Purple Heart is more than a medical or clinical dispute about how to determine the veracity of injury.

PTSD is like punctured eardrums, which do get the PH.

PH "honors sacrifice, not bravery." Injury enough. So what kind of injury?

Wow: one vet's group insists that for PH, soldier must bleed!

Good quote!

At the heart of the disagreement are rival conceptions of <u>moral character and military valor</u>. Those who insist that only bleeding wounds should count believe that post-traumatic stress reflects a weakness of character unworthy of honor. Those who believe that psychological wounds should qualify argue that veterans suffering long-term trauma and severe depression have sacrificed for their country as surely, and as honorably, as those who've lost a limb. The dispute over the Purple Heart illustrates the moral logic of Aristotle's theory of justice. We can't determine who deserves a military medal without asking what virtues the medal properly honors. And to answer that question, we have to assess competing conceptions of character and sacrifice.

— MICHAEL J. SANDEL, Justice: What's the Right Thing to Do?

Argument based on different ideas about what counts as a military virtue.

Coding

You may also find it useful to record your thoughts as you read by using a coding system—for example, using "X" to indicate passages that contradict your assumptions, or "?" for ones that puzzle you. You can make up your own coding system, of course, but you could start with this one*:

- ✔ Confirms what you thought

- X Contradicts what you thought

- ? Puzzles you

- ?? Confuses you

- ! Surprises you

- ☆ Strikes you as important

- → Is new or interesting to you

You might also circle new words that you'll want to look up later and highlight or underline key phrases.

*Adapted from Harvey Daniels and Steven Zemelman, *Subjects Matter: Every Teacher's Guide to Content-Area Reading.*

Summarizing

Writing a summary, boiling down a text to its main ideas, can help you understand it. To do so, you need to identify which ideas in the text are crucial to its meaning. Then you put those crucial ideas into your own words, creating a brief version that accurately sums up the text. Here, for example, is a summary of Sandel's analysis of the Purple Heart debate:

> In "What Wounds Deserve the Purple Heart?," Harvard professor Michael J. Sandel explores the debate over eligibility for the Purple Heart, the medal given to soldiers who die or are wounded in battle. Some argue that soldiers suffering from post-traumatic stress disorder should qualify for the medal because psychological injuries are as serious as physical ones. However, the military disagrees, since PTSD injuries are not "intentionally caused by enemy action" and are hard to diagnose. Sandel observes that the dispute centers on how "character" and "sacrifice" are defined. Those who insist that soldiers must have had physical wounds to be eligible for the Purple Heart see psychological wounds as reflecting "weakness of character," while others argue that veterans with PTSD and other psychological traumas have sacrificed honorably for their country.

Thinking about How the Text Works:
What It Says, What It Does

Sometimes you'll need to think about how a text works, how its parts fit together. You may be assigned to analyze a text, or you may just need to make sense of a difficult text, to think about how the ideas all relate to one another. Whatever your purpose, a good way to think about a text structure is by outlining it, paragraph by paragraph. If you're interested in analyzing its ideas, look at what each paragraph *says*; if, on the other hand, you're concerned with how the ideas are presented, pay attention to what each paragraph *does*.

What it says. Write a sentence that identifies what each paragraph says. Once you've done that for the whole text, look for patterns in the topics the writer addresses. Pay attention to the order in which the topics are presented. Also look for gaps, ideas the writer has left unsaid. Such paragraph-by-paragraph outlining of the content can help you see how the writer has arranged ideas and how that arrangement builds an argument or develops a topic.

What it does. Identify the function of each paragraph. Starting with the first paragraph, ask, What does this paragraph do? Does it introduce a topic? provide background for a topic to come? describe something? define something? entice me to read further? something else? What does the second paragraph do? the third? As you go through the text, you may identify groups of paragraphs that have a single purpose.

Reading Visual Texts

Photos, drawings, graphs, diagrams, and charts are frequently used to help convey important information and often make powerful arguments themselves. So learning to read and interpret visual texts is just as necessary as it is for written texts.

Taking visuals seriously. Remember that visuals are texts themselves, not just decoration. When they appear as part of a written text, they may introduce information not discussed elsewhere in the text. Or they might illustrate concepts hard to grasp from words alone. In either case, it's important to pay close attention to any visuals in a written text.

Looking at any title, caption, or other written text that's part of a visual will help you understand its main idea. It might also help to think about its purpose: Why did the writer include it? What information does it add or emphasize? What argument is it making? See, for example, how a psychology textbook uses visuals to help explain two ways that information can be represented:

Analogical and Symbolic Representations

When we think about information, we use two basic types of internal representations: analogical and symbolic.

Analogical representations usually correspond to images. They have some characteristics of actual objects. Therefore, they are analogous to actual objects. For example, maps correspond to geographical layouts. Family trees depict branching relationships between relatives. A clock corresponds directly to the passage of time. **Figure 2.1a** is a drawing of a violin from a particular perspective. This drawing is an analogical representation.

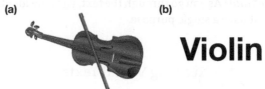

Figure 2.1 Analogical Versus Symbolic Representations

(a)   (b)

(a) Analogical representations, such as this picture of a violin, have some characteristics of the objects they represent.
(b) Symbolic representations, such as the word *violin*, are abstract and do not have relationships to the physical qualities of objects.

By contrast, **symbolic representations** are abstract. These representations usually consist of words or ideas. They do not have relationships to physical qualities of objects in the world. The word *hamburger* is a symbolic representation that usually represents a cooked patty of beef served on a bun. The word *violin* stands for a musical instrument (**Figure 2.1b**).

— Sarah Grison, Todd Heatherton,
and Michael Gazzaniga, *Psychology in Your Life*

The headings tell you the topic: analogical and symbolic representations. The paragraphs define the two types of representation, and the illustrations present a visual example of each type. The visuals make the information in the written text easier to understand by illustrating the differences between the two.

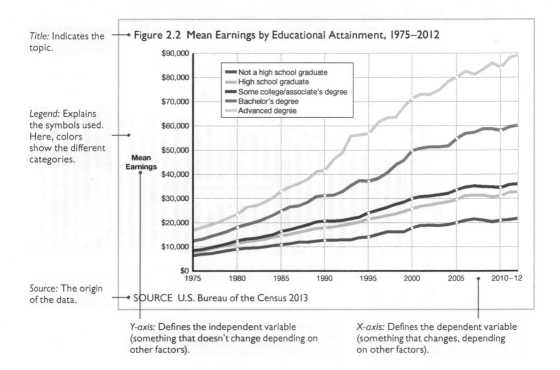

Title: Indicates the topic.

Figure 2.2 Mean Earnings by Educational Attainment, 1975–2012

Legend: Explains the symbols used. Here, colors show the different categories.

Mean Earnings

Not a high school graduate
High school graduate
Some college/associate's degree
Bachelor's degree
Advanced degree

Source: The origin of the data.

SOURCE U.S. Bureau of the Census 2013

Y-axis: Defines the independent variable (something that doesn't change depending on other factors).

X-axis: Defines the dependent variable (something that changes, depending on other factors).

Reading charts and graphs. To read the information in charts and graphs, you need to look for different things depending on what type of chart or graph you're considering. A line graph, for example, usually contains certain elements: title, legend, x-axis, y-axis, and source information. Figure 2.2 shows one such graph taken from a sociology textbook.

Other types of charts and graphs include some of these same elements. But the specific elements vary according to the different kinds of information being presented, and some charts and graphs can be challenging to read. For example, the chart in Figure 2.3, from the same textbook, includes elements of both bar and line graphs to depict two trends at once: the red line shows the percentage of women in the United States who were in the labor force over a sixty-five-year period, and the blue bars show the percentage of U.S. workers who were women during that same period. Both trends are shown in two-year increments. To make sense of this chart, you need to read the title, the *y*-axis labels, and the labels and their definitions carefully.

Figure 2.3 Women's Participation in the Labor Force in the United States, 1948–2012

*Women in the labor force as a percent of all civilian women age sixteen and over.
†Women in the labor force as a percent of the total labor force (both men and women) age sixteen and over.

SOURCE U.S. Bureau of Labor Statistics 2014

Reading Onscreen

Research shows that we tend to read differently onscreen than we do when we read print texts: we skim and sample, often reading a sentence or two and then jumping to another site, another text. If we need to scroll the page to continue, we often don't bother. In general, we don't read as carefully as we do when reading print texts, and we're less likely to reread or take other steps if we find that we don't understand something. Following are some strategies that might help you read effectively onscreen.

Adjust your reading speed and effort to your purpose. Many students use the web to get an overview of a topic and find potential sources. In that case, skimming and browsing are sensible and appropriate tactics. If you're reading to evaluate a source or find specific information on a topic, though, you probably need to read more slowly and carefully.

Keep your purpose in mind as you read. Clicking on hyperlinks and jumping from site to site can be tempting. Resist the temptation! Making a list of specific questions you're seeking to answer can help you stay focused and on task.

Print out longer texts. Some people find reading online to be harder on their eyes than reading pages of print, and many find that they comprehend and remember information in longer texts better if they read them in print. Reading a long text is similar to walking through an unfamiliar neighborhood: we form a mental map of the text as we read and then associate the information with its location in the text, making remembering easier. Since forming such a map is more difficult when reading an electronic text, printing out texts you need to read carefully may be a good strategy.

READING CRITICALLY

To read academic texts effectively, you need to read them critically, to look beyond the words on the page or screen to the rhetorical context of the text and the argument it makes. Academic texts—both the ones you read and the ones you write—are parts of ongoing scholarly conversations, in which writers respond to the ideas and assertions of others in order to advance knowledge. To enter those conversations, you must first read carefully and critically to understand the rhetorical situation and the larger context within which a writer wrote and the argument the text makes.

Considering the Rhetorical Situation

As a reader, you need to think about the message that the writer wants to articulate, including the intended audience and the writer's attitude toward that audience and the topic, as well as about the genre, medium, and design of the text.

Purpose What is the writer's purpose? To entertain? inform? persuade readers to think something or take some action? What is *your* purpose for reading this text?

Audience Who is the intended audience? Are you a member of that group? If not, should you expect that you'll need to look up unfamiliar terms or concepts or that you'll run into assumptions you don't necessarily share? How is the writer addressing the audience—as an expert addressing those less knowledgeable? an outsider addressing insiders?

Genre   What is the genre? Is it a report? an argument? an analysis? something else? Knowing the genre can help you to anticipate certain key features.

Stance   Who is the writer, and what is his or her stance? Critical? Curious? Opinionated? Objective? Passionate? Indifferent? Something else? Knowing the stance affects the way you understand a text, whether you're inclined to agree or disagree with it, to take it seriously, and so on.

Media/ Design   What is the medium, and how does it affect the way you read? If it's a print text, what do you know about the publisher? If it's on the web, who sponsors the site, and when was it last updated? Are there any headings, summaries, or other elements that highlight key parts of the text?

Identifying Patterns

Look for notable patterns in the text—recurring words and their synonyms, as well as repeated phrases, metaphors and other images, and types of sentences. Some readers find it helps to highlight patterns in various colors. Does the author repeatedly rely on any particular writing strategies: narration? comparison? Something else?

Another kind of pattern it might be important to consider is the kind of evidence the text provides. Is it more opinion than facts? nothing but statistics? If many sources are cited, is the information presented in any patterns—as quotations? paraphrases? summaries? Are there repeated references to certain experts or sources?

In visual texts, look for patterns of color, shape, and line. What's in the foreground, and what's in the background? What's completely visible, partly visible, or hidden? In both verbal and visual texts, look for omissions and anomalies: What isn't there that you would expect to find? Is there anything that doesn't really fit in?

If you discover patterns, then you need to consider what, if anything, they mean in terms of what the writer is saying. What do they reveal about the writer's underlying premises and beliefs? What do they tell you about the writer's strategies for persuading readers to accept the truth of what he or she is saying?

See how color-coding an essay by *New York Times* columnist William Safire on the meaning of the Gettysburg Address reveals several patterns in the language Safire uses. In this excerpt from the essay, which was published just before the first anniversary of the September 11, 2001, terrorist attacks, Safire develops his analysis through several patterns. Religious references are colored yellow; references to a "national spirit," green; references to life, death, and rebirth, blue; and places where Safire directly addresses the reader, gray.

> But the selection of this poetic political sermon as the oratorical centerpiece of our observance need not be only an exercise. . . . now, as then, a national spirit rose from the ashes of destruction.
>
> Here is how to listen to Lincoln's all-too-familiar speech with new ears.
>
> In those 266 words, you will hear the word *dedicate* five times. . . .
>
> Those five pillars of dedication rested on a fundament of religious metaphor. From a president not known for his piety—indeed, often criticized for his supposed lack of faith—came a speech rooted in the theme of national resurrection. The speech is grounded in conception, birth, death, and rebirth.
>
> Consider the barrage of images of birth in the opening sentence. . . .
>
> Finally, the nation's spirit rises from this scene of death: "that this nation, under God, shall have a new birth of freedom." Conception, birth, death, rebirth. The nation, purified in this fiery trial of war, is resurrected. Through the sacrifice of its sons, the sundered nation would be reborn as one. . . .
>
> Do not listen on Sept. 11 only to Lincoln's famous words and comforting cadences. Think about how Lincoln's message encompasses but goes beyond paying "fitting and proper" respect to the dead and the bereaved. His sermon at Gettysburg reminds "us the living" of our "unfinished work" and "the great task remaining before us"—to resolve that this generation's response to the deaths of thousands of our people leads to "a new birth of freedom."

The color coding helps us to see patterns in Safire's language, just as Safire reveals patterns in Lincoln's words. He offers an interpretation of Lincoln's address as a "poetic political sermon," and the words he uses throughout support that interpretation. At the end, he repeats the assertion that Lincoln's address is a sermon, inviting us to consider it differently. Safire's repeated commands ("Consider," "Do not listen," "Think about") offer additional insight into how he wishes to position himself in relation to his readers.

Analyzing the Argument

All texts make some kind of argument, claiming something and then offering reasons and evidence as support for any claim. As a critical reader, you need to look closely at the argument a text makes—to recognize all the claims it makes, consider the support it offers for those claims, and decide how you want to respond. What do you think, and why? Here are some questions to consider when analyzing an argument:

- *What claim is the text making?* What is the writer's main point? Is it stated as a thesis, or only implied? Is it limited or qualified somehow? If not, should it have been?

- *How is the claim supported?* What reasons does the writer provide for the claim, and what evidence is given for the reasons? What kind of evidence is it? Facts? Statistics? Examples? Expert opinions? Images? How convincing do you find the reasons and evidence? Is there enough evidence?

- *What appeals besides logical ones are used?* Does the writer appeal to readers' emotions? try to establish common ground? demonstrate his or her credibility as trustworthy and knowledgeable? How successful are these appeals?

- *Are any counterarguments acknowledged?* If so, are they presented accurately and respectfully? Does the writer concede any value to them or try to refute them? How successfully does he or she deal with them?

- *What outside sources of information does the writer cite?* What kinds of sources are they, and how credible do they seem? Are they current and authoritative? How well do they support the argument?

- *Do you detect any fallacies?* Fallacies are arguments that involve faulty reasoning. Because they often seem plausible, they can be persuasive. It is important, therefore, that you question the legitimacy of such reasoning when you run across it.

Believing and Doubting

One way to develop a response to a text is to play the Believing and Doubting Game, sometimes called reading with and against the grain. Your goal is to list or freewrite notes as you read, writing out as many reasons as you can think of for believing what the writer says (reading with the grain) and then as many as you can for doubting it (reading against the grain).

First, try to look at the world through the writer's perspective. Try to understand his or her reasons for arguing as he or she does, even if you strongly disagree. Then reread the text, trying to doubt everything in it: try to find every flaw in the argument, every possible way it can be refuted—even if you totally agree with it. Developed by writing theorist Peter Elbow, the believing and doubting game helps you consider new ideas and question ideas you already have—and at the same time will see where you stand in relation to the ideas in the text you're reading.

Considering the Larger Context

All texts are part of ongoing conversations with other texts that have dealt with the topic of the text. An essay arguing for handgun trigger locks is part of an ongoing conversation on gun control, which is itself part of a conversation on individual rights and responsibilities. Academic texts document their sources in part to show their relationship to the ongoing scholarly conversation on a particular topic. In fact, any time you're reading to learn, you're probably reading for some larger context. Whatever your reading goals, being aware of that larger context can help you better understand what you're reading. Here are some specific aspects of the text to pay attention to:

Who else cares about this topic? Especially when you're reading in order to learn about a topic, the texts you read will often reveal which people or groups are part of the conversation—and might be sources of further reading. For example, an essay describing the formation of Mammoth Cave in Kentucky could be of interest to geologists, spelunkers, travel writers, or tourists. If you're reading such an essay while doing research on the cave, you should consider how the audience to whom the writer is writing determines the nature of the information provided—and its suitability as a source for your research.

What conversations is this text part of? Does the text refer to any concepts or ideas that give you some sense that it's part of a larger conversation? An argument on airport security measures, for example, is part of larger conversations about government response to terrorism, the limits of freedom in a democracy, and the possibilities of using technology to detect weapons and explosives, among others.

What terms does the writer use? Do any terms or specialized language reflect the writer's allegiance to a particular group or academic discipline? If you run across words like *false consciousness*, *ideology*, and *hegemony*, for example, you might guess that the text was written by a Marxist scholar.

What other writers or sources does the writer cite? Do the other writers have a particular academic specialty, belong to an identifiable intellectual school, share similar political leanings? If an article on politics cites Paul Krugman and Barbara Ehrenreich in support of its argument, you might assume that the writer holds liberal opinions; if it cites Ross Douthat and Amity Schlaes, the writer is likely a conservative.

THREE

The Rhetorical Situation

PURPOSE

All writing has a purpose. We write to explore our thoughts and emotions, to express ourselves, to entertain; we write to record words and events, to communicate with others, to try to persuade others to believe as we do or to behave in certain ways. In fact, we often have several purposes at the same time. We may write an essay in which we try to explain something to an audience, but at the same time we may be trying to persuade that audience of something. Look, for example, at this passage from a 2012 *New York Times* op-ed essay by economist and editorial columnist Paul Krugman about so- cial and economic trends among "the traditional working-class family"— declining rates of marriage and of male participation in the labor force and increasing numbers of out-of-wedlock births. Krugman asserts that the pri- mary reason for those statistics is a "drastic reduction in the work opportu- nities available to less-educated men":

> Most of the numbers you see about income trends in America focus on households rather than individuals, which makes sense for some purposes. But when you see a modest rise in incomes for the lower tiers of the income distribution, you have to realize that all—yes, all—of this rise comes from the women, both because more women are in the paid labor force and because women's wages aren't as much below male wages as they used to be.

> For lower-education working men, however, it has been all negative. Adjusted for inflation, entry-level wages of male high school graduates have fallen 23 percent since 1973. Meanwhile, employment benefits have collapsed. In 1980, 65 percent of recent high-school graduates working in the private sector had health benefits, but, by 2009, that was down to 29 percent.
>
> So we have become a society in which less-educated men have great difficulty finding jobs with decent wages and good benefits.
>
> —Paul Krugman, "Money and Morals"

Krugman is reporting information here, outlining how the earnings and benefits of less-educated men have dropped over the last forty years. He is also making an argument, that these economic setbacks are the cause of the social ills among working-class Americans and not, as some would have it, the result of them. (Krugman, writing for a newspaper, is also using a style—including dashes, contractions, and other informal elements—that strives to be engaging while it informs and argues.)

Even though our purposes may be many, knowing our primary reason for writing can help us shape that writing and understand how to proceed with it. Our purpose can determine the genre we choose, our audience, even the way we design what we write.

Identify your purpose.   While a piece of writing often has many purposes, a writer usually focuses on one. When you get an assignment or see a need to write, ask yourself what the primary purpose of the writing task is: to entertain? to inform? to persuade? to demonstrate your knowledge or your writing ability? What are your own goals? What are your audience's expectations, and do they affect the way you define your purpose?

Thinking about Purpose

- *What do you want your audience to do, think, or feel?* How will your readers use what you tell them?

- *What does this writing task call on you to do?* Do you need to show that you have mastered certain content or skills? Do you have an assignment that specifies a particular strategy or genre—to compare two things, perhaps, or to argue a position?

- *What are the best ways to achieve your purpose?* What stance should you take? Should you write in a particular genre? Do you have a choice of medium, and does your text require any special format or design elements?

AUDIENCE

Who will read (or hear) what you are writing? A seemingly obvious but crucially important question. Your audience affects your writing in various ways. Consider a piece of writing as simple as a text from a mother to her son:

> Pls. take chicken out to thaw and feed Annye. Remember Dr. Wong at 4.

On the surface, this brief note is a straightforward reminder to do three things. But in fact it is a complex message filled with compressed information for a specific audience. The writer (the mother) counts on the reader (her son) to know a lot that can be left unsaid. She expects that he knows that the chicken is in the freezer and needs to thaw in time to be cooked for dinner; she knows that he knows who Annye is (a pet?), what he or she is fed, and how much; she assumes that he knows who (and where) Dr. Wong is. She doesn't need to spell out any of that because she knows what her son knows and what he needs to know—and in her text she can be brief. She understands her audience. Think how different such a reminder would be were it written to another audience— a babysitter, perhaps, or a friend helping out while Mom is out of town.

What you write, how much you write, how you phrase it, even your choice of genre (memo, essay, email, note, speech)—all are influenced by the audience you envision. And your audience will interpret your writing according to their own expectations and experiences, not yours.

When you are a student, your audience is most often your teachers, so you need to be aware of their expectations and know the conventions (rules, often unstated) for writing in specific academic fields. You may make statements that seem obvious to you, not realizing that your instructors may consider them assertions that must be proved with evidence of one sort or another. Or you may write more or less formally than teachers expect. Understanding your audience's expectations—by asking outright, by reading materials in your field of study, by trial and error—is important to your success as a college writer.

This point is worth dwelling on. You are probably reading this textbook for a writing course. As a student, you will be expected to produce essays with few or no errors. If you correspond with family, friends, or coworkers using email and texts, you may question such standards; after all, many of the messages you get in these contexts are not grammatically perfect. But in a writing class, the instructor needs to see your best work. Whatever the rhetorical situation, your writing must meet the expectations of your audience.

Identify your audience.   Audiences may be defined as *known, multiple,* or *unknown. Known audiences* can include people with whom you're familiar as well as people you don't know personally but whose needs and expectations you do know. You yourself are a known, familiar audience, and you write to and for yourself often. Class notes, to-do lists, reminders, and journals are all written primarily for an audience of one: you. For that reason, they are often in shorthand, full of references and code that you alone understand.

Other known, familiar audiences include anyone you actually know—friends, relatives, teachers, classmates—and whose needs and expectations you understand. You can also know what certain readers want and need, even if you've never met them personally, if you write for them within a specific shared context. Such a known audience might include PC gamers who read cheat codes that you have posted on the internet for beating a game; you don't know those people, but you know roughly what they know about the game and what they need to know, and you know how to write about it in ways they will understand.

You often have to write for *multiple audiences*. Business memos or reports may be written initially for a supervisor, but he or she may pass them along to others. Grant proposals may be reviewed by four to six levels of readers—each, of course, with its own expectations and perspectives. Even writing for a class might involve multiple audiences: your instructor and your classmates.

Unknown audiences can be the most difficult to address since you can't be sure what they know, what they need to know, how they'll react. Such an audience could be your downstairs neighbor, with whom you've chatted occasionally in the laundry room. How will she respond to your letter asking her to sponsor you in an upcoming charity walk? Another unknown audience—perhaps surprisingly—might be many of your instructors, who want—and expect!—you to write in ways that are new to you. While you can benefit from analyzing any audience, you need to think most carefully about those you don't know.

Thinking about Audience

- *Whom do you want to reach?* To whom are you writing (or speaking)?
- *What is your audience's background—their education and life experiences?* It may be important for you to know, for example, whether your readers attended college, fought in a war, or have young children.

- *What are their interests?* What do they like? What motivates them? What do they care about?

- *Is there any demographic information that you should keep in mind?* Consider whether race, gender, sexual orientation, disabilities, occupation, religious beliefs, economic status, and so on should affect what or how you write. For example, writers for *Men's Health*, *InStyle*, and *Out* must consider the particular interests of each magazine's readers.

- *What political circumstances may affect their reading?* What attitudes—opinions, special interests, biases—may affect the way your audience reads your piece? Are your readers conservative, liberal, or middle of the road? Politics may take many other forms as well—retirees on a fixed income may object to increased school taxes, so a letter arguing for such an increase would need to appeal to them differently than would a similar letter sent to parents of young children.

- *What does your audience already know—or believe—about your topic? What do you need to tell them? What is the best way to do so?* Those retirees who oppose school taxes already know that taxes are a burden for them; they may need to know why schools are justified in asking for more money every few years. A good way to explain this may be with a bar graph showing how property values benefit from good schools with adequate funding. Consider which strategies will be effective—narrative, comparison, something else?

- *What's your relationship with your audience, and how should it affect your language and tone?* Do you know them, or not? Are they friends? colleagues? mentors? adversaries? strangers? Will they likely share your stance? In general, you need to write more formally when you're addressing readers you don't know, and you may address friends and colleagues more informally than you would a boss.

- *What does your audience need and expect from you?* Your history professor, for example, may need to know how well you can discuss the economy of the late Middle Ages in order to assess your learning; he may expect you to write a carefully reasoned argument, drawing conclusions from various sources, with a readily identifiable thesis in the first paragraph. Your boss, on the other hand, may need an informal email that briefly lists your sales contacts for the day; she may expect that you list the contacts in the order in which you saw them, that you clearly identify each one, and that you briefly say how well each contact went. What genre is most appropriate?

- *What kind of response do you want?* Do you want readers to believe or do something? to accept as valid your information on a topic? to understand why an experience you once had matters to you?
- *How can you best appeal to your audience?* Is there a particular medium that will best reach them? Are there any design requirements? (Elderly readers may need larger type, for instance.)

GENRE

Genres are kinds of writing. Letters, profiles, reports, position papers, poems, blog posts, instructions, parodies—even jokes—are genres. For example, here is the beginning of a profile of a mechanic who repairs a specific kind of automobile:

> Her business card reads Shirley Barnes, M.D., and she's a doctor, all right—a Metropolitan Doctor. Her passion is the Nash Metropolitan, the little car produced by Austin of England for American Motors between 1954 and 1962. Barnes is a legend among southern California Met lovers—an icon, a beacon, and a font of useful knowledge and freely offered opinions.

A profile offers a written portrait of someone or something that informs and sometimes entertains, often examining its subject from a particular angle—in this case, as a female mechanic who fixes Nash Metropolitans. While the language in this example is informal and lively ("she's a doctor, all right"), the focus is on the subject, Shirley Barnes, "M.D." If this same excerpt were presented as a poem, however, the new genre would change our reading:

> Her business card reads
> Shirley Barnes, M.D.,
> and she's a doctor, all right
> — a Metropolitan Doctor.
> Her passion is the Nash Metropolitan,
> the little car produced by Austin of England
> for American Motors between 1954 and 1962.
> Barnes is a legend

among southern California Met lovers
— an icon,
a beacon,
and a font of useful knowledge and
freely offered opinions.

The content hasn't changed, but the different presentation invites us to read not only to learn about Shirley Barnes but also to explore the significance of the words and phrases on each line, to read for deeper meaning and greater appreciation of language. The genre thus determines how we read and how we interpret what we read.

Genres help us write by establishing features for conveying certain kinds of content. They give readers clues about what sort of information they're likely to find and so help them figure out how to read ("This article begins with an abstract, so it's probably a scholarly source" or "Thank goodness! I found the instructions for editing videos on my phone"). At the same time, genres are flexible; writers often tweak the features or combine elements of different genres to achieve a particular purpose or connect with an audience in a particular way. Genres also change as writers' needs and available technologies change. For example, computers have enabled us to add audio and video content to texts that once could appear only on paper.

Identify your genre. Does your writing situation call for a certain genre? a memo? a report? a proposal? a letter? Some situations may call for mixing genres. Academic assignments generally specify the genre ("take a position," "analyze the text"), but if not, see Chapter 24 for help choosing genres—or ask your instructor.

Thinking about Genre

- *How does your genre affect what content you can or should include?* Objective information? Researched source material? Your own opinions? Personal experience? A mix?

- *Does your genre call for any specific strategies?* Profiles, for example, usually include some narration; lab reports often explain a process.

- *Does your genre require a certain organization?* Proposals, for instance, usually need to show a problem exists before offering a solution. Some genres leave room for choice. Business letters delivering good news might be organized differently than those making sales pitches.

- *Does your genre affect your tone?* An abstract of a scholarly paper calls for a different tone than a memoir. Should your words sound serious and scholarly? brisk and to the point? objective? opinionated? Sometimes your genre affects the way you communicate your stance.

- *Does the genre require formal (or informal) language?* A letter to the mother of a friend asking for a summer job in her bookstore calls for more formal language than does an email to the friend thanking him for the lead.

- *Do you have a choice of medium?* Some genres call for print; others for an electronic medium. Sometimes you have a choice: a résumé, for instance, can be printed to bring to an interview, or it may be downloaded or emailed. Some teachers want reports turned in on paper; others prefer that they be emailed or posted in the class course management system. If you're not sure what medium you can use, ask.

- *Does your genre have any design requirements?* Some genres call for paragraphs; others require lists. Some require certain kinds of fonts— you wouldn't use impact for a personal narrative, nor would you likely use chiller for an invitation to Grandma's sixty-fifth birthday party. Different genres call for different design elements.

STANCE

Whenever you write, you have a certain stance, an attitude toward your topic. The way you express that stance affects the way you come across to your audience as a writer and a person. This email from a college student to his father, for example, shows a thoughtful, reasonable stance for a carefully researched argument:

> Hi Dad,
> I'll get right to the point: I'd like to buy a car. I saved over $4,500 from working this summer, and I've found three different cars that I can get for under $3,000. That'll leave me $1,400 to cover the insurance. I can park in Lot J, over behind Monte Hall, for $75 for both semesters. And I can earn gas and repair money by upping my hours at the cafeteria. It won't

cost you any more, and if I have a car, you won't have to come and pick
me up when I want to come home. May I buy it?
Love,
Michael

While such a stance can't guarantee that Dad will give permission, it's more
likely to produce results than this version:

Hi Dad,
I'm buying a car. A guy in my Western Civ course has a cool Nissan he
wants to get rid of. I've got $4,500 saved from working this summer, it's
mine, and I'm going to use it to get some wheels. Mom said you'd freak if
I did, but I want this car. OK?
Michael

The writer of the first email respects his reader and offers reasoned
arguments and evidence of research to convince him that buying a car is
an action that will benefit them both. The writer of the second, by contrast,
seems impulsive, ready to buy the first car that comes along, and defiant —
he's picking a fight. Each email reflects a certain stance that shows the writer as a certain kind of person dealing with a topic in a certain way and establishing a certain relationship with his audience.

Identify your stance. What is your attitude toward your topic? Objective?
Critical? Curious? Opinionated? Passionate? Indifferent? Your stance may be
affected by your relationship to your audience. How do you want them to
see you? As a colleague sharing information? As a good student showing
what you can do? As an advocate for a position? Often your stance is affected
by your genre: for example, lab reports require an objective, unemotional
stance that emphasizes the content and minimizes the writer's own attitudes. Memoir, by comparison, allows you to reveal your feelings about your
topic. Your stance is also affected by your purpose, as the two emails about
cars show. Your stance in a piece written to entertain will likely differ from
the stance you'd adopt to persuade.

You communicate (or downplay) your stance through your tone—through
the words you use and other ways your text expresses an attitude toward your
subject and audience. For example, in an academic essay you would state your
position directly—"the *Real Housewives* series reflects the values of American

society today"—a confident, authoritative tone. In contrast, using qualifiers like "might" or "I think" can give your writing a wishy-washy, uncertain tone: "I think the *Real Housewives* series might reflect some of the values of American society today." The following paragraph, from an essay analyzing a text, has a sarcastic tone that might be appropriate for a comment on a blog post but that isn't right for an academic essay:

> In "Just Be Nice," Stephen M. Carter complains about a boy who wore his pants too low, showing his underwear. Is that really something people should worry about? We have wars raging and terrorism happening every day, and he wants to talk about how inconsiderate it is for someone to wear his pants too low? If by that boy pulling his pants up, the world would be a better place and peace would break out in the Middle East, I'm sure everyone would buy a belt.

This writer clearly thinks Carter's complaint is trivial in comparison with the larger issues of the day, but her sarcastic tone belittles Carter's argument instead of answering it with a serious counterargument. Like every other element of writing, your tone must be appropriate for your rhetorical situation.

Just as you likely alter what you say depending on whether you're speaking to a boss, an instructor, a parent, or a good friend, so you need to make similar adjustments as a writer. It's a question of appropriateness: we behave in certain ways in various social situations, and writing is a social situation. You might sign an email to a friend with an XO, but in an email to your supervisor you'll likely sign off with a "Many thanks" or "Sincerely." To write well, you need to write with integrity, to say as much as possible what you wish to say; yet you also must understand that in writing, as in speaking, your stance and tone need to suit your purpose, your relationship to your audience, the way in which you wish your audience to perceive you, and your medium.

In writing as in other aspects of life, the Golden Rule applies: "Do unto audiences as you would have them do unto you." Address readers respectfully if you want them to respond to your words with respect.

Thinking about Stance

- *What is your stance, and how does it relate to your purpose for writing?*
  If you feel strongly about your topic and are writing an argument that
  tries to persuade your audience to feel the same way, your stance and
  your purpose fit naturally together. But suppose you are writing about
  the same topic with a different purpose—to demonstrate the depth of
  your knowledge about the topic, for example, or your ability to consider
  it in a detached, objective way. You will need to adjust your stance to
  meet the demands of this different purpose.

- *How should your stance be reflected in your tone?* Can your tone grow
  directly out of your stance, or do you need to "tone down" your attitude toward the topic or take a different tone altogether? Do you want
  to be seen as reasonable? angry? thoughtful? gentle? funny? ironic? If
  you're writing about something you want to be seen as taking very
  seriously, be sure that your language and even your font reflect that se-
  riousness. Check your writing for words that reflect the tone you want
  to convey—and for ones that do not (and revise as necessary).

- *How is your stance likely to be received by your audience?* Your tone and
  especially the attitude it projects toward your audience will affect how
  they react to the content of what you say.

- *Should you openly discuss your stance?* Do you want or need to announce
  your own perspective on your topic? Will doing so help you reach your
  audience, or would it be better not to say directly where you're coming
  from?

MEDIA / DESIGN

In its broadest sense, a medium is a go-between: a way for information to be
conveyed from one person to another. We communicate through many media, verbal and nonverbal: our bodies (we catch someone's eye, wave, nod);
our voices (we whisper, talk, shout, groan); and various technologies, including handwriting, print, telephone, radio, CD, film, and computer.

Each medium has unique characteristics that influence both what and
how we communicate. As an example, consider this message: "I haven't told
you this before, but I love you." Most of the time, we communicate such a

message in person, using the medium of voice (with, presumably, help from eye contact and touch). A phone call will do, though most of us would think it a poor second choice, and a handwritten letter or note would be acceptable, if necessary. Few of us would break such news on a website, with a tweet, or during a radio call-in program.

By contrast, imagine whispering the following sentence in a darkened room: "By the last decades of the nineteenth century, the territorial expansion of the United States had left almost all Indians confined to reservations." That sentence starts a chapter in a history textbook, and it would be strange indeed to whisper it into someone's ear. It is appropriate, however, in the textbook, in print or in an e-book, or on a *PowerPoint* slide accompanying an oral presentation.

As you can see, we can often choose among various media depending on our purpose and audience. In addition, we can often combine media to create multimedia texts. And different media allow us to use different ways or modes of expressing meaning, from words to images to sound to hyperlinks, that can be combined into multimodal formats.

No matter the medium or media, a text's design affects the way it is received and understood. A typed letter on official letterhead sends a different message than the same words handwritten on pastel stationery. Classic type sends a different message than *flowery italics*. Some genres and media (and audiences) demand photos, diagrams, or color. Some information is easier to explain—and read—in the form of a pie chart or a bar graph than in the form of a paragraph. Some reports and documents are so long and complex that they need to be divided into sections, which are then best labeled with headings. These are some of the elements to consider when you are thinking about how to design what you write.

Identify your media and design needs.　Does your writing situation call for a certain medium and design? A printed essay? An oral report with visual aids? A blog? A podcast? Academic assignments often assume a particular medium and design, but if you're unsure about your options or the degree of flexibility you have, check with your instructor.

Thinking about Media

- *What medium are you using—print?* spoken? electronic? a combination?—and how does it affect the way you will create your text? A printed résumé is usually no more than one page long; a scannable résumé sent via email has no length limits. An oral presentation should contain detailed information; accompanying slides should provide only an outline.

- *How does your medium affect your organization and strategies?* Long paragraphs are fine on paper but don't work well on the web. On presentation slides, phrases or keywords work better than sentences. In print, you need to define unfamiliar terms; on the web, you can sometimes just add a link to a definition found elsewhere.

- *How does your medium affect your language?* Some print documents require a more formal voice than spoken media; email and texting often invite greater informality.

- *How does your medium affect what modes of expression you use?* Should your text include photos, graphics, audio or video files, or links? Do you need slides, handouts, or other visuals to accompany an oral presentation?

Thinking about Design

- *What's the appropriate look for your rhetorical situation?* Should your text look serious? whimsical? personal? something else? What design elements will suit your audience, purpose, stance, genre, and medium?

- *What elements need to be designed?* Is there any information you would like to highlight by putting it in a box? Are there any key terms that should be boldfaced? Do you need navigation buttons? How should you indicate links?

- *What font(s) are appropriate* to your audience, purpose, stance, genre, and medium?

- *Are you including any visuals?* Should you? Will your audience expect or need any? Is there any information in your text that would be easier to understand as a chart or graph? If you need to include video or audio clips, how should the links be presented?

- *Should you include headings?* Would they help you organize your materials and help readers follow the text? Does your genre or medium require them?

- *Should you use a specific format?* MLA? APA?

FOUR

Starting Your Research
Joining the Conversation

WHAT DO YOU FIND MOST DIFFCULT about doing research? Gathering data? Writing it up? Documenting sources? For most students, the hardest part is just getting started. Researchers from Project Information Literacy, an ongoing study at the University of Washington's Information School, have found that U.S. students doing course-related research have the most difficulty with three things: getting started, defining a topic, and narrowing a topic. This chapter will help you tackle these tricky first steps, identify specific questions that will drive your research, and make a schedule to manage the many tasks involved in a research project.

At the same time, we aim to show you that doing research means more than just finding sources. College-level research is a discovery process: it's as much about the search for knowledge and answers as it is about managing sources. When we search, we go down expected and unexpected paths to answer interesting questions, to discover solutions to problems, and to come to new perspectives on old issues. Doing research means learning about something you want to know more about. It means finding out what's been said about that topic, listening to the variety of perspectives (including those that differ from your own)—and then adding your own ideas to that larger conversation when you write about that topic.

While this chapter suggests a sequence of activities for doing research, from finding a topic to coming up with a research question to establishing a schedule, keep in mind that you won't necessarily move through these stages in a fixed order. As you learn more about your topic, you may want to reexamine or change your focus. But first, you have to get started.

Find a Topic That Fascinates You

At its best, research begins as a kind of treasure hunt, an opportunity for you to investigate a subject that you care or wonder about. So finding that topic might be the single most important part of the process.

If you've been assigned a topic, study the instructions carefully so that you understand exactly what you are required to do. Does the assignment give you a list of specific topics to choose from or a general topic or theme to address? Does it specify the research methods? number and kinds of sources? a genre in which to write up your findings? Even if you've been assigned a particular topic and told how to go about researching it, you'll likely still need to decide what aspect of the topic you'll focus on. Consider the following assignment:

> Identify a current language issue that's being discussed and debated nationally or in your local community. Learn as much as you can about this issue by consulting reliable print and online sources. You may also want to interview experts on the issue. Then write a 5-to-7-page informative essay following MLA documentation style. And remember, your task is to report on the issue, not to pick one side over others.

This assignment identifies a genre (a report), research methods (interviews and published sources), a documentation style (MLA), and a general topic (a current language issue), but it leaves the specific issue up to the author. You might investigate how your local school district handles bilingual education for recent immigrants, for example, or you could research the debate about how texting and social media have affected writing habits. While this particular assignment is broad enough to allow you to choose a particular issue that interests you, even assignments that are more specific can be approached in a way that will make them interesting. Is there some aspect of the topic related to your major that you'd like to look into? For example, a political science major might research court cases about the issue.

If you get to choose your topic, think of it as an opportunity to learn about something that intrigues you. Consider topics related to your major, or to personal or professional interests. Are you a hunter who is concerned about legislation that impacts land rights in your hometown? Do the restrictions on downloading files from the internet affect you such that you'd like to understand the multiple sides of the issue? Maybe you're an environmentalist interested in your state's policies on fracking.

In addition to finding a topic that interests you, try to pick one that has not been overdone. Chances are, if you're tired of hearing about an issue—and if you've heard the same things said repeatedly—it's not going to be a good topic to research. Instead, pick a topic that is still being debated: the fact that people are talking about it will ensure that it's something others care about as well.

Think about doing research as an invitation to explore a topic that really matters to you. If you're excited about your topic, that excitement will take you somewhere interesting and lead you to ideas that will in turn inform what you know and think.

For ideas and inspiration, visit TED.com, a site devoted to "ideas worth spreading." While there, check out Steven Johnson's talk, "Where Good Ideas Come From."

Consider Your Rhetorical Situation

As you get started, think about your rhetorical situation, starting with the requirements of the assignment. You may not yet know your genre, and you surely won't know your stance, but thinking about those things now will help you when you're narrowing your topic and figuring out a research question.

- *Audience.* Who will be reading what you write? What expectations might they have, and what will they likely know about your topic? What kinds of sources will they consider credible?

- *Purpose*. What do you hope to accomplish by doing this research? Are you trying to report on the topic? argue a position? analyze the causes of something? something else?

- *Genre.* Have you been assigned to write in a particular genre? Will you argue a position? Narrate a historical event? Analyze some kind of data? Report information? something else?

- *Stance.* What is your attitude toward the topic—and toward your audience? How can you establish your authority with them, and how do you want them to see you? As a neutral researcher? an advocate for a cause? something else?

- *Context.* Do you have any length requirements? When is the due date? What other research has been done on your topic, and how does that affect the direction your research takes?

- *Media.* Are you required to use a certain medium? If not, what media will be most appropriate for your audience, your topic, and what you have to say about it? Will you want or need to include links to other information? audio? video?

- *Design.* Will you include photographs or other illustrations? present any data in charts or graphs? highlight any parts of the text? use headings or lists? Are you working in a discipline with any specific format requirements?

Don't worry if you can't answer all of these questions at this point or if some elements change along the way. Just remember to keep these questions in mind as you work.

Narrow Your Topic

A good academic research topic needs to be substantive enough that you can find adequate information but not so broad that you become overwhelmed by the number of sources you find. The topic "women in sports," for example, is too general; a quick search on *Google* will display hundreds of subtopics, from "Title IX" to "women's sports injuries." One way to find an aspect of a topic that interests you is to scan the subtopics listed in online search results. Additionally, online news sites like *Google News* and *NPR Research News* can give you a sense of current news or research related to your topic. Your goal is to move from a too-general topic to a manageable one, as shown on the facing page:

General topic: women in sports

Narrower topic: injuries among women athletes

Still narrower: injuries among women basketball players

Even narrower: patterns of injuries among collegiate women basketball players compared with their male counterparts

Notice how the movement from a broad topic to one with a much narrower focus makes the number of sources you will consult more manageable. But just as a topic that is too broad will yield an overwhelming number of sources, one that is too narrow will yield too little information. The topic "shin splints among women basketball players at the University of Tennessee," for example, is so narrow that there is probably not enough information available.

Another way of narrowing a topic is to think about what you already know. Have you had any experiences related to your topic? read about it? heard about it? talked with friends about it? Suppose you have been asked to investigate a current health debate for a public health class. You recall a 2015 outbreak of measles in California that prompted a debate about childhood vaccination requirements. Maybe you heard medical experts speaking on the radio about measles and how it spreads. You might also have read about some parents' concern that vaccines cause autism. These are all things that can help you to narrow a topic.

Whatever your topic, write down what you know about it and what you think. Do some brainstorming or some of the other activities for generating ideas. And if it's an issue that's being debated, you could use a search engine to find out what's being said. Exploring your topic in this way can give you an overview of the issue and help you find a focus that you'd like to pursue.

REFLECT. Review your research assignment. Make a list of three topics that you're considering and jot down what you already know about each. Review those notes. What do they suggest to you about your interest in these topics? Finally, narrow each one to a specific, manageable research topic. Which of the three now seems most promising?

Do Some Background Research

Becoming familiar with some existing research on your topic can provide valuable background information and give you an overview of the topic before you dive into more specialized source. It can also help you discover issues that have not been researched—or perhaps even identified. At this point, your goal should be to see your topic in a larger context and to begin formulating questions to guide the rest of your research.

You may want to take a look at some encyclopedias, almanacs, and other reference works, which can provide an overview of your topic and point you toward specific areas where you might want to follow up. Subject-specific encyclopedias provide more detail, including information about scholarly books to check out.

If you don't have access to a university library, see what information you can find online. Though free online encyclopedias such as *Wikipedia* may not be considered appropriate to cite as authoritative sources, such sites can be helpful in the early stages of research because they link to additional sources and will often summarize any controversies around a topic.

Finally, you might begin your background research by reading articles in popular newsmagazines or newspapers to get a sense of who's talking about the topic and what they're saying.

Articulate a Question Your Research Will Answer

Once you have sufficiently narrowed your topic, you will need to turn it into a question that will guide your research. Start by asking yourself what you'd like to know about your topic. A good research question should be simple and focused, but require more than a "yes" or "no" answer. "Yes" or "no" questions are not likely to lead you anywhere—and often obscure the complexity of an issue. Instead, ask an open-ended question that will lead you to gather more information and explore multiple perspectives on your topic. For example:

Topic: injuries among women soccer players

What you'd like to know: What are the current trends in injuries among women soccer players, and how are athletic trainers responding?

Kansas defender Stacy Leeper is tended to after suffering a game-ending injury.

This is a question that's focused, complex—and meaningful. Before settling on a research question, you should consider why the answer to that question matters. Why is it worth looking into and writing about? And why will others want to read about it? Answering the above question, for instance, can help athletic trainers see if their approach can be improved.

Keep your rhetorical context in mind as you work to be sure your research question is manageable in the time you have and narrow or open enough to address in the number of pages you plan to write. Consider also any genre requirements. If you're assigned to argue a position, for example, be sure your research question is one that will lead to an argument. Notice how each question below suggests a different genre:

A question that would lead to a report: What are the current trends in injuries among women soccer players?

A question that would lead to an analysis: Why do women soccer players suffer specific types of injuries during training?

A question that would lead to an argument: At what age should young girls interested in soccer begin serious athletic training to minimize the chance of injury?

Once you've settled on a research question, your next step is to do some more research. Keeping your question in mind will help you stay focused as you search. Your goal at this point is to look for possible answers to your question—to get a sense of the various perspectives on the issue and to start thinking about where you yourself stand.

REFLECT. Write a research question for your narrowed topic that would lead to a report, one that would lead to an analysis, and one that would lead to an argument. Remember, try to avoid "yes" or "no" questions.

Plot Out a Working Thesis

Once you've determined your research question and gathered more information, you should begin to think about what answers are emerging. When you think you've found the best possible answer, the next step is to turn it into a working thesis. Basically, a working thesis is your hypothesis, your best guess about the claim you will make based on your research thus far.

Your working thesis will not necessarily be your final thesis. As you conduct more research, you may find more support for it, but you may find new information that prompts you to rethink the position you take. Consider one working thesis on the question about why women soccer players experience so many injuries during training:

> Female soccer players sustain more injuries than their male counterparts during training because they use training methods that were developed for men; developing training methods to suit female physiology would reduce the incidence of injuries.

This working thesis makes a clear, arguable claim and provides reasons for that position.

Keeping in mind that your working thesis may well change as you learn more about your topic, stay flexible—and expect to revise it as your ideas develop. The more open your mind, the more you'll learn.

Establish a Schedule

A research project can seem daunting if you think of it as one big undertaking from beginning to end, rather than as a series of gradual tasks. Establishing a schedule will help you break your research into manageable steps, stay organized, and focus on the task at hand—and meet all your deadlines along the way. The following template can help you make a plan:

Working title:

Working thesis:

	Due Date
Choose a topic.	_____
Analyze your rhetorical situation.	_____
Do some preliminary research.	_____
Narrow your topic and decide on a research question.	_____
Plot out a working thesis.	_____
Do library and web research.	_____
Start a working bibliography.	_____
Turn in your research proposal and annotated bibliography.	_____
Plan and schedule any field research.	_____
Do any field research.	_____
Draft a thesis statement.	_____
Write out a draft.	_____
Get response.	_____
Do additional research, if needed.	_____
Revise.	_____

Prepare your list of works cited. _____

Edit. _____

Write your final draft. _____

Proofread. _____

Turn in the final draft. _____

FIVE

Evaluating Sources

YOUR RESEARCH QUESTION: Is it racist for a school to use American Indian mascots, symbols, or nicknames for its sports teams? To research this topic, rather than merely giving your opinion, you would need to consult reliable sources. Which do you trust more: the official "Statement of the U.S. Commission on Civil Rights on the Use of Native American Images and Nicknames as Sports Symbols," the *Wikipedia* page on the controversy, or a blog entry on the topic posted on ESPN's blog? Is it possible that they could all be useful? How will you know?

Your integrity as an author rests to some degree on the quality of the sources you cite, so your sources need to be appropriate and reliable. You can probably assume that an article or website recommended by a professor or an expert on your topic is a credible source of information.

But in the absence of such advice, and given the overwhelming amount of information available, it can be difficult to know which sources will be useful, appropriate, and relevant. Or, as media expert Howard Rheingold puts it, the unending stream of information on the internet calls for some serious "crap detection": we have to know how to separate the credible sources from the questionable ones. This chapter provides advice for determining which sources are appropriate for your purposes and then for reviewing those sources with a critical eye.

Which would you trust more: the official "Statement of the U.S. Commission on Civil Rights on the Use of Native American Images and Nicknames as Sports Symbols," the *Wikipedia* page on the Native American mascot controversy, or a *YouTube* video?

Is the Source Worth Your Attention?

A database search turns up fifty articles on your topic. The library catalog shows hundreds. *Google?* Thousands. So how do you decide which sources are worth your time and attention? Here are some questions to consider as you scan your search results.

What's the title? Does it sound relevant to your topic? Does it sound serious? humorous? What does the title tell you about the source's purpose?

Who are the authors? Are they experts on your topic? journalists? staff writers? Are they affiliated with any institution that would indicate their expertise—or affect their viewpoints? Check the source for biographical information, or look for this information elsewhere.

If, for example, you were researching brain injuries among NFL players, you might run across the opinions of two medical experts, Dr. Ann McKee and Dr. Elliott Pellman, each offering very different evidence about the long-term effects of concussions. Looking into their credentials and affiliations, you'd learn that McKee is a neurologist who specializes in brain injuries, while Pellman is a rheumatologist who specializes in the body more than the brain—and chairs a medical committee in the NFL—information that tells you something about each one's stance.

Who's the publisher or sponsor? Is it an academic press? a news organization? a government agency or nonprofit? a business or individual? Knowing the publisher or sponsor can tell you whether the content has been peer reviewed by experts, as is typical for scholarly works and government publications, or fact-checked, as news organizations typically require. Consider also whether the publication or its sponsor has a particular agenda, especially if it presents the opinions of an individual. That said, your topic may call for you to consult the personal blog or even the *Facebook* page of someone with expertise you can trust.

What's the URL, if it's an online source? A site's URL can tell you something about what kind of organization is sponsoring the site: *com* is used by commercial organizations, *edu* by colleges and universities, *org* by nonprofits, *gov* by government agencies.

"On the Internet, nobody knows you're a dog."

When was it published or last updated? Does your topic call for the most current sources or for older historical ones? Even if you're researching a current issue, you may still want to consult older sources to get a sense of the larger context. Likewise, if your topic calls for older sources, you may also want to read the current research on it. And if your source is on a website, check to see that the site itself and any links are still active.

Does it *look* academic? Are there any ads? What impression do you get from the fonts, headings, profile pictures or other images? What does the look of the text suggest about its purpose?

What's the genre? Pay particular attention to whether it's reporting information or arguing some kind of claim. You'll have reason to look for both, but for those that make an argument, you'll need to find multiple sources expressing a number of different perspectives.

Is it cited in other works? Are there links to it in other online sources? Has it been referenced or reposted? You can determine this by searching for the author and title using *Google Scholar*. For instance, if you enter *Susan Miller "Textual Carnivals,"* the search page returns the information shown below, which lets you know the work has been cited in 541 related articles. If many other writers refer or respond to this author's work, you can probably assume they find it credible.

[BOOK] Textual carnivals: The politics of composition
S **Miller** – 1993 – books.google.com
This is the first book-length study of the status of composition in English studies and the uneasy relationship between composition and literature. Composition studies and institutional histories of English studies have long needed this kind of clarification . . .
Cited by 541 Related articles

Imagine that you are conducting research on the controversy over using Native American mascots for athletic teams. You begin your research by doing an online search and come across a report entitled "Ending the Legacy of Racism in Sports & the Era of Harmful 'Indian' Sports Mascots." Looks promising, but will it be worth your attention? The guidelines above can help you make that decision.

Before you look at the report itself, take a moment to examine its origins and the homepage that hosts it. The report is written by the National Congress of American Indians (NCAI) and published on the organization's site. Note that the site URL ends with *org*, which tells you that the NCAI is a nonprofit organization. The "about NCAI" page tells you that the NCAI is an advocacy group whose mission is to represent the interests of American Indians and Alaskan Natives in a variety of legal, social, and economic issues. The organization also researches and reports on topics concerning Native peoples. Some more searching reveals that the NCAI is supported by government agencies and other organizations that can vouch for its credibility, and that its work is mentioned in such sources as *Slate* and the *Washington Post*. You can also see that the website is clean and professionally designed and (if you scroll to the copyright line at the very bottom of the page) has been recently updated. So far, so good.

Now that you've confirmed the report comes from a credible source, look more closely to see if it is relevant to your research topic. The title tells you that the report is arguing against the use of Native American mascots: one important perspective on your topic. The abstract gives a quick summary of how the report goes about advancing this position. Opening to the table of contents gives still more detail:

I. Harmful "Indian" Mascots and Negative Impacts

II. Ending Harmful Mascots—A National Priority for 45 Years

III. National Collegiate Athletic Association (NCAA) Policy on Hostile and Abusive Mascots

IV. State Policy Positions on Harmful Mascots in Schools

V. Professional Sports and Harmful Mascots

VI. Washington Football Team—Ending a Legacy of Racism

VII. Harmful Mascots: Racial Equity and Social Justice

VIII. References

APPENDIX A   Time Line of Race and Change—The Washington Football Team

APPENDIX B   Time Line of Selected College/University Mascot Name Changes and Other Important Events Addressing "Indian" Mascots

APPENDIX C   2009 US Supreme Court Amicus Brief Supporters

APPENDIX D   Groups with Resolutions to End Harmful Mascots

APPENDIX E   Groups Supporting End to Harmful Mascots

End Notes

—NATIONAL CONGRESS OF AMERICAN INDIANS, "Ending the Legacy of Racism in Sports & the Era of Harmful 'Indian' Sports Mascots"

From this overview, you learn that the article examines this topic from a historical perspective ("A National Priority for 45 Years"), in both college and professional sports, and focuses on concerns about "racial equality and social justice." The coverage seems both thorough and detailed—and the references and appendices even more so. Finally, note that the report is dated October 10, 2013, so it is recent enough to be useful.

Given all that you know about this source, is it worth your attention? We would say so. Even if you ultimately argue against the NCAI's position on this issue, the report provides valuable information about the history of the debate and one prominent side's argument.

That said, you should be mindful to research other relevant perspectives on your topic. In this case, another internet search turns up a letter from Washington Redskins owner Dan Snyder arguing for a different point of view from the one put forward by the NCAI. Snyder's letter was published in the *Washington Post* under the title "Letter from Washington Redskins owner Dan Snyder to fans." The title announces his stance as the team's owner writing to "Everyone in Our Washington Redskins Nation." In what follows, Snyder explains why he sees the mascot as a way of honoring Native Americans and the team's heritage. He points out that four players and the head coach of the original Redskins team were Native Americans and cites testimony and data from a 2004 survey conducted by the Annenberg Public Policy Center of the University of Pennsylvania, which found that 90 percent of Native Americans interviewed did not find the term "Redskins" offensive. This letter is definitely relevant to your topic and is probably worth your attention. As you go further in your research, you should seek out other credible sources arguing for or against this perspective.

REFLECT. Read Dan Snyder's letter on everyonesanauthor.tumblr.com and the sources he cites as evidence. Evaluate them to determine if they would be credible sources in this research situation. Describe their strengths and weaknesses.

Reading Sources with a Critical Eye

Once you've determined that a source is credible and appropriate, you'll need to read it closely, thinking carefully about the author's position, how (and how well) it's supported, and how it affects your understanding of the topic as a whole. If the internet has taught us anything, it's to not believe everything that we read. So as you read your sources, approach each one with a critical eye. The following questions can help you do so.

Consider your own rhetorical situation. Will the source help you achieve your purpose? Look at the preface, abstract, or table of contents to determine how extensively and directly it addresses your topic. Will your audience consider the source reliable and credible? Are they expecting you to cite certain kinds of materials, such as historical documents or academic journals?

What is the author's stance? Does the title indicate a certain attitude or perspective? How would you characterize the tone? Is it objective? argumentative? sarcastic? How does the author's stance affect its usefulness for your project?

Who is the audience for this work? Is it aimed at the general public? members of a field? a special interest group? policy makers? Sources written for a general audience may provide useful overviews or explanations. Sources aimed at experts may be more authoritative and provide more detail—but they can be challenging to understand.

What is the main point, and what has motivated the author to write? Is he or she responding to some other argument? What's the larger conversation on this issue? Is it clear why the topic matters?

What reasons and evidence does the author provide as support? Are the reasons fair, relevant, and sound? Is the evidence drawn from credible sources? Is the kind of evidence (statistics, facts, examples, expert testimony, and so on) appropriate to the point it's supporting? How persuasive do you find the argument?

Does the author acknowledge and respond to other viewpoints? Look for mention of multiple perspectives, not just the author's own view. And be sure to consider how fairly any counterarguments are represented. The most trustworthy sources represent other views and information fairly and accurately, even (especially) those that challenge their own.

Have you seen ideas given in this source in any other sources? Information found in multiple sources is more reliable than information you can find in only one place. Do other credible sources challenge this information? If so, you should assume that what's said in this source is controversial.

How might you use this source? Source materials can serve a variety of purposes in both your research and your writing. You might consult some sources for background information or to get a sense of the larger context for your topic. Other sources may provide support for your claims—or for your credibility as an author. Still others will provide other viewpoints, ones that challenge yours or that provoke you to respond. Most of all, they'll give you some sense of what's been said about your topic. Then, in writing up your research, you'll get your chance to say what *you* think—and to add your voice to the conversation.

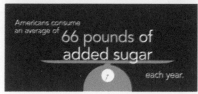

THINK
BEYOND
WORDS

SUPPOSE YOU'RE RESEARCHING current health issues and come across the website SugarScience.org, which claims to be "the authoritative source for evidence-based, scientific information about sugar and its impact on health." A quick look tells you that this site has been developed by a team of health scientists and includes infographics, maps, videos, and "an exhaustive review" of more than 8,000 scientific papers. If you were writing an essay about how sugar consumption has contributed to the obesity crisis, what from this site would you likely cite? How does the way information is presented make it seem more or less credible? For instance, compare the report on sugar "Hidden in Plain Sight" with the infographic shown above. Does one seem more appropriate as a source than the other—and if so, why?

REFLECT. Choose three or four different sources on your chosen topic— possibly one from a government source, one from an academic journal, one from a popular source, and one from a website. Evaluate each of the sources according to the guidelines laid out in this chapter. Explain what makes each source credible (or not).

SIX

Synthesizing Ideas

Moving from What Your Sources Say to What You Say

IT'S SUPER BOWL SUNDAY, just before kickoff and just after the teams have been introduced. The broadcast cuts back from a commercial set to DJ Schmolli's "Super Bowl Anthem" and returns to the stadium where Idina Menzel is singing the "Star-Spangled Banner." So you've just heard two anthems. But what else, if anything, do these tunes have in common? Answer: each is a mash-up—a combination of material from a number of different sources. The "Star-Spangled Banner" combines a poem written by Francis Scott Key with the music of an old British drinking song. DJ Schmolli's effort combines clips from more than a dozen popular stadium anthems, from Madonna's "Celebration" to Queen's "We Will Rock You." And each smoothly integrates its sources into one seamless whole. In academic terms, the authors of these mash-ups have effectively engaged in synthesis, bringing together material from various sources to create something new.

Like a good mash-up artist, you don't just patch together ideas from various sources when you do research. Instead, you synthesize what they say to help you think about and understand the topic you're researching—to identify connections among them and blend them into a coherent whole that at the same time articulates *ideas of your own*. This chapter will help you blend ideas from sources with your own ideas smoothly and effectively—just like a really great mash-up.

An unlikely mash-up: Jane Austen's *Pride and Prejudice* and . . . zombies! With 85% Austen's original text and 15% zombie blood and gore, *Pride and Prejudice and Zombies* became an instant best-seller, setting off a slew of literary monster mash-ups.

Synthesizing the Ideas in Your Sources

Here are some questions to help you synthesize information as you work with your sources:

- What issues, problems, or controversies do your sources address?

- What else do your sources have in common? Any ideas? facts? examples? statistics? Are any people or works cited in more than one source?

- What significant differences do you find among sources? Different stances? positions? purposes? kinds of evidence? conclusions?

- Do any of your sources cite or refer to one another? Does one source provide details, examples, or explanations that build on something said in another? Does any source respond specifically to something said in another?

Your goal is to get a sense of how the information from your various sources fits together—how the sources speak to one another and what's being said about your topic.

One function of a synthesis is to establish context and set the scene for what you yourself have to say. See how the following example from an academic article on high-stakes testing brings together information from a number of sources about the history of testing as context for the discussion of trends in school testing today.

> Although the practice of high-stakes testing gained a prominent position in educational reform with the passage of the No Child Left Behind Act (NCLB) of 2002, its use as a lever for school change preceded NCLB. Tests have been used to distribute rewards and sanctions to teachers in urban schools since the mid 1800s (Tyack, 1974) and for most schools throughout the United States since at least the 1970s (Haertel & Herman, 2005). New York state in particular has led the United States in test-based accountability efforts, "implementing state-developed (1965) and mandated minimal competency testing (MCT) before most other states (1978) and disseminating information to the media about local district performance on the state assessments before it became routinely popular (1985)" (Allington & McGill-Franzen, 1992, p. 398).
>
> —SHARON NICHOLS, GENE GLASS, AND DAVID BERLINER,
> "High-stakes Testing and Student Achievement"

Look now at this dramatic opening to a magazine article on actor-comedian Robin Williams' death:

> If you were keeping an eye on Robin Williams' *Twitter* feed these past few months—along with his 875,000 followers—you would have noticed nothing the least bit worrying about the 63-year-old actor-comedian's state of mind. On June 6, he uploaded a photo of himself visiting the San Francisco Zoo, where one of the monkeys had been named after him ("What an honor!"). On July 30, he posted a plug for his December movie, *Night at the Museum: Secret of the Tomb* ("I hope you enjoy it!"). And then, on July 31, in what would turn out to be his last public comment, he tweeted his daughter Zelda a birthday message ("Quarter of a century old today but always my baby girl").
>
> Eleven days later, he was discovered dead at his home in Marin County, California. —BENJAMIN SVETKEY, "Robin Williams Remembered by Critics, Close Friends"

By synthesizing multiple sources—in this case, Williams' *Twitter* posts—and presenting them as one cohesive whole, Svetkey paints a picture of a seemingly happy man.

While these two examples are quite different—one cites academic sources in an academic publication, the other cites social media sources in a popular magazine—they both synthesize information to give readers context for what the authors go on to say. For all writers, including you, that's the next step.

REFLECT. Try your hand at synthesizing the sources you've consulted so far for something you're writing. What patterns do you see? What's being said about your topic?

Moving from What Your Sources Say to What You Say

As a researcher, you'll always be working to synthesize the ideas and information you find in your research, to see the big picture and make sense of it all. At the same time, you'll be striving to connect the data you gather to your own ideas and to your research goals. You'll be learning a lot about what many others have discovered or said about your topic, and that will surely affect what you yourself think—and write—about it. Here are some questions that can help you move from the ideas you find in your sources to the ideas that you'll then write about:

- How do the ideas and information in your sources address your research question? What answers do they give? What information do you find the most relevant, useful, and persuasive?

- How do they support your tentative thesis? Do they suggest reasons or ways that you should expand, qualify, or otherwise revise it?

- What viewpoints in your sources do you most agree with? disagree with? Why?

- What conclusions can you draw from the ideas and information you've learned from your sources? What discoveries have you made in studying these sources, and what new ideas have they led you to?

- Has your research changed your own views on your topic? Do any of your sources raise questions that you can pursue further?

- Have you encountered any ideas that you would like to build on— or challenge?

- From everything you've read, what is the significance of the topic you're researching? Who cares, and why does it matter?

When you work with your sources in this way, you can count on your ideas to grow—and maybe to change. As we've been saying, research is an act of learning and inquiry, and you never know where it will lead. But as soon as you sit down and write, no matter what you say or how you say it, you will be, as Kenneth Burke says, "putting in your oar," adding your voice *and your ideas* to the very conversation you've been researching.

THINK BEYOND WORDS

WATCH **Cause/Effect: The Unexpected Origins of Terrible Things,** *a video essay by Adam Westbrook that makes a fascinating argument about what caused World War I. (You'll find it at everyonesanauthor.tumblr.com.) As you'll see, Westbrook synthesizes many kinds of sources and information—history books, maps, cartoons, newspapers, archival photographs and video, data from public records, and more—to build a case for his argument. How does he synthesize all these sources in a video? How does he go about introducing each one and weaving them together with his own ideas?*

Entering the Conversation You've Been Researching

Once you've thought carefully about what others have said about your topic, you can add your own voice to the conversation. Look at the following example from the introduction to an essay tracing the changes in political cartoons in the United States between World War II and the Iraq War. See how the writer synthesized ideas from her research into her writing in a way that set up her own questions and thoughts.

A cartoon shows carolers at the White House door making a choral argument to then president George W. Bush that "we gotta get out of this place," referring to America's involvement in the war in Iraq (fig. I). Bush appears completely oblivious to their message.

First published in 2006, this cartoon offered a critique of America's continued presence in Iraq by criticizing the president's actions and attitudes towards the war, exemplifying how political cartoons have long been, and continue to be, a prominent part of wartime propaganda. Combining eye-catching illustrations with textual critique, such cartoons

Fig. I. A cartoon criticizing war in Iraq (Copley News Service, 2006).

do more than merely convey messages about current events. Rather, political cartoons serve as a tool for shaping public opinion. In fact, since the 1500s, political cartoons have used satirical critiques to persuade the general public about matters large and small (McCloud 16–17).

In the United States, the political (or editorial) cartoon is a form of editorializing that began as "scurrilous caricatures," according to Stephen Becker, author of *Comic Art in America*. His book looks, in part, at the social history of political cartoons and states that it was only after "newspapers and magazines came to be published regularly . . . that caricatures, visual allegories, and the art of design were combined to form . . . modern editorial art" (15). As all-encompassing as that description of "modern editorial art" seems to be, it suggests several questions that remain unanswered: Do cartoonists use common themes to send their critical messages? As society and regulations change from generation to generation, do the style and content of political cartoons change as well? Have political cartoons become "modernized" since World War II? The essay that follows aims to answer as well as draw out the implications of these questions.   —JULIA LANDAUER, "War, Cartoons, and Society: Changes in Political Cartoons between World War II and the Iraq War"

Landauer begins with a cartoon (a primary source) that illustrates a point she is making—that editorial cartoons are known for stinging political critiques. She then refers to a source (McCloud) to provide some background information and then another (Becker) to provide additional commentary on the "modern editorial art" she intends to examine in her essay. At that point, she raises questions "that remain unaddressed"—and says that answering them will be the work of her essay. Thus she uses ideas drawn from her sources to introduce her own ideas—and weave them all together into a strong introduction to her essay.

In your college writing, you will have the opportunity to come up with a research question and to dig in and do some research in order to answer it. That digging in will lead you to identify key sources already in conversation about your topic, to read and analyze those sources, and to begin synthesizing them with your own ideas. Before you know it, you won't be just listening in on the conversation: you'll be an active participant in it.

SEVEN

Quoting, Paraphrasing, Summarizing

WHEN YOU'RE TEXTING or talking with friends, you don't usually need to be explicit about where you got your information; your friends trust what you say because they know you. In academic writing, however, it's important to establish your credibility, and one way to do so is by consulting authoritative sources. Doing so shows that you've done your homework on your topic, gives credit to those whose ideas you've relied on, and helps demonstrate your own authority as an author.

Your challenge in much academic writing is to integrate other voices with your own. How do you let your audience hear from expert sources while ensuring that their words don't eclipse yours? How do you pick and choose brief segments from long passages of text—or condense those passages into much briefer statements—without misrepresenting someone's ideas? How do you then introduce these segments and integrate them with your own words and ideas? This chapter provides guidelines on the three ways you can incorporate sources into your writing: quoting, paraphrasing, and summarizing.

A quotation consists of someone's exact words, enclosed in quotation marks or set off as a block from the rest of your text. A paraphrase includes the details of a passage in your own words and syntax. A summary contains the points of a passage that are important to your purpose, leaving out the other details.

Deciding Whether to Quote, Paraphrase, or Summarize

Quote

- Something that is said so well that it's worth repeating
- Complex ideas that are expressed so clearly that paraphrasing or summarizing could distort or oversimplify them
- Experts whose opinions and exact words help to establish your own credibility and authority to write on the topic
- Passages that you yourself are analyzing
- Those who disagree or offer counterarguments—quoting their exact words is a way to be sure you represent their opinions fairly

Paraphrase

- Passages where the details matter, but not the exact words
- Passages that are either too technical or too complicated for your readers to understand

Summarize

- Lengthy passages when the main point is important to your argument but the details are not

Whatever method you use for incorporating the words and ideas of others into your own writing, be sure that they work to support what *you* want to say. You're the author—and whatever your sources say needs to connect to what you say—so be sure to make that connection clear. Don't assume that sources speak for themselves. Introduce any source that you cite, naming the authors and identifying them in some way if your audience won't know who they are. In addition, be sure to follow quotations with a comment that explains how they relate to your point.

And regardless of whether you decide to quote, paraphrase, or summarize, you'll need to credit each source. Even if what you include is not a direct quotation, the ideas are still someone else's, and failing to credit your source can result in plagiarism. Indicate the source in a signal phrase and include in-text documentation.

Quoting

When you include a direct quotation, be sure to use the exact words of the original source. And while you don't want to include too many quotations—you are the author, after all—using the exact words from a source is sometimes the best way to ensure that you accurately represent what was said. Original quotations can also be an effective way of presenting a point, by letting someone speak in his or her own words. But be sure to frame any quotation you include, introducing it and then explaining why it's important to the point that you are making.

Enclose short quotations in quotation marks within your main text. Such quotations should be no longer than four typed lines (in MLA style) or forty words (in APA style).

> Programmer and digital media pioneer Jaron Lanier describes the problems resulting from "lock-in" (in which software becomes difficult to change because it has been engineered to work with existing programs), arguing that lock-in "is an absolute tyrant in the digital world" (8). By that he means, "lock-in" inhibits creativity as new development is constrained by old software.

In MLA style, short quotations of poetry—no more than three lines—should also be enclosed in quotation marks within the main text. Include slashes (with a space on either side) between each line of verse.

> In "When You are Old," poet William Butler Yeats advises Maud Gonne, the radical Irish nationalist, that when she looks back on her youth from old age, she should consider "How many loved your moments of glad grace, / And loved your beauty with love false or true, / But one man loved the pilgrim soul in you." Yeats thus suggests that he is the "one man" who truly loved her so sincerely all these years.

Set off long quotations as a block by indenting them from the left margin. No need to enclose them in quotation marks, but do indent five spaces (or one-half inch) if you are using either MLA or APA style. Use this method for quotations that are more than four lines of prose or three lines of poetry (in MLA) or longer than forty words (in APA).

In her 1976 keynote address to the Democratic National Convention, Texas congresswoman Barbara Jordan reflects on the occasion:

Go to everyones
anauthor.tumblr
.com to listen to
the full text of
Barbara Jordan's
speech.

> Now that I have this grand distinction, what in the world am I supposed to say? I could easily spend this time praising the accomplishments of this party and attacking the Republicans—but I don't choose to do that. I could list the many problems which Americans have. I could list the problems which cause people to feel cynical, angry, frustrated: problems which include lack of integrity in government; the feeling that the individual no longer counts; the reality of material and spiritual poverty; the feeling that the grand American experiment is failing or has failed. I could recite these problems, and then I could sit down and offer no solutions. But I don't choose to do that either. The citizens of America expect more. They deserve and they want more than a recital of problems. (189)

In this passage, Jordan resists the opportunity to attack the opposing party, preferring instead to offer positive solutions rather than simply a list of criticisms and problems.

Notice that with block quotations, the parenthetical citation falls *after* the period at the end of the quotation.

Indicate changes to the text within a quotation by using brackets to enclose text that you add or change and ellipses to indicate text that you omit.

Use brackets to indicate that you have altered the original wording to fit grammatically within your text or have added or changed wording to clarify something that might otherwise be unclear. In this example, the author changed the verb *had* to *should have*:

> John Maeda, president of the Rhode Island School of Design, reacts to America's current emphasis on STEM education with the proposal that "just like STEM is made up of science, technology, engineering and math, we [should have] IDEA, made up of intuition, design, emotion and art—all the things that make us humans feel, well, human" ("On Meaningful Observation").

Use ellipsis marks in place of words, phrases, or sentences that you leave out because they aren't crucial or relevant for your purpose. Use three dots, with a space before each one and after the last, when you omit only words and phrases within a sentence. If you leave out the end of a sentence or a whole sentence or more, put a period after the last word before the ellipsis mark. Note how a writer does both in the example below.

> Warning of the effects of GPS on our relationship to the world around us, Nicholas Carr concludes that "the automation of wayfinding . . . encourages us to observe and manipulate symbols on screens rather than attend to real things in real places. . . . What we should be asking ourselves is, *How far from the world do we want to retreat?* " (137)

When you use brackets or ellipses, make sure your changes don't end up misrepresenting the author's original point, which would damage your own credibility. Mark Twain once joked that "nearly any invented quotation, played with confidence, stands a good chance to deceive." Twain was probably right—it's quite easy to "invent" quotations or twist their meaning by taking them out of context or changing some key word. You don't want to be guilty of this! And of course, be careful that you don't introduce any grammatical errors by altering the quotation.

Set off a quotation within a quotation with single quotation marks. In the following passage, the author quotes Nicholas Carr, who himself quotes the writing of anthropologist Tim Ingold:

> Nicholas Carr sums up the difference between navigating with and without a GPS device using two terms borrowed from Scottish anthropologist Tim Ingold. As Carr explains, Ingold "draws a distinction between two very different modes of travel: wayfaring and transport. Wayfaring, he explains, is 'our most fundamental way of being in the world' " (132). It is navigating by our observations and mental maps of the world around us, as opposed to blindly following GPS-generated directions from point A to point B—the mode Ingold and Carr call "transport."

Punctuate quotations carefully. Parenthetical documentation comes after the closing quotation mark, and any punctuation that is part of your sentence comes after the parentheses (except in the case of a block quote, where the parenthetical documentation goes at the very end).

- *Commas and periods* always go inside the closing quotation marks. If there's parenthetical documentation, however, the period goes after the parentheses.

  > "Everybody worships," said David Foster Wallace in a 2005 commencement speech. "There is no such thing as not worshipping" (8).

- *Colons and semicolons* always go outside closing quotation marks.

  > Wallace warned as well that there are "whole parts of adult American life that nobody talks about in commencement speeches": sometimes, he says, we'll be bored (4).

  > He also once noted that when a lobster is put in a kettle of boiling water, it "behaves very much as you or I would behave if we were plunged into boiling water"; in other words, it acts as if it's in terrible pain (10).

- *Question marks and exclamation points* go inside closing quotation marks if they are part of the original quotation, but outside the quotation marks if they are part of your sentence.

> Wallace opened his speech with a now famous joke about how natural it is to be unaware of the world: an old fish swims by two young fish and says, "Morning, boys. How's the water?" They swim on, and after a while one young fish turns to the other and asks, "What the hell is water?" (I)

> So what, according to David Foster Wallace, is the "capital-T Truth about life" (9)?

Paraphrasing

When you paraphrase, you restate information or ideas from a source using your words, your sentence structure, your style. A paraphrase should cover the same points that the original source does, so it's usually about the same length—but sticking too closely to the sentence structures in your source could be plagiarizing. And even though you're using your own words, don't forget where the ideas came from: you should always name the author and include parenthetical documentation.

Here is a paragraph about the search for other life-forms similar to our own in the universe, followed by three paraphrases.

Original source

> As the romance of manned space exploration has waned, the drive today is to find our living, thinking counterparts in the universe. For all the excitement, however, the search betrays a profound melancholy—a lonely species in a merciless universe anxiously awaits an answering voice amid utter silence. That silence is maddening. Not just because it compounds our feeling of cosmic isolation, but because it makes no sense. As we inevitably find more and more exo-planets where intelligent life *can* exist, why have we found no evidence—no signals, no radio waves—that intelligent life *does* exist?
> —CHARLES KRAUTHAMMER, "Are We Alone in the Universe?"

As the underlined words show, the following paraphrase uses too many words from the original.

Unacceptable paraphrase: wording too close to the original

Charles Krauthammer argues that finding our intelligent <u>counterparts in the universe</u> has become more important as the <u>romance of manned space exploration</u> has declined. Even so, the hunt for similar beings also suggests our sadness as a species waiting in vain for an acknowledgment that we aren't alone in <u>a merciless universe</u>. The lack of response, he says, just doesn't make sense because if we keep finding planets that *could* support life, then we should find evidence—like <u>radio waves or signals</u>—of intelligent life out there (A19).

While the next version uses original language, the sentence structures are much too similar to the original.

Unacceptable paraphrase: sentence structures too close to original

As the allure of adventuring into the unknown cosmos has diminished, the desire to discover beings like us out there has grown. There is a sadness to the search though—the calling out into empty space that brings no response. Nothing. Only a vast silence that not only emphasizes our solitary existence but increases our frustration. How can we continue to discover potentially hospitable planets that could sustain life like ours, yet find no evidence—no signs, no data—that such life exists (Krauthammer A19)?

When you paraphrase, be careful not to simply substitute words and phrases while replicating the same sentence structure. And while it may be necessary to use some of the key terms from the original in order to convey the same concepts, be sure to put them in quotation marks—and not to use too many (which would result in plagiarism).

Acceptable paraphrase

Syndicated columnist Charles Krauthammer observes that our current quest to discover other "intelligent life" in the universe comes just as

the allure of exploring outer space is dimming. It's a search, he says,
that reveals a deep sadness (that we may in fact be living in "cosmic
isolation") and a growing frustration: if scientists continue to discover
more planets where life like ours can be sustainable, why do we find no
actual signs of life (A19)?

Summarizing

Like a paraphrase, a summary presents the source information in your
words. However, a summary dramatically condenses the information, covering only the most important points and leaving out the details. Summaries are therefore much briefer than the original texts, though they vary in
length depending on the size of the original and your purpose for summarizing; you may need only a sentence or two to summarize an essay, or you
may need several paragraphs. In any case, you should always name the author and document the source. The following example appropriately summarizes Krauthammer's passage in one sentence:

> Charles Krauthammer questions whether we will ever find other
> "intelligent life" in the universe—or whether we'll instead discover that
> we do in fact live in "cosmic isolation" (A19).

This summary tells readers Krauthammer's main point, and includes in
quotation marks two key phrases borrowed from the original source. If we
were to work the summary into an essay, it might look like this:

> Many scientists believe that there is a strong probability—given the
> vastness of the universe and how much of it we have yet to explore,
> even with advances like the Hubble telescope—that there is life
> like ours somewhere out there. In a 2011 opinion piece, however,
> syndicated columnist Charles Krauthammer questions whether we
> will ever find other "intelligent life" in the universe—or whether we'll
> instead discover that we do in fact live in "cosmic isolation" (A19).

Three ways a summary can go wrong are if it represents inaccurately the
point of the original source, provides so many details that the summary is too

long, or is so general that readers are left wondering what the source is about. Consider the following unsuccessful summaries of Krauthammer's passage:

Unacceptable summary: misrepresents the source

> Pulitzer Prize–winning columnist Charles Krauthammer extols the virtues of space exploration.

This summary both misses the point of Krauthammer's questioning our troubled search for "intelligent life" beyond earth and claims that the author praises space exploration when at no point in the passage does he do so.

Unacceptable summary: provides too many details

> Award-winning columnist Charles Krauthammer suggests that while sending people into space is no longer as exciting to us as it once was, we are interested in finding out if there is life in the universe beyond Earth. He laments the feeling of being alone in the universe given that all signs point to the very real possibility that intelligent life exists elsewhere. Krauthammer wonders "why we have no evidence . . . of intelligent life" on other habitable planets. He finds this lack of proof confounding.

This summary is almost as long as the original passage and includes as many details. As a summary, it doesn't let readers know what points are most important.

Unacceptable summary: too general

> Charles Krauthammer is concerned about the search for life on other planets.

While the statement above is not false, it does not adequately reflect Krauthammer's main point in a way that will help the reader get the gist of the original passage. A better summary would tell readers what precisely about the search for life concerns Krauthammer.

REFLECT. Return to the quotation from Barbara Jordon on p. 72. First, write an appropriate paraphrase of the quotation; then write an appropriate summary.

Incorporating Source Material

Whether you quote, paraphrase, or summarize source material, you need to be careful to distinguish what you say from what your sources say, while at the same time weaving the two together smoothly in your writing. That is, you must make clear how the ideas you're quoting, paraphrasing, or summarizing relate to your own—why you're bringing them into your text.

Use signal phrases to introduce source materials, telling readers who said what and providing some context if need be. Don't just drop in a quotation or paraphrase or summary; you need to introduce it. And while you can always use a neutral signal phrase such as "he says" or "she claims," try to choose verbs that reflect the stance of those you're citing. In some cases, a simple "she says" does reflect that stance, but usually you can make your writing livelier and more accurate with a more specific signal verb.

Use a signal phrase and parenthetical documentation to clearly distinguish your own words and ideas from those of others. The following paraphrase introduces source material with a signal phrase that includes the author's name and closes with documentation giving the page number from which the information is taken.

> As Ernst Mayr explains, Darwin's theory of evolution presented a
> significant challenge to then-prevalent beliefs about man's centrality in
> the world (9).

If you do not give the author's name in a signal phrase, include it in the parenthetical documentation.

> Darwin's theory of evolution presented a significant challenge to then-
> prevalent beliefs about man's centrality in the world (Mayr 9).

Sometimes you'll want or need to state the author's credentials in the signal phrase, explaining his or her authority on the topic—and at the same time lending credibility to your own use of that source.

> According to music historian Ted Gioia, record sales declined sharply
> during the Great Depression, dropping by almost 90 percent between
> 1927 and 1932 (127).

Choose verbs that reflect the author's stance toward the material—or your own stance in including it. Saying someone "notes" means something different than saying he or she "insists" or "implies."

> Because almost anyone can create a blog, most people assume that blogs give average citizens a greater voice in public dialogue. Political scientist Matthew Hindman questions this assumption: "Though millions of Americans now maintain a blog, only a few dozen political bloggers get as many readers as a typical college newspaper" (103).

Signal phrases do not have to come first. To add variety to your writing, try positioning them in the middle or at the end of a sentence.

> "Attracting attention," observes Richard Lanham, "is what style is all about" (xi).

> "We've got to stop the debates! Enough with the debates!" pleaded John McCain last Sunday on *Meet the Press* (31).

> Noting the importance of literacy in American lives today, rhetorician Deborah Brandt argues, "Writing is at the heart of the knowledge economy" (117).

SOME USEFUL SIGNAL VERBS

acknowledges	contends	replies
adds	declares	reports
agrees	disagrees	responds
asserts	implies	says
believes	notes	suggests
claims	objects	thinks
concludes	observes	writes

Verb tenses. The verb tense you use when referring to a text or researcher in a signal phrase will depend on your documentation style. MLA style requires the present tense (*argues*) or the present perfect (*has argued*). Using

MLA style, you might write, "In *Rhetoric*, Aristotle argues" or "In commenting on Aristotle's *Rhetoric*, scholars have argued." An exception involves sentences that include specific dates in the past. In this case, the past tense is acceptable: "In his introduction to the 1960 edition of Aristotle's *Rhetoric*, Lane Cooper argued."

The past tense is conventional in APA style, as is the present perfect. As in, "In *Rhetoric*, Aristotle argued" or "In commenting on Aristotle's *Rhetoric*, scholars have argued." However, use the present tense when you refer to the results of a study ("the results of Conrad (2012) demonstrate") or when you make a generalization ("writing researchers agree").

Parenthetical documentation. If you're following MLA, you'll need to include page numbers for all quotations, paraphrases, and summaries from print sources in your parenthetical documentation. If you're using APA, page numbers are required for quotations; for paraphrases and summaries, they're optional—but it's always a good idea to include them whenever you can do so.

Incorporating Visual and Audio Sources

Sometimes you will want to incorporate visual or audio elements from sources that you cannot write into a paragraph. For example, you may include charts, tables, photographs, or drawings—and in online writing, you might include audio or video clips as well. Remember that any such materials that come from sources need to be introduced, explained, and documented just as you would a quotation. If you're following MLA or APA style, refer to chapters 17 and 18 for specific requirements.

Tables. Label anything that contains facts or figures displayed in columns as a table. Number all tables in sequence, and provide a descriptive title for each one. Supply source information immediately below the table; credit your data source even if you've created the table yourself. If any information within the table requires further explanation (abbreviations, for example), include a note below the source citation.

Figures. Number and label everything that is not a table (photos, graphs, drawings, maps, and so on) as a figure and include a caption letting readers know what the image illustrates. Unless the visual is a photograph or drawing you created yourself, provide appropriate source information after the caption; graphs, maps, and other figures you produce based on information from other sources should still include a full credit. If the visual is discussed in detail within your text, you can use an abbreviated citation and include full documentation in your works cited or references list.

Audio and video recordings. If your medium allows it, provide a link to any recorded element or embed a media player into the text. If you're working in a medium that won't allow linking or embedding, discuss the recording in your text and provide a full citation in your works cited or references list so your readers can track down the recording themselves.

Captions. Create a clear, succinct caption for each visual or recording: "Fig. 1: The Guggenheim Museum, Spain." The caption should identify and explain the visual—and should reflect your purpose. In an essay about contemporary architecture in Spain, your caption might say "Fig. 1: The Guggenheim

Fig. I: The Guggenheim Museum, Spain.

Museum, Bilbao. Designed by Frank Gehry." If you're blogging about field research in Bilbao, your caption might say something different, perhaps "A roller coaster building: the Guggenheim!"

Sizing and positioning visuals and recordings. Refer to every visual or embedded recording in your text: "(see fig. 1)," "as shown in Table 3," "in the *YouTube* video below." The element may be on the page where it's discussed, but it should not come before you introduce it to your readers. Think carefully about how you will size and position each visual to be most effective: you want to make sure that your visuals are legible, and that they support rather than disrupt the text.

EIGHT

Giving Credit,
Avoiding Plagiarism

WHO OWNS WORDS AND IDEAS? Answers to this question differ from culture to culture: In some societies, they are shared resources, not the property of individuals. In others, using another person's words or ideas may be seen as a tribute or compliment that doesn't require specific acknowledgment. In the United States, however (as well as in much of the Western world), elaborate systems of copyright and patent law have grown up to protect the intellectual property (including words, images, voices, and ideas) of individuals and corporations. This system forms the foundation of the documentation conventions currently followed in U.S. schools. And while these conventions are being challenged today by the open-source movement and others who argue that "information wants to be free," the conventions still hold sway in the academy and in the law. As a researcher, you will need to understand these conventions and to practice them in your own writing. Put simply, these conventions allow you to give credit where credit is due and thereby avoid plagiarism (the use of the words and ideas of others as if they were your own work).

But acknowledging your sources is not simply about avoiding charges of plagiarism (although you would be doing that too). Rather, it helps establish your own credibility as a researcher and an author. It shows that you have consulted other sources of information about your topic and can engage with them in your own work. Additionally, citing and documenting your sources allows readers to locate them for their own purposes if they wish; in effect, it anticipates the needs of your audience.

There are some cases, however, in which you do not need to provide citations for information that you incorporate—for example, if the information is common knowledge. This chapter will help you identify which sources you must acknowledge, explain the basics of documenting your sources, and provide strategies for avoiding plagiarism.

Knowing What You Must Acknowledge

As a general rule, material taken from specific outside sources—whether ideas, texts, images, or sounds—should be cited and documented. But there are some exceptions.

INFORMATION THAT DOES NOT NEED TO BE ACKNOWLEDGED

- *Information that is "common knowledge."* Uncontroversial information ("People today get most of their news and information from the internet"), well-known historical events ("Neil Armstrong was the first person to walk on the moon"), facts ("All mammals are warm-blooded"), and quotations (Armstrong's "That's one small step for man, one giant leap for mankind") that are widely available in general reference sources do not need to be cited.

- *Information well known to your audience.* Keep in mind that what is common knowledge varies depending on your audience. While an audience of pulmonary oncologists would be familiar with the names of researchers who established that smoking is linked to lung cancer, for a general audience you might need to cite a source if you give the names.

- *Information from well-known, easily accessible documents.* You do not need to include the specific location where you accessed texts that are available from a variety of public sources and are widely familiar, such as the United States Constitution.

- *Your own work.* If you've gathered data, come up with an idea, or generated a text (including images, multimedia texts, and so on) entirely on your own, you should indicate that to your readers in some way—but it's not necessary to include a formal citation, unless the material has been previously published elsewhere.

INFORMATION THAT MUST BE ACKNOWLEDGED

- *Direct quotations, paraphrases, and summaries.* Exact wording should always be enclosed in quotation marks and cited. And always cite specific ideas taken from another source, even when you present them using your own words.

- *Controversial information.* If there is some debate over the information you're including, cite the source so readers know whose version or interpretation of the facts you're using.

- *Information given in only a few sources.* If only one or two sources make this information available (that is, it isn't common knowledge widely accessible in general sources), include a citation.

- *Any materials that you did not create yourself*—including tables, charts, images, and audio or video segments. Even if you create a table or chart yourself, if it presents information from an outside source, that's someone else's work that needs to be acknowledged.

A word to the wise: it's always better to cite any information that you've taken from another source than to guess wrong and unintentionally plagiarize. If in doubt, err on the safe side and include a citation.

Fair Use and the Internet

In general, principles of fair use apply to the writing you do for your college classes. These principles allow you to use passages and images from the copyrighted work of others without their explicit permission as long as you do so for educational purposes and you fully cite what you use. When you publish your writing online, however, where that material can be seen by all, then you must have permission from the copyright owner in order to post it.

Students across the country have learned about this limitation on fair use the hard way. One student we know won a prize for an essay she wrote, which was then posted on the writing prize website. In the essay, she included a cartoon that was copyrighted by the cartoonist. Soon after the essay was posted, she received a letter from the copyright holder, demanding that she remove the image and threatening her with a lawsuit. Another student, whose essay was published on a class website, was stunned when his instructor got an angry email from a professor at another university, saying that the student writer had used too much of her work in the essay and that, furthermore, it had not been fully and properly cited. The student, who had intended no dishonesty at all, was embarrassed, to say the least.

Many legal scholars and activists believe that fair use policies and laws should be relaxed and that making these laws more restrictive undermines creativity. While these issues get debated in public forums and legal courts, however, you are well advised to be careful not only in citing and documenting all your sources thoroughly but in getting permission in writing to use any copyrighted text or image in anything you plan to post or publish online.

Avoiding Plagiarism

In U.S. academic culture, incorporating the words, ideas, or materials of others into your own work without giving credit through appropriate citations and documentation is viewed as unethical and is considered plagiarism. The consequences of such unacknowledged borrowing are serious: students who plagiarize may receive failing grades for assignments or courses, be subjected to an administrative review for academic misconduct, or even be dismissed from school.

Certainly, the deliberate and obvious effort to pass off someone else's work as your own, such as by handing in a paper purchased online or written by someone else, is plagiarism and can easily be spotted and punished. More troublesome and problematic, however, is the difficulty some students have using the words and ideas of others fairly and acknowledging them fully. Especially when you're new to a field or writing about unfamiliar ideas, incorporating sources without plagiarizing can be challenging.

In fact, researcher Rebecca Moore Howard has found that even expert writers have difficulty incorporating the words and ideas of others acceptably when they are working with material outside their comfort zone or field of expertise. Such difficulty can often lead to what Howard calls patchwriting: restating material from sources in ways that stick too closely to the original language or syntax.

But patchwriting can help you work with sources. Some call patchwriting plagiarism, even when it's documented, but we believe that it can be a step in the process of learning how to weave the words and thoughts of others into your own work. Assume, for example, that you want to summarize ideas from the following passage:

> Over the past few decades, scholars from a variety of disciplines have devoted considerable attention toward studying evolving public attitudes toward a whole range of LGBT civil rights issues including support for open service in the military, same-sex parent adoption, employment non-discrimination, civil unions, and marriage equality. In the last 10 years in particular, the emphasis has shifted toward studying the various factors that best explain variation in support for same-sex marriage including demographic considerations, religious and ideological predispositions, attitudes toward marriage and family, and social contact (Baunach 2011, 2012; Becker, 2012a, 2012b; Becker & Scheufele, 2009, 2011; Becker and Todd, 2013; Brewer, 2008; Brewer & Wilcox, Lewis, 2005, 2011; Lewis & Gossett, 2008; Lewis & Oh, 2008).
>
> —AMY BECKER, "Employment Discrimination, Local School Boards, and LGBT Civil Rights: Reviewing 25 Years of Public Opinion Data"

This passage includes a lot of detailed information in complex sentences that can be hard to process. See how one student first summarized it, and why this summary would be unacceptable in an essay of his own:

A patchwritten summary

> For more than 20 years, scholars from many disciplines have committed their energies to examining changing public attitudes toward a variety of LGBT civil rights issues. These encompass things like open military service, same-sex parent adoption, equal employment opportunities, civil unions, and marriage equality. Since 2004, focus has moved toward examining those elements that best account for differences in public support for same-sex marriage like demographic considerations, religious and ideological predispositions, attitudes toward marriage and family, and social contact (Baunach 2011, 2012; Becker, 2012a, 2012b; Becker & Scheufele, 2009, 2011; Becker and Todd, 2013; Brewer, 2008; Brewer & Wilcox, Lewis, 2005, 2011; Lewis & Gossett, 2008; Lewis & Oh, 2008).

This is a classic case of patchwriting that would be considered plagiarism. The sentence structure looks very much like Becker's, and even some of the language is taken straight from the original article. While such a summary would not be acceptable in any writing you turn in, this sort of patchwriting can help you understand what a difficult source is saying.

And once you understand the source, writing an acceptable summary gets a lot easier. In the acceptable summary below, the writer focuses on the ideas in the long second sentence of the original passage, turning those ideas into two simpler sentences and using a direct quotation from the original.

Acceptable summary

> Scholars studying changes in public opinion on LGBT issues have increasingly focused on the growing support for same-sex marriage. In looking at the question of why opinions on this issue differ, these scholars have considered factors such as "demographic considerations, religious and ideological predispositions, attitudes toward marriage and family, and social contact" (Becker 342).

An acceptable summary uses the writer's own language and sentence structures, and quotation marks to indicate any borrowed language. To write a summary like this one, you would need to be able to restate the source's main point (that same-sex marriage has gotten greater scholarly attention lately than other LGBT issues) and decide what information is most important for your purposes—what details are worth emphasizing with a quotation or a longer summary. Finally, notice that the citation credits Becker's article, because that is the source this writer consulted, not the research Becker cites.

STEPS YOU CAN TAKE TO AVOID PLAGIARISM

Understand what constitutes plagiarism. Plagiarism includes any unacknowledged use of material from another source that isn't considered common knowledge; this includes phrases, ideas, and materials such as graphs, charts, images, videos, and so on. In a written text, it includes neglecting to put someone else's exact wording in quotation marks; leaving out in-text documentation for sources that you quote, paraphrase, or summarize; and borrowing too many of the original sources' words and sentence structures in paraphrases or summaries. Check to see if your school has any explicit guidelines for what constitutes plagiarism.

Take notes carefully and conscientiously. If you can't locate the source of words or ideas that you've copied down, you may neglect to cite them properly. Technology makes it easy to copy and paste text and materials from electronic sources directly into your own work—and then to move on and forget to put such material in quotation marks or record the source. So keep copies of sources, note documentation information, and be sure to put any borrowed language in quotation marks and to clearly distinguish your own ideas from those of others.

Know where your information comes from. Because information passes quickly and often anonymously through the internet grapevine, you may not always be able to determine the origin of a text or image you find online. If you don't know where something came from, don't include it. Not only would you be unable to write a proper citation, chances are you haven't been able to verify the information either.

Document sources carefully. Below you'll find an overview of the basics of documenting sources. More detail on using MLA and APA documentation is given in the two chapters later in the text.

Plan ahead. Work can pile up in a high-pressure academic environment. Stay on top of your projects by scheduling your work and sticking to the deadlines you set. This way, you'll avoid taking shortcuts that could lead to inadvertent plagiarism.

Consult your instructor if necessary. If you're uncertain about how to acknowledge sources properly or are struggling with a project, talk with your instructor about finding a solution. Even taking a penalty for submitting an assignment late is better than being caught cheating or being accused of plagiarism that you didn't intend to commit.

Documenting Sources

When you document sources, you identify the ones you've used and give information about their authors, titles, and publication. Documenting your sources allows you to show evidence of the research you've done and enables your readers to find those sources if they wish to. Most academic documentation systems include two parts: in-text documentation, which you insert in your text after the specific information you have borrowed, and an end-of-text list of works cited or references, which provides complete bibliographic information for every work you've cited.

This book covers two documentation systems—of the Modern Language Association (MLA) and the American Psychological Association (APA). MLA style is used primarily in English and other humanities subjects, and APA is used mostly in psychology and other social sciences. Chances are that you will be required to use either MLA or APA style or both in your college courses. Note that some disciplines may require other documentation systems, such as CSE (Council of Science Editors) or Chicago.

MLA and APA both call for the same basic information; you'll need to give the author's name (or sometimes the editor's name or the title) in the in-text citation, and your end-of-text list should provide the author, title, and publication information for each source that you cite. But the two systems differ in some ways. In APA, for example, your in-text documentation always includes the date of publication, but that is not generally done in MLA.

REFLECT. Think about the kinds of information you'll need to give when writing about your research. For your topic and your intended audience, what would be considered common knowledge? What might not be common knowledge for a different audience? What do you know about your audience that can help you make that decision?

NINE

Annotated Bibliographies

ANNOTATED BIBLIOGRAPHIES DESCRIBE, give publication information for, and sometimes evaluate each work on a list of sources. When we do research, we may consult annotated bibliographies to evaluate potential sources. In some college courses, you may be assigned to create annotated bibliographies to weigh the potential usefulness of sources and to document your search efforts so that teachers can assess your ability to find, describe, and evaluate sources. There are two kinds of annotations, *descriptive* and *evaluative*; both may be brief, consisting only of phrases, or more formal, consisting of sentences and paragraphs. Sometimes an annotated bibliography is introduced by a short statement explaining its scope.

Descriptive annotations simply summarize the contents of each work, without comment or evaluation. They may be very short, just long enough to capture the flavor of the work, like the examples in the following excerpt from a bibliography of books and articles on teen films, published in the *Journal of Popular Film and Television*.

MICHAEL BENTON, MARK DOLAN, AND REBECCA ZISCH
Teen Film$

In the introduction to his book *The Road to Romance and Ruin*, Jon Lewis points out that over half of the world's population is currently under the age of twenty. This rather startling fact should be enough to make most Hollywood producers drool when they think of the potential profits from a target movie audience. Attracting the largest demographic group is, after all, the quickest way to box-office success. In fact, almost from its beginning, the film industry has recognized the importance of the teenaged audience, with characters such as Andy Hardy and locales such as Ridgemont High and the 'hood.

Beyond the assumption that teen films are geared exclusively toward teenagers, however, film researchers should keep in mind that people of all ages have attended and still attend teen films. Popular films about adolescents are also expressions of larger cultural currents. Studying the films is important for understanding an era's common beliefs about its teenaged population within a broader pattern of general cultural preoccupations.

This selected bibliography is intended both to serve and to stimulate interest in the teen film genre. It provides a research tool for those who are studying teen films and their cultural implications. Unfortunately, however, in the process of compiling this list we quickly realized that it was impossible to be genuinely comprehensive or to satisfy every interest.

> Doherty, Thomas. *Teenagers and Teenpics: The Juvenilization of American Movies in the 1950s*. Unwin Hyman, 1988. Historical discussion of the identification of teenagers as a targeted film market.
>
> Foster, Harold M. "Film in the Classroom: Coping with 'Teenpics.'" *English Journal*, vol. 76, no. 3, Mar. 1987, pp. 86-88. Evaluation of the potential of using teen films such as *Sixteen Candles*, *The Karate Kid*, *Risky Business*, *The Flamingo Kid*, and *The Breakfast Club* to instruct adolescents on the difference between film as communication and film as exploitation.
>
> Washington, Michael, and Marvin J. Berlowitz."Blaxploitation Films and High School Youth: Swat Superfly." *Jump Cut*, vol. 9, Oct.-Dec. 1975, pp. 23-24. Marxist reaction to the trend of youth-oriented black action films. Article seeks to illuminate the negative influences the films have on high school students by pointing out the false ideas about education, morality, and the black family espoused by the heroes in the films.

These annotations are purely descriptive; the authors express none of their own opinions. They describe works as "historical" or "Marxist" but do not indicate whether they're "good." The bibliography entries are documented in MLA style.

Evaluative annotations offer opinions on a source as well as describe it. They are often helpful in assessing how useful a source will be for your own writing. The following evaluative annotations are from a bibliography by Jessica Ann Olson, a student at Wright State University.

JESSICA ANN OLSON

Global Warming

Gore, Al. *An Inconvenient Truth: The Planetary Emergency of Global Warming and What We Can Do about It*. Rodale, 2006.

This publication, which is based on Gore's slide show on global warming, stresses the urgency of the global warming crisis. It centers on how the atmosphere is very thin and how greenhouse gases such as carbon dioxide are making it thicker. The thicker atmosphere traps more infrared radiation, causing warming of the Earth. Gore argues that carbon dioxide, which is created by burning fossil fuels, cutting down forests, and producing cement, accounts for eighty percent of greenhouse gas emissions. He includes several examples of problems caused by global warming. Penguins and polar bears are at risk because the glaciers they call home are quickly melting. Coral reefs are being bleached and destroyed when their inhabitants overheat and leave. Global warming is now affecting people's lives as well. For example, the highways in Alaska are only frozen enough to be driven on fewer than eighty days of the year. In China and elsewhere, record-setting floods and droughts are taking place. Hurricanes are on the rise. This source's goal is to inform its audience about the ongoing global warming crisis and to inspire change across the world. It is useful because it relies on scientific data that can be referred to easily and it provides a solid foundation for me to build on. For example, it explains how carbon dioxide is produced and how it is currently affecting plants and animals. This evidence could potentially help my research on how humans are biologically affected by global warming. It will also help me structure my essay, using its general information to lead into the specifics of my topic. For example, I could introduce the issue by explaining the thinness of the atmosphere and the effect of greenhouse gases, then focus on carbon dioxide and its effects on organisms.

Parmesan, Camille, and Hector Galbraith. "Executive Summary." *Observed Impacts of Global Climate Change in the U.S.*, Pew Center on Global Climate Change, Nov. 2004, c2es.org/docUploads/final_ObsImpact.pdf. Accessed 17 Jan. 2007.

This report summarizes recent scientific findings that document the impact changes in the climate have had on the distribution of plants and animals in the United States and on how they interact within their communities. For example, it explains how a shift has taken place in the blooming period for plants and the breeding period for animals caused by global warming. Because of changes in their geographic range, species may interact differently, possibly resulting in population declines. For example, the red fox is now found in areas dominated by the arctic fox and is threatening its survival. The report stresses that such shifts can harm the world's biodiversity. Plants and animals that are rare now face extinction. The annual cycle of carbon dioxide levels in the atmosphere has also changed, largely due to the lengthening of the growing season, affecting basic ecosystem processes. I did not find this report as helpful as other sources because its information is based only on observations made in the United States. The information appears reliable, though, because it is based on scientific evidence. This essay will be helpful to my essay because it focuses on how plants and animals are currently affected, such as their shifting communities and how they are clashing. I could use this to explain human changes by providing evidence of what is happening to other species. This source will not be as helpful in explaining the climate's effects on human biological function in particular, but it will provide some framework. For example, I could explain how the plants that help convert carbon dioxide into oxygen are being harmed and relate that to how the humans will suffer the consequences.

These annotations not only describe the sources in detail, but also evaluate their usefulness for the writer's own project. They show that the writer understands the content of the sources and can relate it to her own anticipated needs as a researcher and writer.

Key Features / Annotated Bibliographies

A statement of scope. Sometimes you need or are asked to provide a brief introductory statement to explain what you're covering. The authors of the bibliography on teen films introduce their bibliography with three paragraphs establishing a context for the bibliography and announcing their purpose for compiling it.

Complete bibliographic information. Provide all the information about each source using one documentation system (MLA, APA, or another one) so that you, your readers, or other researchers will be able to find the source

easily. It's a good idea to include sources' URLs or permalinks to make access-
ing online sources easier.

A concise description of the work. A good annotation describes each item
as carefully and objectively as possible, giving accurate information and
showing that you understand the source. These qualities will help to build
authority—for you as a writer and for your annotations.

Relevant commentary. If you write an evaluative bibliography, your comments should be relevant to your purpose and audience. The best way to
achieve relevance is to consider what questions a potential reader might have
about each source: What are the main points of the source? What is its argument? How current and reliable is it? Will the source be helpful for your project?

Consistent presentation. All annotations should follow a consistent pattern: if one is written in complete sentences, they should all be. Each annotation in the teen films bibliography, for example, begins with a phrase (not
a complete sentence) characterizing the work.

A BRIEF GUIDE TO WRITING
ANNOTATED BIBLIOGRAPHIES
Considering the Rhetorical Situation

Purpose
: Will your bibliography need to demonstrate the depth
or breadth of your research? Will your readers actually track down and use your sources? Do you need or
want to convince readers that your sources are good?

Audience
: For whom are you compiling this bibliography? What
does your audience need to know about each source?

Stance
: Are you presenting yourself as an objective describer
or evaluator? Or are you expressing a particular point
of view toward the sources you evaluate?

Media/Design
: If you are publishing the bibliography electronically,
will you provide links from each annotation to the
source itself? Online or off, should you distinguish the
bibliographic information from the annotation by using a different font?

Generating Ideas and Text

Decide what sources to include. You may be tempted to include in a bibliography every source you find or look at. A better strategy is to include only those sources that you or your readers may find potentially useful in researching your topic. For an academic bibliography, you need to consider the qualities in the list below. Some of these qualities should not rule a source in or out; they simply raise issues you need to think about.

- *Appropriateness.* Is this source relevant to your topic? Is it a primary source or a secondary source? Is it aimed at an appropriate audience? General or specialized? Elementary, advanced, or somewhere in between?

- *Credibility.* Is the author reputable? Is the publication, publishing company, or sponsor of the site reputable? Do the ideas more or less agree with those in other sources you've read?

- *Balance.* Does the source present enough evidence for its assertions? Does it show any particular bias? Does it present countering arguments fairly?

- *Timeliness.* Is the source recent enough? Does it reflect current thinking or research about the subject?

Compile a list of works to annotate. Give the sources themselves in whatever documentation style is required.

Determine what kind of bibliography you need to write. Descriptive or evaluative? Will your annotations be in the form of phrases? complete sentences? paragraphs? The form will shape your reading and note taking. If you're writing a descriptive bibliography, your reading goal will be just to understand and capture the writer's message as clearly as possible. If you're writing an evaluative bibliography, you will also need to assess the source as you read in order to include your own opinions of it.

Read carefully. To write an annotation, you must understand the source's argument, but when you are writing an annotated bibliography as part of a proposal, you may have neither the time nor the need to read the whole text. Here's a way of quickly determining whether a source is likely to serve your needs:

- Check the publisher or sponsor (university press? scholarly journal? popular magazine? website sponsored by a reputable organization?).

- Read the preface (of a book), abstract (of a scholarly article), introduction (of an article in a nonscholarly magazine or a website).

- Skim the table of contents or the headings.

- Read the parts that relate specifically to your topic.

Research the writer, if necessary. If you are required to indicate the writer's credentials, you may need to do additional research. You may find information by typing the writer's name into a search engine or looking up the writer in *Contemporary Authors*. In any case, information about the writer should take up no more than one sentence in your annotation.

Summarize the work in a sentence or two. describe it as objectively as possible: even if you are writing an evaluative annotation, you can evaluate the central point of a work better by stating it clearly first. *If you're writing a descriptive annotation, you're done.*

Establish criteria for evaluating sources. If you're evaluating sources for a project, you'll need to evaluate them in terms of their usefulness for your project, their stance, and their overall credibility.

Write a brief evaluation of the source. If you can generalize about the worth of the entire work, fine. You may find, however, that some parts are useful while others are not, and what you write should reflect that mix.

Be consistent —in content, sentence structure, and format.

- *Content.* Try to provide about the same amount of information for each entry. If you're evaluating, don't evaluate some sources and just describe others.

- *Sentence structure.* Use the same style throughout — complete sentences, brief phrases, or a mix.

- *Format.* Use one documentation style throughout; use a consistent font for each element in each entry — for example, italicize or underline all book titles.

Ways of Organizing an Annotated Bibliography

Depending on their purpose, annotated bibliographies may or may not include an introduction. Most annotated bibliographies cover a single topic and so are organized alphabetically by author's or editor's last name. When a work lacks a named author, alphabetize it by the first important word in its title. Consult the documentation system you're using for additional details about alphabetizing works appropriately.

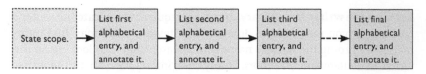

Sometimes an annotated bibliography needs to be organized into several subject areas (or genres, periods, or some other category); if so, the entries are listed alphabetically within each category. For example, a bibliography about terrorism breaks down into subjects such as "Global Terrorism" and "Weapons of Mass Destruction."

[Multicategory bibliography]

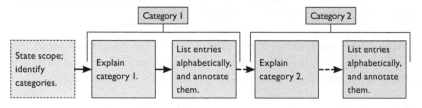

THE ANNOTATED BIBLIOGRAPHY

In ENG 102, all students are required to develop an annotated bibliography. The annotated bibliography is an important tool for students writing a research paper. The primary goal for developing an annotated bibliography is more than simply locating sources. As you conduct your search, evaluating each source for its relevance and usefulness in supporting your thesis is equally important. You are required to include at least three scholarly sources in your annotated bibliography. Other sources may be substantive news sources, government sources or additional scholarly sources. You should consider the annotated bibliography a search record for academic sources that you will consider using to support your discussion in the final research paper. Creating an annotated bibliography helps the writer.

- Discover information about a topic
- Find out which writers are the authorities on a topic
- Find information to help support an argument
- Discover the voice of opposition

You will have the opportunity to learn how to find scholarly sources during the Library Class that is provided for all ENG 102 students. Because the annotated bibliography should be considered a search record, every source that you identify does not have to be used in your final paper. Some sources may provide background information, other sources will help support your discussion or provide the opposing argument. You may also discover that some sources you have identified will not be useful.

EVALUATING SOURCES

Once you have identified sources, it is important to evaluate each source to make sure it is appropriate for an academic paper. You will learn that while certain sources are appropriate for preliminary research, e.g., *Wikipedia* and *CQ Researcher*, these sources should not be used in your final paper.

When you construct your annotated bibliography, sources should be listed alphabetically and include the following elements in each annotation:

1. THE CITATION

MLA Format

> Brookhart, Susan M. "The Public Understanding of Assessment in Educational Reform in the United States." *Oxford Review of Education*, vol. 39, no.1, 2013, pp. 52–71.

APA Format

Brookhart, S. M. (2013). The public understanding of assessment
in educational reform in the United States. *Oxford Review of
Education*, 39(1), 52-71. doi:10.1080/03054985.2013. 764751

2. AUTHOR'S CREDENTIALS

- Who the author is or what organization created your source

- What education, background, and experience makes the author an expert on your research topic. This information can be found at beginning
or end of an article. If you do not find it in either of these places, Google
the author to find out the credentials they had at the time the article
was written

- What other research the author has produced that is related to your
topic

3. SUMMARY

- What the source is about

- What the author's claim is, or whether the source provides information
only

- Whether there is a specific claim, what it is, and how the author comes
to that conclusion

4. RELEVANCE

- How the source relates to your topic

- Whether the source provides background information

- Whether the source supports your thesis or provides a counter claim

The length of the annotation depends on the length of the source but, in
general, each annotation should be approximately 100–200 words long. The
following is an example of one annotation using MLA Format:

DeBoer, George E. "The Scientific Literacy: Another Look at Its Historical and Contemporary Meanings and Its Relationship to Science Education Reform." *Journal of Research in Science Teaching*, vol. 37, no. 6, 2000, pp. 582-601.

In an attempt to define scientific literacy, George E. DeBoer, Emeritus Professor, Colgate, focuses on science in education. As one whose primary interest has been on scientific literacy and the history of secondary school science teaching in the United States, DeBoer contextualizes the inclusion of science in education by providing an historical background that offers readers the shift in approaches to making science part of the general curriculum. In his efforts to provide an extensive overview of the history of science in education, DeBoer includes a discussion about the 1957 launching of Sputnik that became the impetus for the first wave of revising the importance of and approach to teaching science. The goals of science teaching are summarized and the implications of scientific literacy and education reform are discussed. This article provides background information on the events that led to the focus on STEM disciplines in the K–12 experience in the twenty-first century.

Introduction To Annotated Bibliography

As part of the annotated bibliography, you are required to develop an introduction that, if done correctly, will help you discover what you know about your topic, what sources will help you produce the final paper, and what additional work needs to be done. This element of annotated bibliography can also help determine what kind of argument will best serve your purpose. The introduction should include all from the following checklist:

❑ Provide research question

❑ Indicate the kind of paper you intend to write (e.g. position paper, proposal, refutation argument)

❑ Provide thesis/claim/position

❑ Discuss background information readers will need and which sources you will use to supply this information

❑ Identify which sources will be used to support the planned claim

❑ Identify other point(s) of view that you plan to address and which source(s) will be used for this purpose

❑ Discuss strategies in your effort to locate sources (e.g. where you looked, keywords used and the success you had)

❑ Discuss what additional material may be needed

❑ Discuss any problems with the sources listed in the annotated bibliography

❑ Discuss any concerns or difficulties anticipated in writing the essay

STUDENT SAMPLE

Name

Instructor's Name

Course and Section

Date

Introduction: The Role of a Global Economy
on Americans and Their Education

Americans in the twenty-first century are required to compete in
a global market. This reality affects more than the economy – it affects
the education system as well. In order to remain competitors in the job
market, Americans must not only have a high school diploma, but pursue
a higher education as well. My main concern in researching this topic was
how the American education system is preparing its students for one day
obtaining a job and/or career in a highly competitive global job market. I've
found that high dropout rates, a lack of college preparation programs, and
student performance in science, technology, engineering, and math (STEM)
subjects are hurting American job prospects. In terms of education reform,
it is imperative the focus is centered on ensuring that all students, of any
background, are provided with an education allowing them to compete in
the global market. I began with the research questions – How does education
affect America's ability to compete in a global economy? My thesis evolved
into the following statement: With an ever changing economy, the job
market in America no longer holds a place for those without at least a basic
education; therefore, if Americans hope to have a chance at competing in this
new global economy, education must be made a priority.

In researching this topic, I drew from academic articles and
scholarly journals dealing with various topics related to American
dropout rates, dropout job prospects, the global market, and international

STEM education success. "Rising Powers in the Global Economy: Issues and Questions" by Edward Mansfield discusses contrasting elements between the United States and European economies versus Brazil, Russia, India, and China (BRIC) and provides good background information on the global economy. This source is used as material to discuss the opposition. "Barriers to Employment among Out-of-School Youth" by Cynthia Miller and Kristen E. Porter highlights key elements of my argument regarding the struggle for gaining employment for those who have dropped out of school. I use this source as support for my claim of education reform. "Revisiting the Global Market for Higher Education" by Tim Mazzarol and Geoffrey N. Soutar and "Higher Education in the Global Market: Opportunities and Threats" by Navin Singh reinforce my claim that a global economy requires job seekers to have higher education and are also used as evidence to support my thesis. Finally, "U.S. students improving – slowly – in math and science, but still lagging internationally" by Drew Desilver illustrates American shortcomings in math and science education and is used to further supports my point that education reform is needed to improve these areas. The Center on Education and the Workforce and the National Center for Education Statistics both provide reports that analyze national trends in education and labor. I will be using each of the reports as support for my argument using the data discussed. "U.S. Falls in Global Ranking of Young Adults Who Finish College" by Daniel Vise provides background information on U.S. goals to improve higher education attendance and reports evidence of not only a lack of progress, but actual regress. I will use this source as support for my claim that competing countries in the global market are gaining populations that are more highly educated than Americans.

Name

Instructor's Name

Course and Section

Date

Annotated Bibliography: The Role of a Global Economy

on Americans and Their Education

Aspen Institute College Excellence Program. The Aspen Institute, http://
www.aspeninstitute.org/topics/ college-excellence-program.
Accessed 12 October 2015.

    The Aspen Institute is an educational and policy studies
organization based in Washington, DC. The Aspen Institute's
College Excellence Program specifically pursues the goal to
advance higher education practices, policies, and leadership and
bring improvement to U.S. college completion rates, employment
rates after graduation, and education reform ensuring the
success of students in higher education settings. In this report,
the Aspen Institute notes various findings on higher education
and employment after college graduation. This report provides
support for higher education specifically addressing low wages and
unemployment rates.

"Education and Workforce Trends through 2025" Center on Education and
the Workforce. Georgetown University, cew.georgetown.edu/wp-
content/uploads/Iowa_Wrkfrce2025.pdf. Accessed 12 October 2015.

    The Center on Education and the Workforce, an independent,
non-partisan research institute affiliated with Georgetown
University in Washington, DC, focuses on research aimed to

improve education and training for the purpose of gaining a better workforce and decreasing unemployment rates. The research suggests that by the year 2025, over sixty percent of jobs, including those in industry, will require higher education, eight percent of which will actually require a graduate degree. This report provides clear statistics and analysis supporting the claim that the demand for a workforce with higher education is mounting in the twenty-first century – even in positions and industries that traditionally, Americans do not generally think will require a higher education.

DeSilver, Drew. "U.S. Students Improving – Slowly – in Math and Science, but Still Lagging Internationally." Pew Research Center, 2 February 2015. http://www.pewresearch.org/fact-tank/2015/02/02/u-s-students-improving-slowly-in-math-and-science-but-still-lagging-internationally/. Accessed 12 October 2015.

Drew DeSilver, senior writer at the Pew Research Center, a nonpartisan American think-tank based in Washington, D.C., provides information on the U.S. science and math education rankings compared to global counterparts. DeSilver discusses U.S. improvement in two of the four STEM subjects in regards to student education, but goes on to explain that as a nation, America is still falling far behind the other countries across the globe. This report provides statistics showing U.S. STEM education shortcomings and further analyzes the negative trends between American students and their global competitors.

Lastname 3

Mansfield, Edward D. "Rising Powers in the Global Economy: Issues and
Questions." *International Studies Review*, vol. 16, 2014. pp. 437-466.

Edward D. Mansfield, Director of the Christopher H. Browne
Center for International Politics at the University of Pennsylvania,
focuses on the international political economy in his journal
article specifically addressing mounting interest in the growing
economies of Brazil, Russia, India, and China (BRIC). He discusses
the global market and analyzes the U.S. and European economies
compared to those of BRIC. In his discussion of the BRIC economies,
Mansfield provides an argument claiming the BRIC countries do
not pose a threat to Americans as they are not nearly as strong.
This article addresses the opposition of the claim that the global
economy is creating a more competitive job market for Americans.

Mazzarol, Tim and Geoffrey N. Soutar. "Revisiting the Global Market for
Higher Education." *Asia Pacific Journal of Marketing and Logistics*,
vol. 5, 2012, pp. 717-737.

Tim Mazzarol, professor at the University of Western
Australia and an affiliate professor with the Burgundy School of
Business, France, and Geoffrey Soutar, professor at the University
of Western Australia and member of the Australian and New
Zealand Academy of Management, analyze the global market and
the effects of on the higher education around the world in their
journal article. Mazzarol and Soutar contextualize international
industrial reliance and commercialization and further explain how
these elements affect educational requirements and costs across
the globe. This journal article provides strong evidence to support

the idea that a) there is a global economy, b) jobs are now requiring high education to accommodate for international reliance of industry, and finally c) the effects of a and b on education systems around the world.

Miller, Cynthia and Kristin E. Porter. "Barriers to Employment among Out-of-School Youth." *Children and Youth Services Review*, vol. 29, 2007, pp. 572-587.

      Cynthia Miller, economist whose work focuses on policies and programs to increase the employment and earnings of low-wage workers and disadvantaged young adults, and Kristin Porter, statistician with a PhD in biostatistics from the University of California, Berkeley discuss the statistics surrounding youth that dropout of school and further analyze their obstacles to employment thereafter. Miller and Porter found that youth without at least a GED or high school diploma face extreme unemployment rates and often very low wages. Furthermore, those with children had the longest unemployment spells and often faced the most instability. This journal article supports education reform to improve dropout rates and favors the claim that pursuing higher education will improve the status of Americans in the job market.

"Projections of Education Statistics to 2021" National Center for Education Statistics. U.S. Department of Education, http://nces.ed.gov/ programs/projections/projections2021/. Accessed 12 October 2015.

The National Center for Education Statistics, the primary
federal institution for collecting and analyzing data related to
education, reports various educational statistics from 1996 to 2013
and further projects data through 2021. This report gives specific
statistics for current college attendance rates and anticipated
enrollment for the next six years. This source provides great
background and support for the claim that other nations have been
more highly educated in 2015, and America is falling behind in
terms of students pursuing college degrees.

Vise, Daniel. "U.S. Falls in Global Ranking of Young Adults Who
　　Finish College." *The Washington Post*, 13 September 2011. www.
　　washingtonpost.com/local/education/us-falls-in-global-ranking-of-
　　young-adults-who-finish-college/2011/08/22/gIQAAsU3OK_story.
　　html. Accessed 12 October 2015.

　　　　Daniel Vise, higher education reporter at the Washington Post
and author of College Inc., discusses the United States' dropping
ranking among other countries across the globe regarding
college attendance and graduation rates. Vise contextualizes
the educational goals of the U.S. government, specifically Barack
Obama, and further analyzes the shortcomings of such goals.
This article provides support for the claim that other nations in
the world better prepare their students for college and are now
benefiting from a highly educated populations, whereas, the U.S. is
falling behind further every year.

TEN

Arguing

FOOTBALL FANS ARGUE about who's better, Eli or Peyton Manning. Political candidates argue that they have the most experience or best judgment. A toilet paper ad argues that "you deserve a little luxury in your life, and so does your bottom." As you likely realize, we are surrounded by arguments, and much of the work you do as a college student requires you to read and write arguments. When you write a literary analysis, for instance, you argue for a particular interpretation. In a proposal, you argue for a particular solution to a problem. Even a profile argues that a subject should be seen in a certain way. This chapter offers advice on some of the key elements of making an argument, from developing an arguable thesis and identifying good reasons and evidence that supports those reasons to building common ground and dealing with viewpoints other than your own.

Reasons for Arguing

We argue for many reasons, and they often overlap: to convince others that our position on a subject is reasonable, to influence the way they think about a subject, to persuade them to change their point of view or to take some sort of action. In fact, many composition scholars and teachers believe that all writing makes an argument.

As a student, you'll be called upon to make arguments continually: when you participate in class discussions, when you take an essay exam, when you post a comment to an online discussion or a blog. In all these instances, you are adding your opinions to some larger conversation, arguing for what you believe — and why.

Arguing Logically: Claims, Reasons, and Evidence

The basic building blocks of argument are claims, reasons, and evidence that supports those reasons. Using these building blocks, we can construct a strong logical argument.

Claims. Good arguments are based on arguable claims — statements that reasonable people may disagree about. Certain kinds of statements cannot be argued:

- *Verifiable statements of fact.* Most of the time, there's no point in arguing about facts like "The earth is round" or "George H. W. Bush was America's forty-first president." Such statements contain no controversy, no potential opposition — and so no interest for an audience. However, you might argue about the basis of a fact. For example, until recently it was a fact that our solar system had nine planets, but when further discoveries led to a change in the definition of *planet*, Pluto no longer qualified.

- *Issues of faith or belief.* By definition, matters of faith cannot be proven or refuted. If you believe in reincarnation or don't believe there is an afterlife, there's no way I can convince you otherwise. However, in a philosophy or religion course you may be asked to argue, for example, whether or not the universe must have a cause.

- *Matters of simple opinion or personal taste.* If you think cargo pants are ugly, no amount of arguing will convince you to think otherwise. If you own every Taylor Swift CD and think she's the greatest singer ever, you won't convince your Nirvana-loving parents to like her, too. If matters of taste are based on identifiable criteria, though, they may be argued in an evaluation, where "Tom Cruise is a terrible actor" is more than just your opinion—it's an assertion you can support with evidence.

You may begin with an opinion: "I think wearing a helmet makes riding a bike more dangerous, not less." As it stands, that statement can't be considered a claim—it needs to be made more reasonable and informed. To do that, you might reframe it as a question—"Do bike riders who wear helmets get injured more often than those who don't?"—that may be answered as you do research and start to write. Your opinion or question should lead you to an arguable claim, however, one that could be challenged by another thoughtful person. In this case, for example, your research might lead you to a focused, qualified claim: *Contrary to common sense, wearing a helmet while riding a bicycle increases the chances of injury, at least to adult riders.*

Qualifying a claim. According to an old saying, there are two sides to every story. Much of the time, though, arguments don't sort themselves neatly into two sides, pro and con. No matter what your topic, your argument will rarely be a simple matter of being for or against; in most cases, you'll want to qualify your claim — that it is true in certain circumstances, with certain conditions, with these limitations, and so on. Qualifying your claim shows that you're reasonable and also makes your topic more manageable by limiting it. The following questions can help you qualify your claim.

- *Can it be true in some circumstances or at some times but not others?* For example, freedom of speech should generally be unrestricted, but individuals can sue for slander or libel.

- *Can it be true only with certain conditions?* For instance, cell phones and computer monitors should be recycled, but only by licensed, domestic recyclers.

- *Can it be true for some groups or individuals but not others?* For example, nearly everyone should follow a low-carb diet, but some people, such as diabetics, should avoid it.

SOME WORDS FOR QUALIFYING A CLAIM

sometimes	nearly	it seems/seemingly
rarely	usually	some
in some cases	more or less	perhaps
often	for the most part	possibly
routinely	in many cases	in most cases

Drafting a thesis statement. Once your claim is focused and appropriately qualified, it can form the core of your essay's thesis statement, which announces your position and forecasts the path your argument will follow. For example, here is the opening paragraph of an essay by the executive director of the National Congress of American Indians arguing that the remains of Native Americans should be treated with the same respect given to others. The author outlines the context of her argument and then presents her thesis (here, in italics):

> What if museums, universities and government agencies could put your dead relatives on display or keep them in boxes to be cut up and otherwise studied? What if you believed that the spirits of the dead could not rest until their human remains were placed in a sacred area? The ordinary American would say there ought to be a law—and there is, for ordinary Americans. *The problem for American Indians is that there are too many laws of the kind that make us the archeological property of the United States and too few of the kind that protect us from such insults.*
> —Susan Shown Harjo, "Last Rites for Indian Dead: Treating Remains Like Artifacts Is Intolerable"

Reasons. Your claim must be supported by reasons that your audience will accept. A reason can usually be linked to a claim with the word because:

CLAIM +	*BECAUSE* +	REASON
College students	*because*	they will earn far more
should strive		over their lifetimes
to graduate		than those who do not.

Keep in mind that you likely have a further reason, a rule or principle that underlies the reason you link directly to your claim. In this argument, the underlying reason is that isolation from other people is bad. If your audience doesn't accept that principle, you may have to back it up with further reasons or evidence.

To come up with good reasons, start by stating your position and then answering the question *why?*

CLAIM: College students should strive to graduate. Why?
REASON: (Because) They will earn far more over their lifetimes than those who do not. *Why?*
UNDERLYING REASON: The economy values college graduates and pays them more.

As you can see, this exercise can continue indefinitely as the underlying reasons grow more and more general and abstract. You can do the same with other positions:

CLAIM: Smoking should be banned. *Why?*
REASON: (Because) It is harmful to smokers and also to nonsmokers.
UNDERLYING REASON: People should be protected from harmful substances.

Evidence. Evidence to support your reasons can come from various sources. In fact, you may need to use several kinds of evidence to persuade your audience that your claim is true. Some of the most common types of evidence include facts, statistics, examples, authorities, anecdotes, scenarios, case studies, textual evidence, and visuals.

Facts are ideas that are proven to be true. Facts can include observations or scholarly research (your own or someone else's), but they need to be accepted as true. If your audience accepts the facts you present, they can be powerful means of persuasion. For example, an essay on junk email offers these facts to demonstrate the seasonal nature of spam:

> The flow of spam is often seasonal. It slows in the spring, and then, in the month that technology specialists call "black September" — when hundreds of thousands of students return to college, many armed with new computers and access to fast Internet connections — the levels rise sharply.
> —Michael Specter, "Damn Spam"

Specter offers this fact with only a general reference to its origin ("technology specialists"), but given what most people know — or think they know — about college students, it rings true. A citation from a study published by a "technology specialist" would offer even greater credibility.

Statistics are numerical data, usually produced through research, surveys, or polls. Statistics should be relevant to your argument, as current as possible, accurate, and from a reliable source. An argument advocating that Americans should eat less meat presents these data to support the writer's contention that we eat far too much of it:

Americans are downing close to 200 pounds of meat, poultry, and fish per capita per year (dairy and eggs are separate, and hardly insignificant), an increase of 50 pounds per person from 50 years ago. We each consume something like 110 grams of protein a day, about twice the federal government's recommended allowance; of that, about 75 grams come from animal protein. (The recommended level is itself considered by many dietary experts to be higher than it needs to be.) It's likely that most of us would do just fine on around 30 grams of protein a day, virtually all of it from plant sources.

— Mark Bittman, "Rethinking the Meat-Guzzler"

Bittman's statistics demonstrate the extent to which Americans have increased their meat consumption over the last half century, the proportion of our diets that comes from meat, and, by comparison, how much protein our bodies require — and summarize the heart of his argument in stark numeric terms.

Examples are specific instances that illustrate general statements. In a book on life after dark in Europe, a historian offers several examples to demonstrate his point that three hundred years ago, night — without artificial lighting — was treacherous:

Even sure-footed natives on a dark night could misjudge the lay of the land, stumbling into a ditch or off a precipice. In Aberdeenshire, a fifteen-year-old girl died in 1739 after straying from her customary path through a churchyard and tumbling into a newly dug grave. The Yorkshireman Arthur Jessop, returning from a neighbor's home on a cold December evening, fell into a stone pit after losing his bearings.

— A. Roger Ekirch, *At Day's Close: Night in Times Past*

Ekirch illustrates his point and makes it come alive for readers by citing two specific individuals' fates.

Authorities are experts on your subject. To be useful, authorities must be reputable, trustworthy, and qualified to address the subject. You should evaluate any authorities you consult carefully to be sure they have the credentials necessary for readers to take them seriously. When you cite experts, you should clearly identify them and the origins of their authority in a signal phrase, as does the author of an argument that deforested land can be reclaimed:

> Reed Funk, professor of plant biology at Rutgers University, believes that the vast areas of deforested land can be used to grow millions of genetically improved trees for food, mostly nuts, and for fuel. Funk sees nuts used to supplement meat as a source of high-quality protein in developing-country diets.
> —Lester R. Brown, *Plan B 2.0: Rescuing a Planet under Stress and a Civilization in Trouble*

Brown cites Funk, an expert on plant biology, to support his argument that humans need to rethink the global economy in order to create a sustainable world. Without the information on Funk's credentials, though, readers would have no reason to take his proposal seriously.

Anecdotes are brief narratives that your audience will find believable and that contribute directly to your argument. Anecdotes may come from your personal experience or the experiences of others. In an essay arguing that it's understandable when athletes give in to the temptation to use performance-enhancing drugs, sports blogger William Moller uses an anecdote to show that the need to perform can outweigh the potential negative consequences of using drugs:

> I spent my high school years at a boarding school hidden among the apple orchards of Massachusetts. Known for a spartan philosophy regarding the adolescent need for sleep, the school worked us to the bone, regularly slamming us with six hours of homework. I pulled a lot more all-nighters (of the scholastic sort) in my years there than I ever did in college. When we weren't in class, the library, study hall, or formal sit-down meals, we were likely found on a sports field. We also had school on Saturday, beginning at 8 a.m. just like every other non-Sunday morning.
>
> Adding kindling to the fire, the students were not your laid-back types; everyone wanted that spot at the top of the class, and social life was rife with competition. The type A's that fill the investment banking, legal, and political worlds — those are the kids I spent my high school years with.

And so it was that midway through my sophomore year, I found myself on my third all-nighter in a row, attempting to memorize historically significant pieces of art out of E. H. Gombrich's *The Story of Art*. I had finished a calculus exam the day before, and the day before that had been devoted to world history. And on that one cold night in February, I had had enough. I had hit that point where you've had so little sleep over such a long time that you start seeing spots, as if you'd been staring at a bright light for too long. The grade I would compete for the next day suddenly slipped in importance, and I began daydreaming about how easy the real world would be compared to the hell I was going through.

But there was hope. A friend who I was taking occasional study breaks with read the story in the bags beneath my eyes, in the slump of my shoulders, the nervous drumming of my fingers on the chair as we sipped flat, warm Coke in the common room. My personal *deus ex machina*,* he handed me a small white pill.

I was very innocent. I matured way after most of my peers, and was probably best known for being the kid who took all the soprano solos away from the girls in the choir as a first-year student. I don't think I had ever been buzzed, much less drunk. I'd certainly never smoked a cigarette. And knowing full well that what I was doing could be nothing better than against the rules (and less importantly, illegal) I did what I felt I needed to do, to accomplish what was demanded of me. And it worked. I woke up and regained focus like nothing I'd ever experienced. Unfortunately, it also came with serious side effects: I was a hypersensitized, stuffed-up, sweaty, wide-eyed mess, but I studied until the birds started chirping. And I aced my test.

Later I found out the pill was Ritalin, and it was classified as a class 3 drug.[†] I did it again, too — only a handful of times, as the side effects were so awful. But every time it was still illegal, still against the rules. And as emphasized above, I was much more worried about the scholastic consequences if I were discovered abusing a prescription drug than the fact that I was breaking the law. Though I was using it in a far different manner than the baseball players who would later get caught with it in their systems, it was still very clearly a "performance-enhancing drug."

Deus ex machina: In ancient Greek and Roman drama, a god introduced into the plot to resolve complications.
†*Class 3 drug:* Drug that is illegal to possess without a prescription.

Just like every other person on this planet, I was giving in to the incentive scheme that was presented to me. The negative of doing poorly on the test was far greater than the negative of getting caught, discounted by the anesthetic of low probability.

—William Moller, "We, the Public, Place the Best Athletes on Pedestals"

Moller uses this anecdote to demonstrate the truth of his argument, that given the choice between "breaking the rules and breaking my grades" or "getting an edge" in professional sports, just about everyone will choose to break the rules.

Scenarios are hypothetical situations. Like anecdotes, "what if" scenarios can help you describe the possible effects of particular actions or offer new ways of looking at a particular state of affairs. For example, a mathematician presents this lighthearted scenario about Santa Claus in a tongue-in-cheek argument that Christmas is (almost) pure magic:

Let's assume that Santa only visits those who are children in the eyes of the law, that is, those under the age of 18. There are roughly 2 billion such individuals in the world. However, Santa started his annual activities long before diversity and equal opportunity became issues, and as a result he doesn't handle Muslim, Hindu, Jewish and Buddhist children. That reduces his workload significantly to a mere 15% of the total, namely 378 million. However, the crucial figure is not the number of children but the number of homes Santa has to visit. According to the most recent census data, the average size of a family in the world is 3.5 children per household. Thus, Santa has to visit 108,000,000 individual homes. (Of course, as everyone knows, Santa only visits good children, but we can surely assume that, on an average, at least one child of the 3.5 in each home meets that criterion.)

—Keith Devlin, "The Mathematics of Christmas"

Devlin uses this scenario, as part of his mathematical analysis of Santa's yearly task, to help demonstrate that Christmas is indeed magical — because if you do the math, it's clear that Santa's task is physically impossible.

Case studies and observations feature detailed reporting about a subject. Case studies are in-depth, systematic examinations of an occasion, a person, or a group. For example, in arguing that class differences exist in the

United States, sociologist Gregory Mantsios presents studies of three "typical" Americans to show "enormous class differences" in their lifestyles.

Observations offer detailed descriptions of a subject. Here's an observation of the emergence of a desert stream that flows only at night:

> At about 5:30 water came out of the ground. It did not spew up, but slowly escaped into the surrounding sand and small rocks. The wet circle grew until water became visible. Then it bubbled out like a small fountain and the creek began.
>
> —Craig Childs, *The Secret Knowledge of Water*

Childs presents this and other observations in a book that argues (among other things) that even in harsh, arid deserts, water exists, and knowing where to find it can mean the difference between life and death.

Textual evidence includes quotations, paraphrases, and summaries. Usually, the relevance of textual evidence must be stated directly, as excerpts from a text may carry several potential meanings. For example, here is an excerpt from a student essay analyzing the function of the raft in Huckleberry Finn as "a platform on which the resolution of conflicts is made possible":

> [T]he scenes where Jim and Huck are in consensus on the raft contain the moments in which they are most relaxed. For instance, in chapter twelve of the novel, Huck, after escaping capture from Jackson's Island, calls the rafting life "solemn" and articulates their experience as living "pretty high" (Twain 75–76). Likewise, subsequent to escaping the unresolved feud between the Grangerfords and Shepherdsons in chapter eighteen, Huck is unquestionably at ease on the raft: "I was powerful glad to get away from the feuds. . . . We said there warn't no home like a raft, after all. Other places do seem so cramped up and smothery, but a raft don't. You feel mighty free and easy and comfortable on a raft" (Twain 134).
>
> —Dave Nichols, "'Less All Be Friends': Rafts as Negotiating Platforms in Twain's *Huckleberry Finn*"

Huck's own words support Nichols's claim that he can relax on a raft. Nichols strengthens his claim by quoting evidence from two separate pages, suggesting that Huck's opinion of rafts pervades the novel.

Visuals can be a useful way of presenting evidence. Remember, though, that charts, graphs, photos, drawings, and other visual texts seldom speak for themselves and thus must be explained in your text. Below, for example, is a photograph of a poster carried by demonstrators at the 2008 Beijing Summer Olympics, protesting China's treatment of Tibetans.

If you were to use this photo in an essay, you would need to explain that the poster combines the image of a protester standing before a tank during the 1989 Tiananmen Square uprising with the Olympic logo, making clear to your readers that the protesters are likening China's treatment of Tibetans to its brutal actions in the past. Similarly, the poster for a recycling campaign below uses an American flag made from household waste to argue that recycling is patriotic.

Choosing appropriate evidence. The kinds of evidence you provide to support your argument depends on your rhetorical situation. If your purpose is, for example, to convince readers to accept the need for a proposed solution, you'd be likely to include facts, statistics, and anecdotes. If you're writing for an academic audience, you'd be less likely to rely on anecdotes, preferring authorities, textual evidence, statistics, and case studies instead. And even within academic communities different disciplines and genres may focus primarily on different kinds of evidence. If you're not sure what counts as appropriate evidence, ask your instructor for guidance.

Convincing Readers You're Trustworthy

For your argument to be convincing, you need to establish your own credibility with readers — to demonstrate your knowledge about your topic, to show that you and your readers share some common ground, and to show yourself to be evenhanded in the way you present your argument.

Building common ground. One important element of gaining readers' trust is to identify some common ground, some values you and your audience share. For example, to introduce a book arguing for the compatibility of science and religion, author Chet Raymo offers some common memories:

> Like most children, I was raised on miracles. Cows that jump over the moon; a jolly fat man that visits every house in the world in a single night; mice and ducks that talk; little engines that huff and puff and say, "I think I can"; geese that lay golden eggs. This lively exercise of credulity on the part of children is good practice for what follows — for believing in the miracle stories of traditional religion, yes, but also for the practice of poetry or science.
>
> — Chet Raymo, *Skeptics and True Believers: The Exhilarating Connection between Science and Religion*

Raymo presents childhood stories and myths that are part of many people's shared experiences to help readers find a connection between two realms that are often seen as opposed.

Incorporating other viewpoints. To show that you have carefully considered the viewpoints of others, including those who may agree or disagree with you, you should incorporate those viewpoints into your argument by acknowledging, accommodating, or refuting them.

Acknowledging other viewpoints. One essential part of establishing your credibility is to acknowledge that there are viewpoints different from yours and to represent them fairly and accurately. Rather than weakening your argument, acknowledging possible objections to your position shows that you've thought about and researched your topic thoroughly. For example, in an essay about his experience growing up homosexual, writer Andrew Sullivan admits that not every young gay man or woman has the same experience:

> I should add that many young lesbians and homosexuals seem to have had a much easier time of it. For many, the question of sexual identity was not a critical factor in their life choices or vocation, or even a factor at all.   —Andrew Sullivan, "What Is a Homosexual?"

In response to a reasonable objection, Sullivan qualifies his assertions, making his own stance appear to be reasonable.

Accommodating other viewpoints. You may be tempted to ignore views you don't agree with, but in fact it's important to demonstrate that you are aware of them and have considered them carefully. You may find yourself conceding that opposing views have some merit and qualifying your claim or even making them part of your own argument. See, for example, how a philosopher arguing that torture is sometimes "not merely permissible but morally mandatory" addresses a major objection to his position:

> The most powerful argument against using torture as a punishment or to secure confessions is that such practices disregard the rights of the individual. Well, if the individual is all that important—and he is—it is correspondingly important to protect the rights of individuals threatened by terrorists. If life is so valuable that it must never be taken, the lives of the innocents must be saved even at the price of hurting the one who endangers them.
> —Michael Levin, "The Case for Torture"

Levin acknowledges his critics' argument that the individual is indeed important but then asserts that if the life of one person is important, the lives of many people must be even more important. In effect, he uses an opposing argument to advance his own.

Refuting other viewpoints. Often you may need to refute other arguments and make a case for why you believe they are wrong. Are the values underlying the argument questionable? Is the reasoning flawed? Is the evidence inadequate or faulty? For example, an essay arguing for the elimination of college athletics scholarships includes this refutation:

> Some argue that eliminating athletics scholarships would deny opportunity and limit access for many students, most notably black athletes. The question is, access to what? The fields of competition or an opportunity

to earn a meaningful degree? With the six-year graduation rates of black basketball players hovering in the high 30-percent range, and black football players in the high 40-percent range, despite years of "academic reform," earning an athletics scholarship under the current system is little more than a chance to play sports. —John R. Gerdy, "For True Reform, Athletics Scholarships Must Go"

Gerdy bases his refutation on statistics showing that for more than half of African American college athletes, the opportunity to earn a degree by playing a sport is an illusion.

When you incorporate differing viewpoints, be careful to avoid the fallacies of attacking the person making the argument or refuting a competing position that no one seriously entertains. It is also important that you not distort or exaggerate opposing viewpoints. If your argument is to be persuasive, other arguments should be represented fairly.

Appealing to Readers' Emotions

Logic and facts, even when presented by someone who seems reasonable and trustworthy, may not be enough to persuade readers. Many successful arguments include an emotional component that appeals to readers' hearts as well as to their minds. Advertising often works by appealing to its audience's emotions, as in this paragraph from a Volvo ad:

Choosing a car is about the comfort and safety of your passengers, most especially your children. That's why we ensure Volvo's safety research examines how we can make our cars safer for everyone who travels in them—from adults to teenagers, children to babies. Even those who aren't even born yet.   —Volvo.com

This ad plays on the fear that children — or a pregnant mother — may be injured or killed in an automobile accident.

Keep in mind that emotional appeals can make readers feel as though they are being manipulated and, consequently, less likely to accept an argument. For most kinds of academic writing, use emotional appeals sparingly.

Checking for Fallacies

Fallacies are arguments that involve faulty reasoning. It's important to avoid fallacies in your writing because they often seem plausible but are usually unfair or inaccurate and make reasonable discussion difficult. Here are some of the most common fallacies:

- *Ad hominem* arguments attack someone's character rather than address the issues. (*Ad hominem* is Latin for "to the man.") It is an especially common fallacy in political discourse and elsewhere: "Jack Turner has no business talking about the way we run things in this city. He's just another flaky liberal." Whether or not Turner is a "flaky liberal" has no bearing on the worth of his argument about "the way we run things in this city"; insulting one's opponents isn't an argument against their positions.

- *Bandwagon appeals* argue that because others think or do something, we should, too. For example, an advertisement for a rifle association suggests that "67 percent of voters support laws permitting concealed weapons. You should, too." It assumes that readers want to be part of the group and implies that an opinion that is popular must be correct.

- *Begging the question* is a circular argument. It assumes as a given what is trying to be proved, essentially supporting an assertion with the assertion itself. Consider this statement: "Affirmative action can never be fair or just because you cannot remedy one injustice by committing another." This statement begs the question because to prove that affirmative action is unjust, it assumes that it is an injustice.

- *Either-or* arguments, also called *false dilemmas*, are oversimplifications that assert there can be only two possible positions on a complex issue. For example, "Those who oppose our actions in this war are enemies of freedom" inaccurately assumes that if someone opposes the war in question, he or she opposes freedom. In fact, people might have many other reasons for opposing the war.

- *False analogies* compare things that resemble each other in some ways but not in the most important respects — for example, "Trees pollute the air just as much as cars and trucks do." Although it's true that plants emit hydrocarbons, and hydrocarbons are a component of smog, they also produce oxygen, whereas motor vehicles emit gases that combine with hydrocarbons to form smog. Vehicles pollute the air; trees provide the air that vehicles' emissions pollute.

- *Faulty causality,* also known as *post hoc, ergo propter hoc* (Latin for "after this, therefore because of this"), assumes that because one event followed another, the first event caused the second — for example, "Legalizing same-sex marriage in Sweden led to a decline in the marriage rate of opposite-sex couples." The statement contains no evidence to show that the first event caused the second.

- *Straw man* arguments misrepresent an opposing position to make it ridiculous or extreme and thus easy to refute, rather than dealing with the actual position. For example, if someone argues that funding for food stamps should be cut, a straw man response would be, "You want the poor to starve," transforming a proposal to cut a specific program into an exaggerated argument that the proposer hasn't made.

- *Hasty generalizations* are conclusions based on insufficient or inappropriately qualified evidence. This summary of a research study is a good example: "Twenty randomly chosen residents of Brooklyn, New York, were asked whether they found graffiti tags offensive; fourteen said yes, five said no, and one had no opinion. Therefore, 70 percent of Brooklyn residents find tagging offensive." In Brooklyn, a part of New York City with a population of over two million, twenty residents is far too small a group from which to draw meaningful conclusions. To be able to generalize, the researcher would have had to survey a much greater percentage of Brooklyn's population.

- *Slippery slope* arguments assert that one event will inevitably lead to another, often cataclysmic event without presenting evidence that such a chain of causes and effects will in fact take place. Here's an example: "If the state legislature passes this 2 percent tax increase, it won't be long before all the corporations in the state move to other states and leave thousands unemployed." According to this argument, if taxes are raised, the state's economy will be ruined — not a likely scenario, given the size of the proposed increase.

Considering the Rhetorical Situation

To argue effectively, you need to think about the message that you want to articulate, the audience you want to persuade, the effect of your stance, and the larger context you are writing in.

Purpose	What do you want your audience to do? To think a certain way? To take a certain action? To change their minds? To consider alternative views to their current ones? To accept your position as plausible? To see that you have thought carefully about an issue and researched it appropriately?
Audience	Who is your intended audience? What do they likely know and believe about your topic? How personal is it for them? To what extent are they likely to agree or disagree with you? Why? What common ground can you find with them? How should you incorporate other viewpoints they have? What kind of evidence are they likely to accept?
Genre	What genre will help you achieve your purpose? A position paper? An evaluation? A review? A proposal? An analysis?
Stance	What's your attitude toward your topic, and why? What strategies will help you to convey that stance? How do you want your audience to perceive you? As an authority on your topic? As someone much like them? As calm? reasonable? impassioned or angry? something else?
Media/ Design	What media will you use, and how do your media affect your argument? If you're writing on paper, does your argument call for photos or charts? If you're giving an oral presentation, should you put your reasons and support on slides? If you're writing online, should you add links to sites representing other positions or containing evidence that supports your position?

ELEVEN

Arguing a Position

Everything we say or do presents some kind of argument, takes some kind of position. Often we take overt positions: "Everyone in the United States is entitled to affordable health care." "The university needs to offer more language courses." "Photoshopped images should carry disclosure notices." But arguments can be less direct and specific as well, from yellow ribbons that honor U.S. troops to a yellow smiley face, which might be said to argue for a good day.

In college course work, you are constantly called on to argue positions: in an English class, you may argue for a certain interpretation of a poem; in a business course, you may argue for the merits of a flat tax; in a linguistics class, you may argue that English is now a global language. All of those positions are arguable—people of goodwill can agree or disagree with them and present reasons and evidence to support their positions.

This chapter provides guidelines for writing an essay that argues a position. We'll begin with three good examples, the first one annotated to point out key features of this kind of writing.

JOANNA MacKAY
Organ Sales Will Save Lives

In this essay, written for a class on ethics and politics in science, MIT student Joanna MacKay argues that the sale of human organs should be legal.

Clear and arguable position.

There are thousands of people dying to buy a kidney and thousands of people dying to sell a kidney. It seems a match made in heaven. So why are we standing in the way? Governments should not ban the sale of human organs; they should regulate it. Lives should not be wasted; they should be saved.

About 350,000 Americans suffer from end-stage renal disease, a state of kidney disorder so advanced that the organ stops functioning altogether. There are no miracle drugs that can revive a failed kidney, leaving dialysis and kidney transplantation as the only possible treatments (McDonnell and Mallon, pars. 2 and 3).

Dialysis is harsh, expensive, and, worst of all, only temporary. Acting as an artificial kidney, dialysis mechanically filters the blood of a patient. It works, but not well. With treatment sessions lasting three hours, several times a week, those dependent on dialysis are, in a sense, shackled to a machine for the rest of their lives. Adding excessive stress to the body, dialysis causes patients to feel increasingly faint and tired, usually keeping them from work and other normal activities.

Necessary background information.

Kidney transplantation, on the other hand, is the closest thing to a cure that anyone could hope for. Today the procedure is both safe and reliable, causing few complications. With better technology for confirming tissue matches and new anti-rejection drugs, the surgery is relatively simple.

But those hoping for a new kidney have high hopes indeed. In the year 2000 alone, 2,583 Americans died while waiting for a kidney transplant; worldwide the number of deaths is around 50,000 (Finkel 27). With the sale of organs outlawed in almost every country, the number of living donors willing to part with a kidney for free is small. When no family member is a suitable candidate for donation, the patient is placed on a deceased donors list, relying on the organs from people dying of old age or accidents. The list is long. With over 60,000 people in line in the United States alone, the average wait for a cadaverous kidney is ten long years.

Daunted by the low odds, some have turned to an alternative solution: purchasing kidneys on the black market. For about $150,000, they can buy a fresh kidney from a healthy, living donor. There are no lines, no waits. Arranged through a broker, the entire procedure is carefully planned out. The buyer, seller, surgeons, and nurses are flown to a predetermined hospital in a foreign country. The operations are performed, and then all are flown back to their respective homes. There is no follow-up, no paperwork to sign (Finkel 27).

The illegal kidney trade is attractive not only because of the promptness but also because of the chance at a living donor. An organ from a cadaver will most likely be old or damaged, estimated to function for about ten years at most. A kidney from a living donor can last over twice as long. Once a person's transplanted cadaverous kidney stops functioning, he or she must get back on the donor list, this time probably at the end of the line. A transplanted living kidney, however, could last a person a lifetime.

While there may seem to be a shortage of kidneys, in reality there is a surplus. In third-world countries, there are people willing to do anything for money. In such extreme poverty these people barely have enough to eat, living in shacks and sleeping on dirt floors. Eager to pay off debts, they line up at hospitals, willing to sell a kidney for about $1,000. The money will go toward food and clothing, or perhaps to pay for a family member's medical operation (Goyal et al. 1590–91). Whatever the case, these people need the money.

Reason (donors need the money) supported by evidence.

There is certainly a risk in donating a kidney, but this risk is not great enough to be outlawed. Millions of people take risks to their health every day for money, or simply for enjoyment. As explained in *The Lancet*, "If the rich are free to engage in dangerous sports for pleasure, or dangerous jobs for high pay, it is difficult to see why the poor who take the lesser risk of kidney selling for greater rewards . . . should be thought so misguided as to need saving from themselves" (Radcliffe-Richards et al. 1951). Studies have shown that a person can live a healthy life with only one kidney. While these studies might not apply to the poor living under strenuous conditions in unsanitary environments, the risk is still theirs to take. These people have decided that their best hope for money is to sell a kidney. How can we deny them the best opportunity they have?

Counterargument (donating a kidney is risky) acknowledged.

*Counterargument
(selling organs
is wrong)
acknowledged.*

Some agree with Pope John Paul II that the selling of organs is mor- 10 ally wrong and violates "the dignity of the human person" (qtd. in Finkel 26), but this is a belief professed by healthy and affluent individuals. Are we sure that the peasants of third-world countries agree? The morals we hold are not absolute truths. We have the responsibility to protect and help those less fortunate, but we cannot let our own ideals cloud the issues at hand.

*Reason (altruism
is not enough)
supported by
evidence.*

In a legal kidney transplant, everybody gains except the donor. The doctors and nurses are paid for the operation, the patient receives a new kidney, but the donor receives nothing. Sure, the donor will have the warm, uplifting feeling associated with helping a fellow human being, but this is not enough reward for most people to part with a piece of themselves. In an ideal world, the average person would be altruistic enough to donate a kidney with nothing expected in return. The real world, however, is run by money. We pay men for donating sperm, and we pay women for donating ova, yet we expect others to give away an entire organ for no compensation. If the sale of organs were allowed, people would have a greater incentive to help save the life of a stranger.

*Counterargument
(poor people
are exploited)
acknowledged.*

While many argue that legalizing the sale of organs will exploit the poorer people of third-world countries, the truth of the matter is that this is already the case. Even with the threat of a $50,000 fine and five years in prison (Finkel 26), the current ban has not been successful in preventing illegal kidney transplants. The kidneys of the poor are still benefiting only the rich. While the sellers do receive most of the money promised, the sum is too small to have any real impact on their financial situation. A study in India discovered that in the long run, organ sellers suffer. In the illegal kidney trade, nobody has the interests of the seller at heart. After selling a kidney, their state of living actually worsens. While the $1,000 pays off one debt, it is not enough to relieve the donor of the extreme poverty that placed him in debt in the first place (Goyal et al. 1591).

*Reason (regulating
organ sales would
lead to better
decisions).*

These impoverished people do not need stricter and harsh-er penalties against organ selling to protect them, but quite the opposite. If the sale of organs were made legal, it could be regulated and closely monitored by the government and other responsible organizations. Under a regulated system, education would be incorpo-rated into the application process. Before deciding to donate a kidney, the seller should know the details of the operation and any hazards involved. Only with an understanding of the long-term physical health risks can a person make an informed decision (Radcliffe-Richards et al. 1951).

Regulation would ensure that the seller is fairly compensated. In the illegal kidney trade, surgeons collect most of the buyer's money in return for putting their careers on the line. The brokers arranging the procedure also receive a modest cut, typically around ten percent. If the entire practice were legalized, more of the money could be directed toward the person who needs it most, the seller. By eliminating the middleman and allowing the doctors to settle for lower prices, a regulated system would benefit all those in need of a kidney, both rich and poor. According to Finkel, the money that would otherwise be spent on dialysis treatment could not only cover the charge of a kidney transplant at no cost to the recipient, but also reward the donor with as much as $25,000 (32). This money could go a long way for people living in the poverty of third-world countries.

Reason (fairness to sellers) followed by evidence.

Critics fear that controlling the lawful sale of organs would be too difficult, but could it be any more difficult than controlling the unlawful sale of organs? Governments have tried to eradicate the kidney market for decades to no avail. Maybe it is time to try something else. When "desperately wanted goods" are made illegal, history has shown that there is more opportunity for corruption and exploitation than if those goods were allowed (Radcliffe-Richards et al. 1951). (Just look at the effects of the prohibition of alcohol, for example.) Legalization of organ sales would give governments the authority and the opportunity to closely monitor these live kidney operations.

15

Counterargument (controlling organ sales would be difficult) acknowledged.

Regulation would also protect the buyers. Because of the need for secrecy, the current illegal method of obtaining a kidney has no contracts and, therefore, no guarantees. Since what they are doing is illegal, the buyers have nobody to turn to if something goes wrong. There is nobody to point the finger at, nobody to sue. While those participating in the kidney market are breaking the law, they have no other choice. Without a new kidney, end-stage renal disease will soon kill them. Desperate to survive, they are forced to take the only offer available. It seems immoral to first deny them the opportunity of a new kidney and then to leave them stranded at the mercy of the black market. Without laws regulating live kidney transplants, these people are subject to possibly hazardous procedures. Instead of turning our backs, we have the power to ensure that these operations are done safely and efficiently for both the recipient and the donor.

Reason (fairness to buyers) supported by examples.

Concludes by
asking a question for
readers to
consider.

Those suffering from end-stage renal disease would do anything for the chance at a new kidney, take any risk or pay any price. There are other people so poor that the sale of a kidney is worth the profit. Try to tell someone that he has to die from kidney failure because selling a kidney is morally wrong. Then turn around and try to tell another person that he has to remain in poverty for that same reason. In matters of life and death, our stances on moral issues must be reevaluated. If legalized and regulated, the sale of human organs would save lives. Is it moral to sentence thousands to unnecessary deaths?

Works Cited

Finkel, Michael. "This Little Kidney Went to Market." *The New York Times Magazine,* 27 May 2001, pp. 26+.

Goyal, Madhav, et al. "Economic and Health Consequences of Selling a Kidney in India." *Journal of the American Medical Association,* vol. 288, 2002, pp. 1589–92.

McDonnell, Michael B., and William K. Mallon. "Kidney Transplant." *eMedicine Health,* 18 Aug. 2008, www.emedicinehealth.com/articles/24500-1.asp. Accessed 30 Nov. 2008.

Radcliffe-Richards, J., et al. "The Case for Allowing Kidney Sales." *The Lancet,* vol. 351, no. 9120, 27 June 1998, pp. 1950-52.

MacKay clearly states her position at the beginning of her text: "Governments should not ban the sale of human organs; they should regulate it." Her argument appeals to her readers' sense of fairness; when kidney sales are legalized and regulated, both sellers and buyers will benefit from the transaction. She uses MLA style to document her sources.

NICHOLAS KRISTOF
Our Blind Spot about Guns

In this essay, which first appeared in the New York Times in 2014, columnist Nicholas Kristof argues that if guns and their owners were regulated in the same way that cars and their drivers are, thousands of lives could be saved each year.

If we had the same auto fatality rate today that we had in 1921, by my calculations we would have 715,000 Americans dying annually in vehicle accidents.

Instead, we've reduced the fatality rate by more than 95 percent — not by confiscating cars, but by regulating them and their drivers sensibly.

We could have said, "Cars don't kill people. People kill people," and there would have been an element of truth to that. Many accidents are a result of alcohol consumption, speeding, road rage or driver distraction. Or we could have said, "It's pointless because even if you regulate cars, then people will just run each other down with bicycles," and that, too, would have been partly true.

Yet, instead, we built a system that protects us from ourselves. This saves hundreds of thousands of lives a year and is a model of what we should do with guns in America.

Whenever I write about the need for sensible regulation of guns,   5
some readers jeer: *Cars kill people, too, so why not ban cars? Why are you so hypocritical as to try to take away guns from law-abiding people when you don't seize cars?*

That question is a reflection of our national blind spot about guns. The truth is that we regulate cars quite intelligently, instituting evidence-based measures to reduce fatalities. Yet the gun lobby is too strong, or our politicians too craven, to do the same for guns. So guns and cars now each kill more than 30,000 in America every year.

One constraint, the argument goes, is the Second Amendment. Yet the paradox is that a bit more than a century ago, there was no universally recognized individual right to bear arms in the United States, but there was widely believed to be a "right to travel" that allowed people to drive cars without regulation.

A court struck down an early attempt to require driver's licenses, and initial attempts to set speed limits or register vehicles were met with resistance and ridicule. When authorities in New York City sought in 1899 to ban horseless carriages in the parks, the idea was lambasted in the *New York Times* as "devoid of merit" and "impossible to maintain."

Yet, over time, it became increasingly obvious that cars were killing and maiming people, as well as scaring horses and causing accidents. As a distinguished former congressman, Robert Cousins, put it in 1910: "Pedestrians are menaced every minute of the days and nights by a wanton recklessness of speed, crippling and killing people at a rate that is appalling."

Courts and editorial writers alike saw the carnage and agreed that   10
something must be done. By the 1920s, courts routinely accepted driver's license requirements, car registration and other safety measures.

That continued in recent decades with requirements of seatbelts and air bags, padded dashboards and better bumpers. We cracked down on drunken drivers and instituted graduated licensing for young people, while also improving road engineering to reduce accidents. The upshot is that there is now just over 1 car fatality per 100 million miles driven.

Yet as we've learned to treat cars intelligently, we've gone in the opposite direction with guns. In his terrific new book, *The Second Amendment: A Biography,* Michael Waldman, the president of the Brennan Center for Justice at the New York University School of Law, notes that "gun control laws were ubiquitous" in the nineteenth century. Visitors to Wichita, Kansas, for example, were required to check their revolvers at police headquarters.

And Dodge City, symbol of the Wild West? A photo shows a sign on the main street in 1879 warning: "The Carrying of Fire Arms Strictly Prohibited."

Dodge City, Kansas, 1878. The sign reads, "The Carrying of Fire Arms strictly prohibited."

The National Rifle Association supported reasonable gun control for most of its history and didn't even oppose the landmark Gun Control Act of 1968. But, since then, most attempts at safety regulation have stalled or gone backward, and that makes the example of cars instructive.

"We didn't ban cars, or send black helicopters to confiscate them," 15 notes Waldman. "We made cars safer: air bags, seatbelts, increasing the drinking age, lowering the speed limit. There are similar technological and behavioral fixes that can ease the toll of gun violence, from expanded background checks to trigger locks to smart guns that recognize a thumbprint, just like my iPhone does."

Some of these should be doable. A Quinnipiac poll this month found 92 percent support for background checks for all gun buyers.

These steps won't eliminate gun deaths any more than seatbelts eliminate auto deaths. But if a combination of measures could reduce the toll by one-third, that would be 10,000 lives saved every year.

A century ago, we reacted to deaths and injuries from unregulated vehicles by imposing sensible safety measures that have saved hundreds of thousands of lives a year. Why can't we ask politicians to be just as rational about guns?

Kristof argues that because regulating cars has made them much safer, guns should be regulated similarly. He supports his argument with data on fatality rates and the history of automobile and gun regulation in the United States.

ANDREW LEONARD
Black Friday: Consumerism Minus Civilization

This essay arguing that advertising for day-after-Thanksgiving sales has gone too far first appeared on Salon, *where it includes several videos and links to other websites, which are underlined in this text. The online version may be accessed via* wwnorton.com/write/fieldguidelinks.

Here's a Thanksgiving recipe guaranteed to deliver a nervous breakdown impervious to even the most bleeding-edge psychopharma-ceutical wonder drug. Go to *YouTube*, search for "Black Friday

Grown men scream at Justin Bieber in the Macy's Black Friday ad.

commercials," start watching, and then, once you've sated yourself on grown men screaming at Justin Bieber, remakes of Rebecca Black's "Friday," and, most distressingly, the continuing adventures of the Crazy Target Lady, ask yourself this question:

What does it all mean?

I stared into this heart of retail panic darkness, and the more I clicked and pondered, the more confused — (mind-boggled? fascinated? flabbergasted?) — I became. The Crazy Target Lady, so proud of her OCD — obsessive Christmas disorder — is not funny. She's scary. She's why people trample each other to death. She is wrong.

There is a point in our culture beyond which camp and kitsch no longer make the least ironic sense, where consumerism loses its last mooring to civilization, where even seemingly legitimate protest devolves into farce. That point is Black Friday.

Let me be clear. I am not opposed to vigorous sprees of retail   5
spending. For the sake of the U.S. economy, I would love to see a robust Christmas shopping season and I plan to do my part. I find the notion that we should "occupy Black Friday" and withhold our consumer dollars as a way of hitting back at the 1 percent just nutty. Voluntarily subtracting demand from the economy hurts *us*. A general consumer strike would

result in more layoffs and pay cuts and bankruptcies and foreclosures. Sure, Wal-Mart would take a hit, but so would Wal-Mart employees.

But there's also a point where healthy consumerism becomes out-of-control marketing-driven commodity fetishism, and when we find ourselves checking our smartphones for last minute online deals while standing in line for a chain store opening at midnight on Thanksgiving, we are clearly too far gone. That's insanity.

And corporate America knows this. The retail moguls are counting on it. They are outright encouraging it — and role-modeling the appropriate behavior for us. The Crazy Target Lady is not a joke. Watch her cannibalize her gingerbread man, or strategize her reverse psychology shopping techniques, or show off her shopping utility belt: You cannot avoid the dual conclusion that a) she is not a healthy woman, and b) she is *America*. She might be a lunatic, but it's a culturally approved lunacy — the kind that keeps the American engine of capitalism all stoked up. The message that keeps getting blasted across my TV is that we should all be more like her — doing our patriotic duty to boost fourth-quarter retail sales. Sure, you can laugh at her. But then get in line and keep your credit card handy.

The Crazy Target Lady models her shopping utility belt.

But, of course, the big story of this year's Black Friday has been the welcome news that at least some subsection of the population of the United States has come to the realization that it's time to step back from the brink. The budding protests against the decision by some of the country's biggest retailers — Target, Macy's, Best Buy, Kohl's — to move the start of their Black Friday sales to midnight Thanksgiving, or even earlier, is laudable.

The nearly 200,000 signatures on part-time Target employee Anthony Hardwick's petition to "Save Thanksgiving" is proof that both employees and customers of Target are beginning to see this endless race by retailers to one-up each other as dehumanizing and ridiculous. What does a Target employee forced to go to work at 11 p.m. on Thanksgiving have to give thanks for?

The "Friday" parody used in the Kohl's campaign.

(Although, even here, in the protest arena, it's hard to know what to make of the "Respect the Bird" campaign hosted at AllRecipes.com that mixes pledges to "take back Thanksgiving" with KitchenAid mixer promotions and ads for pop-up turkey timers. Even the protests are inseparable from consumerist mania.) 10

The chains are lamely defending their move as a response to forces beyond their control:

"As that is the busiest shopping day of the year, it is imperative that we be competitive," said Anahita Cameron, a Target human resources director, in a statement quoted by the *L.A. Times*. "Our guests have expressed that they would prefer to kick off their holiday shopping by heading out after their holiday celebrations rather than getting up in the middle of the night."

Guests? Pre-programmed automatons would be more accurate. I am undoubtedly reading too much into the "Black Friday" parody of Rebecca Black's "Friday" currently touting the midnight Thanksgiving sale at Kohl's, but there is an awfully revealing moment at the very end of the ad.

After the perky Stepford-wife shopper sings joyfully about how she's "been in line since yesterday" and how everybody's going to Kohl's at "midnight, midnight" the ad ends with her observing, with a mild air of perturbance, that she "can't get this darn song out of my head."

Ladies and gentlemen, there's your winner of the 2011 award for   15 honesty in advertising. A commercial attempting to brainwash consumers into lining up for a midnight sale manages also to explicitly reference the difficulty of shaking free from mindless jingles.

That's kind of brilliant. But also very wrong. Which makes it the perfect commercial for summing up the culture-wide psychotic spasm that is Black Friday. Stay home Thanksgiving night. Go shopping after getting a full night's rest. Sure, you might miss a sale or two. But you'll be a better human being.

Leonard's claim, that Black Friday represents "out-of-control marketing-driven commodity fetishism" or, more concisely, "insanity," is vividly illustrated by several videos of commercials that provide both background information and evidence for his argument. He acknowledges the need for "vigorous sprees of retail spending" while decrying the "psychotic spasm that is Black Friday."

Key Features / Arguments

A clear and arguable position. At the heart of every argument is a claim with which people may reasonably disagree. Some claims are not arguable because they're completely subjective, matters of taste or opinion ("I hate sauerkraut"), because they are a matter of fact ("The first *Star Wars* movie came out in 1977"), or because they are based on belief or faith ("There is life after death"). To be arguable, a position must reflect one of at least two points of view, making reasoned argument necessary: Guns should (or should not) be regulated; selling human organs should be legal (or illegal). In college writing, you will often argue not that a position is correct but that it is plausible—that it is reasonable, supportable, and worthy of being taken seriously.

Necessary background information. Sometimes we need to provide some background on a topic we are arguing so that readers can understand what is being argued. MacKay establishes the need for kidney donors before launching her argument for legalizing the selling of organs; Kristof describes the history of automobile regulation.

Good reasons. By itself, a position does not make an argument; the argument comes when a writer offers reasons to back up the position. There are many kinds of good reasons. Kristof makes his argument by comparing cars to guns. MacKay bases her argument in favor of legalizing the sale of human organs on the grounds that doing so would save more lives, that impoverished people should be able to make risky choices, and that regulation would protect such people who currently sell their organs on the black market as well as desperate buyers.

Convincing evidence. Once you've given reasons for your position, you then need to offer evidence for your reasons: facts, statistics, expert testimony, anecdotal evidence, case studies, textual evidence. All three arguments use a mix of these types of evidence. MacKay cites statistics about Americans who die from renal failure to support her argument for legalizing organ sales; Kristof shows how regulating cars led to dramatic decreases in driving deaths and injuries. Leonard presents several videos to demonstrate how excessive Black Friday advertising has become.

Appeals to readers' values. Effective arguers try to appeal to readers' values and emotions. MacKay appeals to basic values of compassion and fairness. These are deeply held values that we may not think about very much and as a result may see as common ground we share with the writers. And some of MacKay's evidence appeals to emotion—her descriptions of people dying from kidney disease and of poor people selling their organs are likely to evoke an emotional response in many readers.

A trustworthy tone. Arguments can stand or fall on the way readers perceive the writer. Very simply, readers need to trust the person who's making the argument. One way of winning this trust is by demonstrating that you know what you're talking about. Kristof offers plenty of facts to show his knowledge of the history of automotive regulation — and he does so in a self-assured tone. There are many other ways of establishing yourself (and your argument) as trustworthy — by showing that you have some experience with your subject, that you're fair, and of course that you're honest. Occasionally, an outraged tone such as Leonard's is appropriate, especially when it is tempered by good reasons and qualified as he does in noting that he is "undoubtedly reading too much into the Kohl's . . . parody."

Careful consideration of other positions. No matter how reasonable and careful we are in arguing our positions, others may disagree or offer counterarguments. We need to consider those other views and to acknowledge and, if possible, refute them in our written arguments. MacKay, for example, acknowledges that some believe that selling organs is unethical, but she counters that it's usually healthy, affluent people who say this — not people who need either an organ or the money they could get by selling one.

A GUIDE TO WRITING ARGUMENTS

Choosing a Topic

A fully developed argument requires significant work and time, so choosing a topic in which you're interested is very important. Students often find that widely debated topics such as "animal rights" or "abortion" can be difficult to write on because they don't feel any personal connection to them. Better topics include those that

- interest you right now
- are focused but not too narrowly
- have some personal connection to your life

One good way to generate ideas for a topic that meets those three criteria is to explore your own roles in life.

Start with your roles in life. Make four columns with the headings "Personal," "Family," "Public," and "School." Then list the roles you play that relate to it. Here is a list one student wrote:

Personal	Family	Public	School
gamer	son	voter	college student
dog owner	younger	homeless-shelter	work-study
old-car owner	brother	volunteer	employee
male	grandson	American	dorm resident
white		resident	primary-education
middle class		of Texas	major

Identify issues that interest you. Think, then, about issues or controversies that may concern you as a member of one or more of those groups. For instance, as a primary-education major, this student cares about the controversy over whether teachers' jobs should be focused on preparing kids for high-stakes standardized tests. As a college student, he cares about the costs of a college education. Issues that stem from these subjects could include the following: Should student progress be measured by standardized tests? Should college cost less than it does?

Pick four or five of the roles you list. In five or ten minutes, identify issues that concern or affect you as a member of each of those roles. It might help to word each issue as a question starting with *Should*.

Frame your topic as a problem. Most position papers address issues that are subjects of ongoing debate—their solutions aren't easy, and people disagree on which ones are best. Posing your topic as a problem can help you think about the topic, find an issue that's suitable to write about, and find a clear focus for your essay.

For example, if you wanted to write an argument on the lack of student parking at your school, you could frame your topic as one of several problems: What causes the parking shortage? Why are the university's parking garages and lots limited in their capacity? What might alleviate the shortage?

Choose one issue to write about. Remember that the issue should be interesting to you and have some connection to your life. It is a tentative choice; if you find later that you have trouble writing about it, simply go back to your list of roles or issues and choose another.

Considering the Rhetorical Situation

Purpose   Do you want to persuade your audience to do something? Change their minds? Consider alternative views? Accept your position as plausible — see that you have thought carefully about an issue and researched it appropriately?

Audience   Who is your intended audience? What do they likely know and believe about this issue? How personal is it for them? To what extent are they likely to agree or disagree with you — and with one another? Why? What common ground can you find with them?

Stance   What's your attitude toward your topic, and why? How do you want your audience to perceive your attitude? How do you want your audience to perceive you? As an authority on your topic? As someone much like them? As calm? reasonable? impassioned or angry? something else?

Media/   What media will you use, and how do your media affect
Design   your argument? Does your print or online argument call for photos or charts? If you're giving an oral presentation, should you put your reasons and support on slides? If you're writing electronically, should you include audio or video evidence or links to counterarguments or your sources?

Generating Ideas and Text

Most essays that successfully argue a position share certain features that make them interesting and persuasive. Remember that your goal is to stake out a position and convince your readers that it is plausible.

Explore what you already know about the issue. Write out whatever you know about the issue by freewriting or as a list or outline. Why are you interested in this topic? What is your position on it at this point, and why? What aspect do you think you'd like to focus on? Where do you need to focus your research efforts? This activity can help you discover what more you need to learn. Chances are you'll need to learn a lot more about the issue before you even decide what position to take.

Do some research. At this point, try to get an overview. Start with one general source of information that will give you a sense of the ins and outs of your issue, one that isn't overtly biased. The atlantic.com, Time.com, Slate, and other online newspapers and magazines can be good starting points on current issues. For some issues, you may need to interview an expert. For example, one student who wanted to write about chemical abuse of animals at 4-H competitions interviewed an experienced show competitor. Use your overview source to find out the main questions raised about your issue and to get some idea about the various ways in which you might argue it.

Explore the issue strategically. Most issues may be argued from many different perspectives. You'll probably have some sense of the different views that exist on your issue, but you should explore multiple perspectives before deciding on your position. The following methods are good ways of exploring issues:

- As a matter of definition. What is it? How should it be defined? How can *organic* or *genetically modified food* be defined? How do proponents of *organic food* define it—and how do they define *genetically modified food*? How do advocates of genetically modified food define it—and how do they define *organic food*? Considering such definitions is one way to identify different perspectives on the topic.

- As a matter of classification. Can the issue be divided into categories? Are there different kinds of, or different ways of, producing organic foods and genetically modified foods? Do different categories suggest particular positions or perhaps a way of supporting a certain position? Are there other ways of categorizing foods?

- As a matter of comparison. Is one subject being considered better than another? Is organic food healthier or safer than genetically modified food? Is genetically modified food healthier or safer than organic? Is the answer somewhere in the middle?

- As a matter of process. Should somebody do something? What? Should people buy and eat more organic food? More genetically modified food? Should they buy and eat some of each?

Reconsider whether the issue can be argued. Is this issue worth discussing? Why is it important to you and to others? What difference will it make if one position or another prevails? Is it arguable? At this point, you want to be sure that your topic is worth arguing about.

Draft a thesis. Having explored the possibilities, decide your position, and write it out as a complete sentence. For example:

> Parents should be required to have their children vaccinated.
>
> Pod-based coffeemakers should be banned.
>
> Genetically modified foods should be permitted in the United States.

Qualify your thesis. Rather than taking a strict pro or con position, in most cases you'll want to qualify your position — in certain circumstances, with certain conditions, with these limitations, and so on. This is not to say that we should settle, give in, sell out; rather, it is to say that our position may not be the only "correct" one and that other positions may be valid as well. qualifying your thesis also makes your topic manageable by limiting it. For example:

> Parents should be required to have their children vaccinated, with only medical exemptions allowed.
>
> Pod-based coffeemakers should be banned unless the pods are recyclable.
>
> Genetically modified foods should be permitted in the United States if they are clearly labeled as such.

Come up with good reasons. Once you have a thesis, you need to come up with good reasons to convince your readers that it's plausible. Write out your position, and then list several reasons. For instance, if your thesis is that pod-based coffeemakers should be banned, two of your reasons might be:

> The pods cannot be recycled.
>
> Other methods of making coffee are more environmentally sound.

Think about which reasons are best for your purposes. Which seem the most persuasive? Which are most likely to be accepted by your audience? Which seem to matter the most now? If your list of reasons is short or you think you'll have trouble developing them enough to write an appropriate essay, this is a good time to rethink your topic — before you've invested too much time in it.

Develop support for your reasons. Next you have to come up with evidence to support your reasons: facts, statistics, examples, testimony by authorities and experts, anecdotal evidence, scenarios, case studies and observation, and textual evidence. For some topics, you may want or need to use evidence in visual form like photos, graphs, and charts; online, you could also use video or audio evidence and links to evidence in other websites.

What counts as evidence varies across audiences. Statistical evidence may be required in certain disciplines but not in others; anecdotes may be accepted as evidence in some courses but not in engineering. Some audiences will be persuaded by emotional appeals while others will not. For example, if you argue that foods produced from genetically modified organisms (GMOs) should be allowed to be sold because they're safe, you could support that reason with *facts*: GMOs are tested thoroughly by three separate U.S. government agencies. Or you could support it with statistics: A study of 29 years of data on livestock fed GMO feed found that GMO-fed cattle had no adverse health effects. *Expert testimony* might include R. E. Goodman of the Department of Food Science and Technology at the University of Nebraska–Lincoln, who writes that "there is an absence of proof of harm to consumers from commercially available GMOs."

Identify other positions. Now think about positions other than yours and the reasons people are likely to give for those positions. Be careful to represent their points of view as accurately and fairly as you can. Then decide whether you need to acknowledge or to refute each position.

Acknowledging other positions. Some positions can't be refuted but are too important to ignore, so you need to acknowledge concerns and objections they raise to show that you've considered other perspectives. For example, in an essay arguing that vacations are necessary to maintain good health, medical writer Alina Tugend acknowledges that "in some cases, these trips — particularly with entire families in tow — can be stressful in their own way. The joys of a holiday can also include lugging around a ridiculous amount of paraphernalia, jet-lagged children sobbing on airplanes, hotels that looked wonderful on the Web but are in reality next to a construction site." Tugend's acknowledgment moderates her position and makes her argument appear more reasonable.

Refuting other positions. State the position as clearly and as fairly as you can, and then refute it by showing why you believe it is wrong. Perhaps the reasoning is faulty or the supporting evidence inadequate. Acknowledge the merits of the position, if any, but emphasize its shortcomings. Avoid the fallacy of attacking the person holding the position or bringing up a competing position that no one seriously entertains.

Ways of Organizing an Argument

Readers need to be able to follow the reasoning of your argument from beginning to end; your task is to lead them from point to point as you build your case. Sometimes you'll want to give all the reasons for your argument first, followed by discussion of any other positions. Alternatively, you might discuss each reason and any opposing arguments together.

[Reasons to support your argument, followed by opposing arguments]

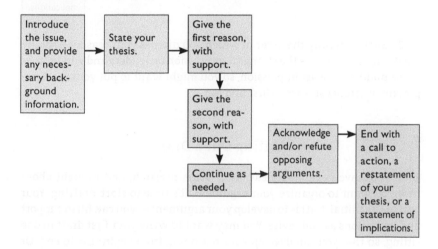

[Reason/opposing argument, reason/opposing argument]

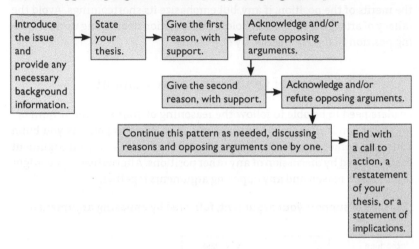

Consider carefully the order in which you discuss your reasons. Usually what comes last makes the strongest impression on readers and what comes in the middle the least impression, so you might want to put your most important or strongest reasons first and last.

Writing Out a Draft

Once you have generated ideas, done some research, and thought about how you want to organize your argument, it's time to start drafting. Your goal in the initial draft is to develop your argument — you can fill in support and transitions as you revise. You may want to write your first draft in one sitting, so that you can develop your reasoning from beginning to end. Or you may write the main argument first and the introduction and conclusion after you've drafted the body of the essay; many writers find that beginning and ending an essay are the hardest tasks they face. Here is some advice on how you might begin and end your argument:

Draft a beginning. There are various ways to begin an argument essay, depending on your audience and purpose. Here are a few suggestions:

- *Offer background information.* You may need to give your readers information to help them understand your position. MacKay outlines the extent of kidney failure in the United States and the limits of dialysis as treatment.

- *Define a key term.* You may need to show how you're using certain keywords. MacKay, for example, defines *end-stage renal disease* as "a state of kidney disorder so advanced that the organ stops functioning altogether," a definition that is central to her argument.

- *Begin with something that will get readers' attention.* MacKay begins emphatically: "There are thousands of people dying to buy a kidney and thousands of people dying to sell a kidney . . . So why are we standing in the way?" Leonard offers still photos from two commercials and links to two more available online.

- *Explain the context for your position.* All arguments are part of a larger, ongoing conversation, so you might begin by showing how your position fits into the arguments others have made. Kristof places his argument about guns in the context of government regulation of other dangerous technologies.

Draft an ending. Your conclusion is the chance to wrap up your argument in such a way that readers will remember what you've said. Here are a few ways of concluding an argument essay:

- *Summarize your main points.* Especially when you've presented a complex argument, it can help readers to summarize your main point. MacKay sums up her argument with the sentence "If legalized and regulated, the sale of human organs would save lives."

- *Call for action.* Kristof does this by asking politicians to consider "sensible safety measures." Leonard presents an alternative to Black Friday's excesses: "Stay home Thanksgiving night. Go shopping after getting a full night's rest."

- *Frame your argument by referring to the introduction.* MacKay does this when she ends by reiterating that selling organs benefits both seller and buyer.

Come up with a title. Most often you'll want your title to tell readers something about your topic—and to make them want to read on. MacKay's "Organ Sales Will Save Lives" tells us both her topic and position. Kristof's title, "Our Blind Spot about Guns," entices us to find out what that blind spot is. See the chapter on guiding your reader for more advice on composing a good title.

Considering Matters of Design

You'll probably write the main text of your argument in paragraph form, but think about what kind of information you're presenting and how you can design it to make your argument as easy as possible for your readers to understand. Think also about whether any visual or audio elements would be more persuasive than written words.

- What would be an appropriate font? Something serious like Times Roman? Something traditional like Courier? Something else?

- Would it help your readers if you divided your argument into shorter sections and added headings?

- If you're making several points, would they be easier to follow if you set them off in a list?

- Do you have any supporting evidence that would be easier to understand in the form of a bar graph, line graph, or pie chart?

- Would illustrations—photos, diagrams, or drawings—add support for your argument? Online, would video, audio, or links help?

Getting Response and Revising

At this point you need to look at your draft closely, and if possible get response from others as well. Following are some questions for looking at an argument with a critical eye.

- Is there sufficient background or context?

- Have you defined terms to avoid misunderstandings?

- Is the thesis clear and appropriately qualified?

- Are the reasons plausible?

- Is there enough evidence to support these reasons? Will readers accept the evidence as valid and sufficient?

- Can readers follow the steps in your reasoning?

- Have you considered potential objections or other positions? Are there any others that should be addressed?

- Have you cited enough sources, and are these sources credible?

- Are source materials documented carefully and completely, with in-text citations and a works cited or references section?

- Are any visuals or links that are included used effectively and integrated smoothly with the rest of the text? If there are no visuals or links, would using some strengthen the argument?

Next it's time to revise, to make sure your argument offers convincing evidence, appeals to readers' values, and achieves your purpose.

Editing and Proofreading

Readers equate correctness with competence. Once you've revised your draft, follow these guidelines for editing an argument:

- Check to see that your tone is appropriate and consistent throughout, reflects your stance accurately, and enhances the argument you're making.

- Be sure readers will be able to follow the argument; check to see you've provided transitions and summary statements where necessary.

- Make sure you've smoothly integrated quotations, paraphrases, and summaries from source material into your writing and documented them accurately.

- Look for phrases such as "I think" or "I feel" and delete them; your essay itself expresses your opinion.

- Make sure that illustrations have captions and that charts and graphs have headings—and that all are referred to in the main text.

- If you're writing online, make sure all your links work.

- Proofread and spell-check your essay carefully.

Taking Stock of Your Work

Take stock of what you've written by writing out answers to these questions:

- What did you do well in this piece?

- What could still be improved?

- How did you go about researching your topic?

- How did others' responses influence your writing?

- How did you go about drafting this piece?

- Did you use visual elements (tables, graphs, diagrams, photographs), audio elements, or links effectively? If not, would they have helped?

- What would you do differently next time?

- What have you learned about your writing ability from writing this piece? What do you need to work on in the future?

TWELVE

Beginning and Ending

Whenever we pick up something to read, we generally start by looking at the first few words or sentences to see if they grab our attention, and based on them we decide whether to keep reading. Beginnings, then, are important, both attracting readers and giving them some information about what's to come. When we get to the end of a text, we expect to be left with a sense of closure, of satisfaction — that the story is complete, our questions have been answered, the argument has been made. So endings are important, too. This chapter offers advice on how to write beginnings and endings.

Beginning

How you begin depends on your rhetorical situation, especially your purpose and audience. Academic audiences generally expect your introduction to establish context, explaining how the text fits into some larger conversation, addresses certain questions, or explores an aspect of the subject. Most introductions also offer a brief description of the text's content, often in the form of a thesis statement. The following opening of an essay on the effect of texting on student writing does all of this:

> It's taking over our lives. We can do it almost anywhere—walking to class, waiting in line at the grocery store, or hanging out at home. It's quick, easy, and convenient. It has become a concern of doctors, parents, and teachers alike. What is it? It's texting!

Text messaging—or texting, as it's more commonly called—is the process of sending and receiving typed messages via a cellular phone. It is a common means of communication among teenagers and is even becoming popular in the business world because it allows quick messages to be sent without people having to commit to a telephone conversation. A person is able to say what is needed, and the other person will receive the information and respond when it's convenient to do so.

In order to more quickly type what they are trying to say, many people use abbreviations instead of words. The language created by these abbreviations is called textspeak. Some people believe that using these abbreviations is hindering the writing abilities of students, and others argue that texting is actually having a positive effect on writing. In fact, it seems likely that texting has no significant effect on student writing.

—Michaela Cullington, "Does Texting Affect Writing?"

If you're writing for a nonacademic audience or genre — for a newspaper or a website, for example — your introduction may need to entice your readers to read on by connecting your text to their interests through shared experiences, anecdotes, or some other attention-getting device. Cynthia Bass, writing a newspaper article about the Gettysburg Address on its 135th anniversary, connects that date — the day her audience would read it — to Lincoln's address. She then develops the rationale for thinking about the speech and introduces her specific topic: debates about the writing and delivery of the Gettysburg Address:

November 19 is the 135th anniversary of the Gettysburg Address. On that day in 1863, with the Civil War only half over and the worst yet to come, Abraham Lincoln delivered a speech now universally regarded as both the most important oration in U.S. history and the best explanation—"government of the people, by the people, for the people"—of why this nation exists.

We would expect the history of an event so monumental as the Gettysburg Address to be well established. The truth is just the opposite. The only thing scholars agree on is that the speech is short—only ten sentences—and that it took Lincoln under five minutes to stand up, deliver it, and sit back down.

Everything else—when Lincoln wrote it, where he wrote it, how quickly he wrote it, how he was invited, how the audience reacted—has been open to debate since the moment the words left his mouth.

—Cynthia Bass, "Gettysburg Address: Two Versions"

Ways of Beginning

Explain the larger context of your topic. Most essays are part of an ongoing conversation, so you might begin by outlining the context of the subject to which your writing responds. An essay exploring the "emotional climate" of the United States after Barack Obama became president begins by describing the national moods during some of his predecessors' administrations:

> Every president plays a symbolic, almost mythological role that's hard to talk about, much less quantify—it's like trying to grab a ball of mercury. I'm not referring to using the bully pulpit to shape the national agenda but to the way that the president, as America's most inescapably powerful figure, colors the emotional climate of the country. John Kennedy and Ronald Reagan did this affirmatively, expressing ideals that shaped the whole culture. Setting a buoyant tone, they didn't just change movies, music, and television; they changed attitudes. Other presidents did the same, only unpleasantly. Richard Nixon created a mood of angry paranoia, Jimmy Carter one of dreary defeatism, and George W. Bush, especially in that seemingly endless second term, managed to do both at once.
>
> —John Powers, "Dreams from My President"

State your thesis. Sometimes the best beginning is a clear thesis stating your position, like the following statement in an essay arguing that fairy tales and nursery rhymes introduce us to "the rudiments and the humanness of engineering":

> We are all engineers of sorts, for we all have the principles of machines and structures in our bones. We have learned to hold our bodies against the forces of nature as surely as we have learned to walk. We calculate the paths of our arms and legs with the computer of our brain, and we catch baseballs and footballs with more dependability than the most advanced weapons systems intercept missiles. We may wonder if human evolution may not have been the greatest engineering feat of all time. And though many of us forget how much we once knew about the principles and practices of engineering, the nursery rhymes and fairy tales of our youth preserve the evidence that we did know quite a bit.
>
> —Henry Petroski, "Falling Down Is Part of Growing Up"

Forecast your organization. You might begin by briefly outlining the way in which you will organize your text. The following example from a scholarly

paper on the role of immigrants in the U.S. labor market offers background
on the subject and describes the points that the writer's analysis will discuss:

> Debates about illegal immigration, border security, skill levels of work-
> ers, unemployment, job growth and competition, and entrepreneurship
> all rely, to some extent, on perceptions of immigrants' role in the U.S.
> labor market. These views are often shaped as much by politics and
> emotion as by facts.
>
> To better frame these debates, this short analysis provides data on
> immigrants in the labor force at the current time of slowed immigration,
> high unemployment, and low job growth and highlights eight industries
> where immigrants are especially vital. How large a share of the labor
> force are they and how does that vary by particular industry? How do
> immigrants compare to native-born workers in their educational attain-
> ment and occupational profiles?
>
> The answers matter because our economy is dependent on immi-
> grant labor now and for the future. The U.S. population is aging rapidly
> as the baby boom cohort enters old age and retirement. As a result, the
> labor force will increasingly depend upon immigrants and their children
> to replace current workers and fill new jobs. This analysis puts a spotlight
> on immigrant workers to examine their basic trends in the labor force
> and how these workers fit into specific industries and occupations of
> interest.
>
> —Audrey Singer, "Immigrant Workers in the U.S. Labor Force"

Offer background information. If your readers may not know as much as
you do about your topic, giving them information to help them understand
your position can be important, as David Guterson does in an essay on the
Mall of America:

> Last April, on a visit to the new Mall of America near Minneapolis, I car-
> ried with me the public-relations press kit provided for the benefit of re-
> porters. It included an assortment of "fun facts" about the mall: 140,000
> hot dogs sold each week, 10,000 permanent jobs, 44 escalators and 17
> elevators, 12,750 parking places, 13,300 short tons of steel, $1 million in
> cash disbursed weekly from 8 automatic-teller machines. Opened in the
> summer of 1992, the mall was built on the 78-acre site of the former Met-
> ropolitan Stadium, a five-minute drive from the Minneapolis–St. Paul In-
> ternational Airport. With 4.2 million square feet of floor space—including
> twenty-two times the retail footage of the average American shopping

center—the Mall of America was "the largest fully enclosed combination retail and family entertainment complex in the United States."
—David Guterson, "Enclosed. Encyclopedic. Endured. One Week at the Mall of America"

The rotunda of the Mall of America.

Visuals can also help provide context. For example, this essay on the Mall of America might have included a photo like the one on the preceding page to convey the size of the structure.

Define key terms or concepts. The success of an argument often hinges on how key terms are defined. You may wish to provide definitions up front, as an advocacy website, Health Care without Harm, does in a report on the hazards of fragrances in health-care facilities:

> To many people, the word "fragrance" means something that smells nice, such as perfume. We don't often stop to think that scents are chemicals. Fragrance chemicals are organic compounds that volatilize, or vaporize into the air—that's why we can smell them. They are added to products to give them a scent or to mask the odor of other ingredients. The volatile organic chemicals (VOCs) emitted by fragrance products can contribute to poor indoor air quality (IAQ) and are associated with a variety of adverse health effects.
>
> —"Fragrances," *Health Care without Harm*

Connect your subject to your readers' interests or values. You'll always want to establish common ground with your readers, and sometimes you may wish to do so immediately, in your introduction, as in this example:

> We all want to feel safe. Most Americans lock their doors at night, lock their cars in parking lots, try to park near buildings or under lights, and wear seat belts. Many invest in expensive security systems, carry pepper spray or a stun gun, keep guns in their homes, or take self-defense classes. Obviously, safety and security are important issues in American life.
>
> —Andy McDonie, "Airport Security: What Price Safety?"

Start with something that will provoke readers' interest. Anna Quindlen opens an essay on feminism with the following eye-opening assertion:

> Let's use the F word here. People say it's inappropriate, offensive, that it puts people off. But it seems to me it's the best way to begin, when it's simultaneously devalued and invaluable.
>
> Feminist. Feminist, feminist, feminist.
>
> —Anna Quindlen, "Still Needing the F Word"

Start with an anecdote. Sometimes a brief narrative helps bring a topic to life for readers. See, for example, how an essay on the dozens, a type of verbal contest played by some African Americans, begins:

Alfred Wright, a nineteen-year-old whose manhood was at stake on Longwood Avenue in the South Bronx, looked fairly calm as another teenager called him Chicken Head and compared his mother to Shamu the whale.

He fingered the gold chain around his thin neck while listening to a detailed complaint about his sister's sexual abilities. Then he slowly took the toothpick out of his mouth; the jeering crowd of young men quieted as he pointed at his accuser.

"He was so ugly when he was born," Wright said, "the doctor smacked his mom instead of him."

— John Tierney, "Playing the Dozens"

Ask a question. Instead of a thesis statement, you might open with a question about the topic your text will explore, as this study of the status of women in science does:

Are women's minds different from men's minds? In spite of the women's movement, the age-old debate centering around this question continues. We are surrounded by evidence of de facto differences between men's and women's intellects — in the problems that interest them, in the ways they try to solve those problems, and in the professions they choose. Even though it has become fashionable to view such differences as environmental in origin, the temptation to seek an explanation in terms of innate differences remains a powerful one.

— Evelyn Fox Keller, "Women in Science: A Social Analysis"

Jump right in. Occasionally you may wish to start as close to the key action as possible. See how one writer jumps right into his profile of a blues concert:

Long Tongue, the Blues Merchant, strolls onstage. His guitar rides side-saddle against his hip. The drummer slides onto the tripod seat behind the drums, adjusts the high-hat cymbal, and runs a quick, off-beat tattoo on the tom-tom, then relaxes. The bass player plugs into the amplifier, checks the settings on the control panel, and nods his okay. Three horn players stand off to one side, clustered, lurking like brilliant sorcerer-wizards waiting to do magic with their musical instruments.

— Jerome Washington, "The Blues Merchant"

Ending

Endings are important because they're the last words readers read. How you end a text will depend in part on your rhetorical situation. You may end by wrapping up loose ends, or you may wish to give readers something to think about. Some endings do both, as Cynthia Bass does in a report on the debate over the Gettysburg Address. In her two final paragraphs, she first summarizes the debate and then shows its implications:

> What's most interesting about the Lincoln-as-loser and Lincoln-as-winner versions is how they marshal the same facts to prove differ-ent points. The invitation asks Lincoln to deliver "a few appropriate re-marks." Whether this is a putdown or a reflection of the protocol of the time depends on the "spin"—an expression the highly politicized Lincoln would have readily understood—which the scholar places on it.
>
> These diverse histories should not in any way diminish the power or beauty of Lincoln's words. However, they should remind us that history, even the history of something as deeply respected as the Gettysburg Address, is seldom simple or clear. This reminder is especially useful today as we watch expert witnesses, in an effort to divine what the founders meant by "high crimes and misdemeanors," club one another with conflicting interpretations of the same events, the same words, the same precedents, and the same laws.
>
> —Cynthia Bass, "Gettysburg Address: Two Versions"

Bass summarizes the dispute about Lincoln's address and then moves on to discuss the role of scholars in interpreting historical events. Writing during the Clinton impeachment hearings, she concludes by pointing out the way in which expert government witnesses often offer conflicting interpretations of events to suit their own needs. The ending combines several strategies to bring various strands of her essay together, leaving readers to interpret her final words themselves.

Ways of Ending

Restate your main point. Sometimes you'll simply summarize your central idea, as in this example from an essay arguing that we have no "inner" self and that we should be judged by our actions alone:

The inner man is a fantasy. If it helps you to identify with one, by all means, do so; preserve it, cherish it, embrace it, but do not present it to others for evaluation or consideration, for excuse or exculpation, or, for that matter, for punishment or disapproval.

Like any fantasy, it serves your purposes alone. It has no standing in the real world which we share with each other. Those character traits, those attitudes, that behavior — that strange and alien stuff sticking out all over you — *that's the real you!*

—Willard Gaylin, "What You See Is the Real You"

Discuss the implications of your argument. The following conclusion of an essay on the development of Post-it notes leads readers to consider how failure sometimes leads to innovation:

Post-it notes provide but one example of a technological artifact that has evolved from a perceived failure of existing artifacts to function without frustrating. Again, it is not that form follows function but, rather, that the form of one thing follows from the failure of another thing to function as we would like. Whether it be bookmarks that fail to stay in place or taped-on notes that fail to leave a once-nice surface clean and intact, their failure and perceived failure is what leads to the true evolution of artifacts. That the perception of failure may take centuries to develop, as in the case of loose bookmarks, does not reduce the importance of the principle in shaping our world.

—Henry Petroski, "Little Things Can Mean a Lot"

End with an anecdote, maybe finishing a narrative that was begun earlier in your text or adding one that illustrates the point you are making. See how Sarah Vowell uses a story to end an essay on students' need to examine news reporting critically:

I looked at Joanne McGlynn's syllabus for her media studies course, the one she handed out at the beginning of the year, stating the goals of the class. By the end of the year, she hoped her students would be better able to challenge everything from novels to newscasts, that they would come to identify just who is telling a story and how that person's point of view affects the story being told. I'm going to go out on a limb here and say that this lesson has been learned. In fact, just recently, a student came up to McGlynn and told her something all teachers dream of

hearing. The girl told the teacher that she was listening to the radio, singing along with her favorite song, and halfway through the sing-along she
stopped and asked herself, "What am I singing? What do these words
mean? What are they trying to tell me?" And then, this young citizen of
the republic jokingly complained, "I can't even turn on the radio without
thinking anymore."

—Sarah Vowell, "Democracy and Things Like That"

Refer to the beginning. One way to bring closure to a text is to bring up
something discussed in the beginning; often the reference adds to or even
changes the original meaning. For example, Amy Tan opens an essay on her
Chinese mother's English by establishing herself as a writer and lover of language who uses many versions of English in her writing:

I am not a scholar of English or literature. I cannot give you much more
than personal opinions on the English language and its variations in this
country or others.

I am a writer. And by that definition, I am someone who has always
loved language. I am fascinated by language in daily life. I spend a great
deal of my time thinking about the power of language—the way it can
evoke an emotion, a visual image, a complex idea, or a simple truth. Language is the tool of my trade. And I use them all—all the Englishes I grew
up with.

At the end of her essay, Tan repeats this phrase, but now she describes language not in terms of its power to evoke emotions, images, and ideas but
in its power to evoke "the essence" of her mother. When she began to write
fiction, she says,

[I] decided I should envision a reader for the stories I would write. And
the reader I decided upon was my mother, because these were stories
about mothers. So with this reader in mind—and in fact she did read my
early drafts—I began to write stories using all the Englishes I grew up
with: the English I spoke to my mother, which for lack of a better term
might be described as "simple"; the English she used with me, which for
lack of a better term might be described as "broken"; my translation of
her Chinese, which could certainly be described as "watered down"; and
what I imagined to be her translation of her Chinese if she could speak in
perfect English, her internal language, and for that I sought to preserve

the essence, but neither an English nor a Chinese structure. I wanted to capture what language ability tests can never reveal: her intent, her passion, her imagery, the rhythms of her speech and the nature of her thoughts.

—Amy Tan, "Mother Tongue"

Note how Tan not only repeats "all the Englishes I grew up with" but also provides parallel lists of what those Englishes can do for her: "evoke an emotion, a visual image, a complex idea, or a simple truth," on the one hand, and, on the other, capture her mother's "intent, her passion, her imagery, the rhythms of her speech and the nature of her thoughts."

Propose some action, as in the following conclusion of a report on the consequences of binge drinking among college students:

The scope of the problem makes immediate results of any interventions highly unlikely. Colleges need to be committed to large-scale and long-term behavior-change strategies, including referral of alcohol abusers to appropriate treatment. Frequent binge drinkers on college campuses are similar to other alcohol abusers elsewhere in their tendency to deny that they have a problem. Indeed, their youth, the visibility of others who drink the same way, and the shelter of the college community may make them less likely to recognize the problem. In addition to addressing the health problems of alcohol abusers, a major effort should address the large group of students who are not binge drinkers on campus who are adversely affected by the alcohol-related behavior of binge drinkers.

—Henry Wechsler et al., "Health and Behavioral Consequences of Binge Drinking in College: A National Survey of Students at 140 Campuses"

Considering the Rhetorical Situation

As a writer or speaker, think about the message that you want to articulate, the audience you want to reach, and the larger context you are writing in.

Purpose   Your purpose will affect the way you begin and end. If you're trying to persuade readers to do something, you may want to open by clearly stating your thesis and end by calling for a specific action.

Audience   Who do you want to reach, and how does that affect the way you begin and end? You may want to open with an intriguing fact or anecdote to entice your audience to read a profile, for instance, whereas readers of a report may expect it to conclude with a summary of your findings.

Genre   Does your genre require a certain type of beginning or ending? Arguments, for example, often provide a statement of the thesis near the beginning; proposals typically end with a call for some solution.

Stance   What is your stance, and can your beginning and ending help you convey that stance? For example, beginning an argument on the distribution of AIDS medications to underdeveloped countries with an anecdote may demonstrate concern for the human costs of the disease, whereas starting with a statistical analysis may suggest the stance of a careful researcher. Ending a proposal by weighing the advantages and disadvantages of the solution you propose may make you seem reasonable.

Media/   Your medium may affect the way you begin and end. A web
Design   text, for instance, may open with a homepage listing a menu of the site — and giving readers a choice of where they will begin. With a print text, you get to decide how it will begin and end.

THIRTEEN

Guiding Your Reader

Traffic lights, street signs, and lines on the road help drivers find their way. Readers need similar guidance — to know, for example, whether they're reading a report or an argument, an evaluation or a proposal. They also need to know what to expect: What will the report be about? What perspective will it offer? What will this **paragraph cover**? What about the next one? How do the two paragraphs relate to each other?

When you write, then, you need to provide cues to help your readers navigate your text and understand the points you're trying to make. This chapter offers advice on guiding your reader and, specifically, on using *titles*, *thesis statements*, *topic sentences*, and *transitions*.

Titles

A title serves various purposes, naming a text and providing clues to the content. It also helps readers decide whether they want to read further, so it's worth your while to come up with a title that attracts interest. Some titles include subtitles. You generally have considerable freedom in choosing a title, but always you'll want to consider the rhetorical situation to be sure your title serves your purpose and appeals to the audience you want to reach.

Some titles simply announce the subject of the text:

> "Black Men and Public Space"
> *The Pencil*
> "Why Colleges Shower Their Students with A's"
> "Does Texting Affect Writing?"

Some titles provoke readers or otherwise entice them to read:

> "Kill 'Em! Crush 'Em! Eat 'Em Raw!"
> "Thank God for the Atom Bomb"
> "What Are Homosexuals For?"

Sometimes writers add a subtitle to explain or illuminate the title:

> *Aria: Memoir of a Bilingual Childhood*
> "It's in Our Genes: The Biological Basis of Human Mating Behavior"
> "From Realism to Virtual Reality: Images of America's Wars"

Sometimes when you're starting to write, you'll think of a title that helps you generate ideas and write. More often, though, a title is one of the last things you'll write, when you know what you've written and can craft a suitable name for your text.

Thesis Statements

A thesis identifies the topic of your text along with the claim you are making about it. A good thesis helps readers understand an essay. Working to create a sharp thesis can help you focus both your thinking and your writing. Here are three steps for moving from a topic to a thesis statement:

1. State your topic as a question. You may have an idea for a topic, such as "gasoline prices," "analysis of 'real women' ad campaigns," or "famine." Those may be good topics, but they're not thesis statements, primarily because none of them actually makes a statement. A good way to begin moving from topic to thesis statement is to turn your topic into a question:

What causes fluctuations in gasoline prices?

Are ads picturing "real women" who aren't models effective?

What can be done to prevent famine in Africa?

2. Then turn your question into a position. A thesis statement is an assertion — it takes a stand or makes a claim. Whether you're writing a report or an argument, you are saying, "This is the way I see . . . ," "My research shows . . . ," or "This is what I believe about . . ." Your thesis statement announces your position on the question you are raising about your topic, so a relatively easy way of establishing a thesis is to answer your own question:

Gasoline prices fluctuate for several reasons.

Ads picturing "real women" instead of models are effective because women can easily identify with them.

The most recent famine in Somalia could have been avoided if certain measures had been taken.

3. Narrow your thesis. A good thesis is specific, guiding you as you write and showing your audience exactly what your essay will cover. The preceding thesis statements need to be qualified and focused — they need to be made more specific. For example:

Gasoline prices fluctuate because of production procedures, consumer demand, international politics, and oil companies' policies.

Dove's "Campaign for Self-Esteem" and Cover Girl's ads featuring Queen Latifah work because consumers can identify with the women's bodies and admire their confidence in displaying them.

The 2012 famine in Somalia could have been avoided if farmers had received training in more effective methods and had had access to certain technology and if other nations had provided more aid more quickly.

A good way to narrow a thesis is to ask questions about it: Why do gasoline prices fluctuate? How could the Somalia famine have been avoided? The answers will help you craft a narrow, focused thesis.

4. Qualify your thesis. Sometimes you want to make a strong argument and to state your thesis bluntly. Often, however, you need to acknowledge that your assertions may be challenged or may not be unconditionally true. In those cases, consider limiting the scope of your thesis by adding to it such terms as *may, probably, apparently, very likely, sometimes,* and *often.*

Gasoline prices *very likely* fluctuate because of production procedures, consumer demand, international politics, and oil companies' policies.

Dove's and Cover Girl's ad campaigns featuring "real women" *may* work because consumers can identify with the women's bodies and admire their confidence in displaying them.

The 2012 famine in Somalia could *probably* have been avoided if farmers had received training in more effective methods and had had access to certain technology and if other nations had provided more aid more quickly.

Thesis statements are typically positioned at or near the end of a text's introduction, to let readers know at the outset what is being claimed and what the text will be aiming to prove. A thesis doesn't necessarily forecast your organization, which may be more complex than the thesis itself. For example, Carolyn Stonehill's research paper, "It's in Our Genes: The Biological Basis of Human Mating Behavior," contains this thesis statement:

While cultural values and messages clearly play a part in the process of mate selection, the genetic and psychological predispositions developed by our ancestors play the biggest role in determining to whom we are attracted.

However, the paper that follows includes sections on "Women's Need to Find a Capable Mate" and "Men's Need to Find a Healthy Mate," in which the "genetic and psychological predispositions" are discussed, followed by sections titled "The Influence of the Media on Mate Selection" and "If Not Media, Then What?" discussing "cultural values and messages." The paper delivers what the thesis includes without following the order in which the thesis presents the topics.

Topic Sentences

Just as a thesis statement announces the topic and position of an essay, a topic sentence states the subject and focus of a paragraph. Good paragraphs focus on a single point, which is summarized in a topic sentence. Usually, but not always, the topic sentence begins the paragraph:

*Graduating from high school or college is an exciting, occasionally even trau-
matic event.* Your identity changes as you move from being a high school
teenager to a university student or a worker; your connection to home
loosens as you attend school elsewhere, move to a place of your own,
or simply exercise your right to stay out later. You suddenly find yourself
doing different things, thinking different thoughts, fretting about different matters. As recent high school graduate T. J. Devoe puts it, "I wasn't
really scared, but having this vast range of opportunity made me uneasy.
I didn't know *what* was gonna happen." Jenny Petrow, in describing her
first year out of college, observes, "It's a tough year. It was for all my
friends."

—Sydney Lewis, *Help Wanted: Tales from the First Job Front*

Sometimes the topic sentence may come at the end of the paragraph or
even at the end of the preceding paragraph, depending on the way the paragraphs relate to one another. Other times a topic sentence will summarize
or restate a point made in the previous paragraph, helping readers understand what they've just read as they move on to the next point. See how the
linguist Deborah Tannen does this in the first paragraphs of an article on
differences in men's and women's conversational styles:

I was addressing a small gathering in a suburban Virginia living room—a
women's group that had invited men to join them. Throughout the evening, one man had been particularly talkative, frequently offering ideas
and anecdotes, while his wife sat silently beside him on the couch. Toward the end of the evening, I commented that women frequently complain that their husbands don't talk to them. This man quickly concurred.
He gestured toward his wife and said, "She's the talker in our family." The
room burst into laughter; the man looked puzzled and hurt. "It's true,"
he explained. "When I come home from work I have nothing to say. If
she didn't keep the conversation going, we'd spend the whole evening
in silence."

*This episode crystallizes the irony that although American men tend to
talk more than women in public situations, they often talk less at home.* And
this pattern is wreaking havoc with marriage.

—Deborah Tannen, "Sex, Lies, and Conversation:
Why Is It So Hard for Men and Women to Talk to Each Other?"

Transitions

Transitions help readers move from thought to thought—from sentence to sentence, paragraph to paragraph. You are likely to use a number of transitions as you draft; when you're editing, you should make a point of checking transitions. Here are some common ones:

- *To signal causes and effects:* accordingly, as a result, because, consequently, hence, so, then, therefore, thus
- *To signal comparisons:* also, in the same way, like, likewise, similarly
- *To signal changes in direction or expections:* although, but, even though, however, in contrast, instead, nevertheless, nonetheless, on the contrary, on the one hand . . . on the other hand, still, yet
- *To signal examples:* for example, for instance, indeed, in fact, such as
- *To signal sequences or similarities:* again; also; and; and then; besides; finally; furthermore; last; moreover; next; too; first, second, third, etc.
- *To signal time relations:* after, as soon as, at first, at the same time, before, eventually, finally, immediately, later, meanwhile, next, simultaneously, so far, soon, then, thereafter
- *To signal a summary or conclusion:* as a result, as we have seen, finally, in a word, in any event, in brief, in conclusion, in other words, in short, in the end, in the final analysis, on the whole, therefore, thus, to summarize

FOURTEEN

Assessing Your Own Writing

In school and out, our work is continually assessed by others. Teachers determine whether our writing is strong or weak; supervisors decide whether we merit raises or promotions; even friends and relatives size up in various ways the things we do. As writers, we need to assess our own work — to step back and see it with a critical eye. By developing standards of our own and being conscious of the standards others use, we can assess — and shape — our writing, making sure it does what we want it to do. This chapter will help you assess your own written work.

What we write for others must stand on its own because we usually aren't present when it is read — we rarely get to explain to readers why we did what we did and what it means. So we need to make our writing as clear as we can before we submit, post, display, or publish it. It's a good idea to assess your writing in two stages, first considering how well it meets the needs of your particular rhetorical situation, then studying the text itself to check its focus, argument, organization, and clarity. Sometimes some simple questions can get you started:

What works?
What still needs work?
Where do I need to say more (or less)?

Considering the Rhetorical Situation

Purpose
: What is your purpose for writing? If you have multiple purposes, list them, and then note which ones are the most important. How well does your draft achieve your purpose(s)? If you're writing for an assignment, what are the requirements of the assignment, and does your draft meet those requirements?

Audience
: To whom are you writing? What do those readers need and expect, as far as you can tell? Does your draft answer their needs? Do you define any terms and explain any concepts they won't know?

Genre
: What is the genre, and what are the key features of that genre? Does your draft include each of those features? If not, is there a good reason?

Stance
: Is your attitude toward your topic and your audience clear? Does your language project the personality and tone that you want?

Media/
Design
: What medium (print? spoken? electronic?) or combination of media is your text intended for, and how well does your writing suit it? How well does the design of the text suit your purpose and audience? Does it meet any requirements of the genre or of the assignment, if you're writing for one?

Examining the Text Itself

Look carefully at your text to see how well it says what you want it to say. Start with its focus, and then examine its reasons and evidence, organization, and clarity, in that order. If your writing lacks focus, the revising you'll do to sharpen the focus is likely to change everything else; if it needs more reasons and evidence, the organization may well change.

Consider your focus. Your writing should have a clear point, and every part of the writing should support that point. Here are some questions that can help you see if your draft is adequately focused:

- What is your thesis? Even if it is not stated directly, you should be able to summarize it for yourself in a single sentence.

- Is your thesis narrow or broad enough to suit the needs and expectations of your audience?

- How does the beginning focus attention on your thesis or main point?

- Does each paragraph support or develop that point? Do any paragraphs or sentences stray from your focus?

- Does the ending leave readers thinking about your main point? Is there another way of concluding the essay that would sharpen your focus?

Consider the support you provide for your argument. Your writing needs to give readers enough information to understand your points, follow your argument, and see the logic of your thinking. How much information is enough will vary according to your audience. If they already know a lot about your subject or are likely to agree with your point of view, you may need to give less detail. If, however, they are unfamiliar with your topic or are skeptical about your views, you will probably need to provide much more.

- What reasons and evidence do you give to support your thesis? Where might more information be helpful? If you're writing online, could you provide links to it?

- What key terms and concepts do you define? Are there any other terms your readers might need to have explained? Could you do so by providing links?

- Where might you include more description or other detail?

- Do you make any comparisons? Especially if your readers will not be familiar with your topic, it can help to compare it with something more familiar.

- If you include narrative, how is it relevant to your point?

Consider the organization. As a writer, you need to lead readers through your text, carefully structuring your material so that they will be able to follow your argument.

- Analyze the structure by outlining it. An informal outline will do since you mainly need to see the parts, not the details.

- Is your text complete? Does your genre require an abstract, a works-cited list, or any other elements?
- What transitions help readers move from idea to idea and paragraph to paragraph? Do you need more?
- If there are no headings, would adding them help orient readers?

Check for clarity. Nothing else matters if readers can't understand what you write. Following are some questions that can help you see whether your meaning is clear and your text is easy to read:

- Does your title announce the subject of your text and give some sense of what you have to say? If not, would a more direct title strengthen your argument?
- Do you state your thesis directly? If not, will readers easily understand what your main point is? Try stating your thesis outright, and see if it makes your argument easier to follow.
- Does your beginning tell readers what they need to understand your text, and does your ending help them make sense of what they've just read?
- How does each paragraph relate to the ones before and after? Are those relationships clear — or do you need to add transitions?
- Do you vary your sentences? If all the sentences are roughly the same length or follow the same subject-verb-object pattern, your text probably lacks any clear emphasis and might even be difficult to read.
- Are visuals clearly labeled, positioned near the text they relate to, and referred to clearly in the text?
- If you introduce materials from other sources, have you clearly distinguished quoted, paraphrased, or summarized ideas from your own?
- Do you define all the words that your readers may not know?
- Does your punctuation make your writing more clear or less? Incorrect punctuation can make writing difficult to follow or, worse, change the meaning from what you intended. As a best-selling punctuation manual reminds us, there's a considerable difference between "eats, shoots, and leaves" and "eats shoots and leaves."

Thinking about Your Process

Your growth as a writer depends on how well you understand what you do when you write so that you can build on good habits. After you finish a writing project, considering the following questions can help you see the process that led to its creation — and find ways to improve the process next time.

- How would you tell the story of your thinking? Try writing these sentences: "When I first began with my topic, I thought _____ . But as I did some thinking, writing, and research about the topic, my ideas changed and I thought _____ ."

- At some point in your writing, did you have to choose between two or more alternatives? What were they, and how did you choose?

- What was the most difficult problem you faced while writing? How did you go about trying to solve it?

- Whose advice did you seek while researching, organizing, drafting, revising, and editing? What advice did you take, and what did you ignore? Why?

FIFTEEN

Getting Response
and Revising

If we want to learn to play a song on the guitar, we play it over and over again until we get it right. If we play basketball or baseball, we likely spend hours shooting foul shots or practicing a swing. Writing works the same way. Making meaning clear can be tricky, and you should plan on revising and, if need be, rewriting in order to get it right. When we speak with someone face-to-face or on the phone or text a friend, we can get immediate response and restate or adjust our message if we've been misunderstood. In most other situations when we write, that immediate response is missing, so we need to seek out responses from readers to help us revise. This chapter includes a list of things for those readers to consider, along with various strategies for subsequent revising and rewriting.

Getting Response

Sometimes the most helpful eyes belong to others: readers you trust, including trained writing-center tutors. They can often point out problems (and strengths) that you simply cannot see in your own work. Ask your readers to consider the specific elements in the list below, but don't restrict them to those elements. Caution: if a reader says nothing about any of these elements, don't be too quick to assume that you needn't think about them yourself.

- What did you think when you first saw the title? Is it interesting? informative? appropriate? Will it attract other readers' attention?

- Does the beginning grab your attention? If so, how does it do so? Does it give enough information about the topic? offer necessary background information? How else might the piece begin?

- Is there a clear thesis? What is it?

- Is there sufficient support for the thesis? Is there anywhere you'd like to have more detail? Is the supporting material sufficiently documented?

- Does the text have a clear pattern of organization? Does each part relate to the thesis? Does each part follow from the one preceding it? Was the text easy to follow? How might the organization be improved?

- Is the ending satisfying? What did it leave you thinking? How else might the piece end?

- Can you tell the writer's stance or attitude toward the subject and audience? What words convey that attitude? Is it consistent throughout?

- How well does the text meet the needs and expectations of its audience? Where might readers need more information, guidance, or clarification? How well does it achieve its purpose? Does every part of the text help achieve the purpose? Could anything be cut? Should anything be added? Does the text meet the requirements of its genre? Should anything be added, deleted, or changed to meet those requirements?

Revising

Once you have studied your draft with a critical eye and, if possible, gotten responses from other readers, it's time to revise. Major changes may be necessary, and you may need to generate new material or do some rewriting. But assume that your draft is good raw material that you can revise to achieve your purposes. Revision should take place on several levels, from global (whole-text issues) to particular (the details). Work on your draft in that order, starting with the elements that are global in nature and gradually moving to smaller, more particular aspects. This allows you to use your time most efficiently and take care of bigger issues first. In fact, as you deal with the larger aspects of your writing, many of the smaller ones will be taken care of along the way.

Give yourself time to revise. When you have a due date, set deadlines for yourself that will give you time — preferably several days but as much as your schedule permits — to work on the text before it has to be delivered. Also, get some distance. Often when you're immersed in a project, you can't see the big picture because you're so busy creating it. If you can, get away from your writing for a while and think about something else. When you return to it, you're more likely to see it freshly. If there's not time to put a draft away for several days or more, even letting it sit overnight or for a few hours can help.

As you revise, assume that nothing is sacred. Bring a critical eye to all parts of a draft, not only to those parts pointed out by your reviewers. Content, organization, sentence patterns, individual words — all are subject to improvement. Be aware that a change in one part of the text may require changes in other parts.

At the same time, don't waste energy struggling with writing that simply doesn't work; you can always discard it. Look for the parts of your draft that do work — the parts that match your purpose and say what you want to say. Focus your efforts on those bright spots, expanding and developing them.

Revise to sharpen your focus. Examine your thesis to make sure it matches your purpose as you now understand it. Read each paragraph to ensure that it contributes to your main point; you may find it helpful to outline your draft to help you see all the parts. One way to do this is to highlight one sentence in each paragraph that expresses the paragraph's main idea. Then copy and paste the highlighted sentences into a new document. Does one state the thesis of the entire essay? Do the rest relate to the thesis? Are they in the best order? If not, you need to either modify the parts of the draft that don't advance your thesis or revise your thesis to reflect your draft's focus and to rearrange your points so they advance your discussion more effectively.

Read your beginning and ending carefully; make sure that the first paragraphs introduce your topic and provide any needed contextual information and that the final paragraphs provide a satisfying conclusion.

Revise to strengthen the argument. If readers find some of your claims unconvincing, you need to provide more information or more support. You may need to define terms you've assumed they will understand, offer additional examples, or provide more detail by describing, explaining processes, adding dialogue, or using some other strategies. Make sure you show as well as tell — and don't forget that you might need to do so literally, with visuals like photos, graphs, or charts. You might try freewriting, clustering, or other ways of generating ideas and text. If you need to provide additional evidence, you might need to do additional research.

Revise to improve the organization. If you've outlined your draft, number each paragraph, and make sure each one follows from the one before. If anything seems out of place, move it, or if necessary, cut it completely. Check to see if you've included appropriate transitions or headings to help readers move through the text, and add them as needed. Check to make sure your text meets readers' expectations of the genre you're writing in.

Revise for clarity. Be sure readers will be able to understand what you're saying. Look closely at your title to be sure it gives a sense of what the text is about and at your thesis: will readers recognize your main point? If you don't state a thesis directly, consider whether you should. Provide any necessary background information and define any key terms. Make sure you've integrated any quotations, paraphrases, or summaries into your text smoothly. Are all paragraphs focused around one main point? Do the sentences in each paragraph contribute to that point? Finally, consider whether there are any data that would be more clearly presented in a chart, table, or graph.

One way to test whether your text is clear is to switch audiences: write what you're trying to express as if you were talking to an eight-year-old. Your final draft probably won't be written that way, but the act of explaining your ideas to a young audience or readers who know nothing about your topic can help you discover any points that may be unclear.

Read and reread—and reread. Take some advice from writing theorist Donald Murray:

> Nonwriters confront a writing problem and look away from the text to rules and principles and textbooks and handbooks and models. Writers look at the text, knowing that the text itself will reveal what needs to be done and what should not yet be done or may never be done. The writer reads and rereads and rereads, standing far back and reading quickly from a distance, moving in close and reading slowly line by line, reading again and again, knowing that the answers to all writing problems lie within the evolving text.
>
> — Donald Murray, *A Writer Teaches Writing*

Rewriting

Some writers find it useful to try rewriting a draft in various ways or from various perspectives just to explore possibilities. Try it! If you find that your original plan works best for your purpose, fine. But you may find that another way will work better. Especially if you're not completely satisfied with your draft, consider the following ways of rewriting. Experiment with your rhetorical situation:

- Rewrite your draft from different points of view, through the eyes of different people perhaps or through the eyes of an animal or even from the perspective of an object. See how the text changes (in the information it presents, its perspective, its voice).

- Rewrite for a different audience. How might an email detailing a recent car accident be written to a friend, an insurance agent, a parent?

- Rewrite in a different tone. If the first draft was temperate and judicious, be extreme; if it was polite, be more direct. If the first draft was in standard English, rewrite it more informally.

- Rewrite the draft in a different genre or medium. Rewrite an essay as a letter, story, poem, speech, comic strip, PowerPoint presentation. Which genre and medium work best to reach your intended audience and achieve your purpose?

Ways of rewriting a narrative

- Rewrite one scene completely in dialogue.

- Start at the end of the story and work back to the beginning, or start in the middle and fill in the beginning as you work toward the end.

Ways of rewriting a textual analysis

- Compare the text you're analyzing with another text (which may be in a completely different genre — film, TV, song lyrics, computer games, poetry, fiction, whatever).

- Write a parody of the text you're analyzing. Be as silly and as funny as you can while maintaining the structure of the original text. Alternatively, write a parody of your analysis, using evidence from the text to support an outrageous analysis.

Ways of rewriting a report

- Rewrite for a different audience. For example, explain a concept to your grandparents; describe the subject of a profile to a visitor from another planet.
- Be silly. Rewrite the draft as if for The Daily Show or the Onion, or rewrite it as if it were written by Bart Simpson.

Ways of rewriting an argument

- Rewrite taking another position. Argue as forcefully for that position as you did for your actual one, acknowledging and refuting your original position. Alternatively, write a rebuttal to your first draft from the perspective of someone with different beliefs.
- Rewrite your draft as a story—make it real in the lives of specific individuals. (For example, if you were writing about abortion rights, you could write a story about a young pregnant woman trying to decide what she believes and what to do.) Or rewrite the argument as a fable or parable.
- Rewrite the draft as a letter responding to a hostile reader, trying at least to make him or her understand what you have to say.
- Rewrite the draft as an angry letter to someone or as a table-thumping dinner-with-the-relatives discussion. Write from the most extreme position possible.
- Write an analysis of the topic of your argument in which you identify, as carefully and as neutrally as you can, the various positions people hold on the issue.

Once you've rewritten a draft in any of these ways, see whether there's anything you can use. Read each draft, considering how it might help you achieve your purpose, reach your audience, convey your stance. Revise your actual draft to incorporate anything you think will make your text more effective, whether it's other genres or a different perspective.

SIXTEEN

Editing and Proofreading

Your ability to produce clear, error-free writing shows something about your ability as a writer and also leads readers to make assumptions about your intellect, your work habits, even your character. Readers of job-application letters and résumés, for example, may reject applications if they contain a single error, for no other reason than it's an easy way to narrow the field of potential candidates. In addition, they may well assume that applicants who present themselves sloppily in an application will do sloppy work on the job. This is all to say that you should edit and proofread your work carefully.

Editing

Editing is the stage when you work on the details of your paragraphs, sentences, words, and punctuation to make your writing as clear, precise, correct—and effective—as possible. Your goal is not to achieve "perfection" (whatever that may be) so much as to make your writing as effective as possible for your particular purpose and audience. Check a good writing handbook for detailed advice, but the following guidelines can help you check your drafts systematically for some common errors with paragraphs, sentences, and words.

Editing paragraphs

- Does each paragraph focus on one point? Does it have a topic sentence that announces that point, and if so, where is it located? If it's not the first sentence, should it be? If there's no clear topic sentence, should there be one?

- Does every sentence relate to the main point of the paragraph? If any sentences do not, should they be deleted, moved, or revised?

- Is there enough detail to develop the paragraph's main point? How is the point developed — with narrative? definition? some other strategy?

- Where have you placed the most important information—at the beginning? the end? in the middle? The most emphatic spot is at the end, so in general that's where to put information you want readers to remember. The second most emphatic spot is at the beginning.

- Are any paragraphs especially long or short? Consider breaking long paragraphs if there's a logical place to do so—maybe an extended example should be in its own paragraph, for instance. If you have paragraphs of only a sentence or two, see if you can add to them or combine them with another paragraph, unless you're using a brief paragraph to provide emphasis.

- Check the way your paragraphs fit together. Does each one follow smoothly from the one before? Do you need to add any transitions?

- Does the beginning paragraph catch readers' attention? In what other ways might you begin your text?

- Does the final paragraph provide a satisfactory ending? How else might you conclude your text?

Editing sentences

- Is each sentence complete? Does it have someone or something (the subject) performing some sort of action or expressing a state of being (the verb)? Does each sentence begin with a capital letter and end with a period, question mark, or exclamation point?

- Check your use of the passive voice. Although there are some rhetorical situations in which the passive voice ("The emperor was assassinated by an anarchist") is more appropriate than the active voice ("An anarchist assassinated the emperor") because you want to emphasize an action rather than who performed it, you'll do well to edit it out unless you have a good reason for using it.

- Check for parallelism. Items in a list or series should be parallel in form—all nouns (lions, tigers, bears), all verbs (hopped, skipped, jumped), all clauses (he came, he saw, he conquered), and so on.

- Do many of your sentences begin with it or there? Too often these words make your writing wordy and vague or even conceal needed information. Why write "There are reasons we voted for him" when you can say "We had reasons to vote for him"?

- Are your sentences varied? If they all start with the subject or are the same length, your writing might be dull and maybe even hard to read. Try varying your sentence openings by adding transitions, introductory phrases or clauses. Vary sentence lengths by adding detail to some or combining some sentences.

- Make sure you've used commas correctly. Is there a comma after each introductory element? ("After the lead singer quit, the group nearly disbanded. However, they then produced a string of hits.") Do commas set off nonrestrictive elements—parts that aren't needed to understand the sentence? ("The books I read in middle school, like the Harry Potter series, became longer and more challenging.") Are compound sentences connected with a comma? ("I'll eat broccoli steamed, but I prefer it roasted.")

Editing words

- Are you sure of the meaning of every word? Use a dictionary; be sure to look up words whose meanings you're not sure about. And remember your audience — do you use any terms they'll need to have defined?

- Is any of your language too general or vague? Why write that you competed in a race, for example, if you could say you ran the 4 × 200 relay?

- What about the tone? If your stance is serious (or humorous or critical or something else), make sure that your words all convey that attitude.

- Do any pronouns have vague or unclear antecedents? If you use "he" or "they" or "it" or "these," will readers know whom or what the words refer to?

- Have you used any clichés—expressions that are used so frequently that they are no longer fresh? "Live and let live," avoiding something "like the plague," and similar expressions are so predictable that your writing will almost always be better off without them.

- Be careful with language that refers to others. Make sure that your words do not stereotype any individual or group. Mention age, gender, race, religion, sexual orientation, and so on only if they are relevant to your subject. When referring to an ethnic group, make every effort to use the terms members of the group prefer.

- Edit out language that might be considered sexist. Do you say "he" when you mean "he and she"? Have you used words like *manpower* or *policeman* to refer to people who may be female? If so, substitute less gendered words such as *personnel* or *police officer*. Do your words reflect any gender stereotypes—for example, that all engineers are male, or all nurses female? If you mention someone's gender, is it even necessary? If not, eliminate the unneeded words.

- How many of your verbs are forms of *be* and *do*? If you rely too much on these words, try replacing them with more specific verbs. Why write "She did a proposal for" when you could say "She proposed"?

- Do you ever confuse *its* and *it's*? Use *it's* when you mean *it is* or *it has*. Use *its* when you mean *belonging to it*.

Proofreading

Proofreading is the final stage of the writing process, the point where you clean up your work to present it to your readers. Proofreading is like checking your appearance in a mirror before going into a job interview: being neat and well groomed looms large in creating a good first impression, and the same principle applies to writing. Misspelled words, missing pages, mixed-up fonts, and other lapses send a negative message about your work — and about you. Most readers excuse an occasional error, but by and large readers are an intolerant bunch: too many errors will lead them to declare your writing — and maybe your thinking — flawed. There goes your credibility. So proofread your final draft with care to ensure that your message is taken as seriously as you want it to be.

Up to this point, you've been told *not* to read individual words on the page and instead to read for meaning. Proofreading demands the opposite: you must slow down your reading so that you can see every word, every punctuation mark.

- Use your computer's grammar checker and spelling checker, but only as a first step, and know that they're not very reliable. Computer programs don't read writing; instead, they rely on formulas and banks of words, so what they flag (or don't flag) as mistakes may or may not be accurate. If you were to write, "my brother was diagnosed with a leaning disorder," leaning would not be flagged as misspelled because it is a word, even though it's the wrong word in that sentence.

- To keep your eyes from jumping ahead, place a ruler or piece of paper under each line as you read. Use your finger or a pencil as a pointer.

- Some writers find it helpful to read the text one sentence at a time, beginning with the last sentence and working backward.

- Read your text out loud to yourself—or better, to others, who may hear problems you can't see. Alternatively, have someone else read your text aloud to you while you follow along on the screen or page.

- Ask someone else to read your text. The more important the writing is, the more important this step is.

- If you find a mistake after you've printed out your text and are unable to print out a corrected version, make the change as neatly as possible in pencil or pen.

SEVENTEEN

MLA Style

MLA STYLE CALLS for (1) brief in-text documentation and (2) complete bibliographic information in a list of works cited at the end of your text. The models and examples in this chapter draw on the eighth edition of the *MLA Handbook*, published by the Modern Language Association in 2016. For additional information, visit style.mla.org.

A DIRECTORY TO MLA STYLE

In-Text Documentation   196

1. Author named in a signal phrase 196
2. Author named in parentheses 196
3. Two or more works by the same author 197
4. Authors with the same last name 197
5. Two or more authors 197
6. Organization or government as author 198
7. Author unknown 198
8. Literary works 198
9. Work in an anthology 199
10. Encyclopedia or dictionary 199
11. Legal and historical documents 200
12. Sacred text 200
13. Multivolume work 200
14. Two or more works cited together 201
15. Source quoted in another source 201
16. Work without page numbers 201
17. An entire work or a one-page article 202

Notes   202

List of Works Cited   203

Core Elements   203
Authors and Other
Contributors 203
Titles 204
Publisher 204

Dates 205
Location 205
Punctuation 206

Authors and Other Contributors   207
1. One author 207
2. Two authors 207
3. Three or more authors 207
4. Two or more works by the same author 207

5. Author and editor or translator 208
6. No author or editor 208
7. Organization or government as author 209

Articles and Other Short Works   209
8. Article in a journal 209
9. Article in a magazine 210
10. Article in a newspaper 212
11. Article accessed through a database 212
12. Entry in a reference work 215

13. Editorial 215
14. Letter to the editor 216
15. Review 216
16. Comment on an online article 217

Books and Parts of Books   217
17. Basic entries for a book 217
18. Anthology 218
19. Work in an anthology 218
20. Multivolume work 220
21. Book in a series 220
22. Graphic narrative 221
23. Sacred text 221
24. Edition other than the first 221

25. Republished work 221
26. Foreword, introduction, preface, or afterword 222
27. Published letter 222
28. Paper at a conference 222
29. Dissertation 223

Websites   223
30. Entire website 223
31. Work on a website 225
32. Blog entry 225
33. Wiki 225

Personal Communication and Social Media   225
34. Personal letter 225
35. Email 226
36. Text message 226
37. Post to an online forum 226
38. Post to *Twitter, Facebook*, or other social media 226

Audio, Visual, and Other Sources   227
39. Advertisement 227
40. Art 227
41. Cartoon 228
42. Supreme Court case 229
43. Film 229
44. Interview 230
45. Map 230
46. Musical score 230
47. Online video 231
48. Oral presentation 231
49. Podcast 231
50. Radio program 232
51. Sound recording 232
52. TV show 232
53. Video game 233

Formatting a Research Paper   233

Sample Research Paper   235

Throughout this chapter, you'll find models and examples that are color coded to help you see how writers include source information in their texts and in their lists of works cited: tan for author, editor, translator, and other contributors; yellow for titles; gray for publication information — publisher, date of publication, page number(s) or other location information, and so on.

IN-TEXT DOCUMENTATION

Brief documentation in your text makes clear to your reader what you took from a source and where in the source you found the information.

In your text, you have three options for citing a source: QUOTING, PARAPHRASING, and SUMMARIZING. As you cite each source, you will need to decide whether or not to name the author in a signal phrase—"as Toni Morrison writes"—or in parentheses—(Morrison 24).

The first examples below show basic in-text documentation of a work by one author. Variations on those examples follow. The examples illustrate the MLA style of using quotation marks around titles of short works and italicizing titles of long works.

1. Author named in a signal phrase

If you mention the author in a SIGNAL PHRASE, put only the page number(s) in parentheses. Do not write *page* or *p*.

> McCullough describes John Adams' hands as those of someone used to manual labor (18).

2. Author named in parentheses

If you do not mention the author in a signal phrase, put his or her last name in parentheses along with the page number(s). Do not use punctuation between the name and the page number(s).

> Adams is said to have had "the hands of a man accustomed to pruning his own trees, cutting his own hay, and splitting his own firewood" (McCullough 18).

Whether you use a signal phrase and parentheses or parentheses only, try to put the parenthetical documentation at the end of the sentence or as close as possible to the material you've cited — without awkwardly interrupting the sentence. Notice that in the example above, the parenthetical reference comes after the closing quotation marks but before the period at the end of the sentence.

3. Two or more works by the same author

If you cite multiple works by one author, include the title of the work you are citing either in the signal phrase or in parentheses. Give the full title if it's brief; otherwise, give a short version.

> Kaplan insists that understanding power in the Near East requires
> "Western leaders who know when to intervene, and do so
> without illusions" (*Eastward* 330).

Put a comma between author and title if both are in the parentheses.

> Understanding power in the Near East requires "Western
> leaders who know when to intervene, and do so without
> illusions" (Kaplan, *Eastward* 330).

4. Authors with the same last name

Give the author's first and last names in any signal phrase, or add the author's first initial in the parenthetical reference.

> *Imaginative* applies not only to modern literature but also to
> writing of all periods, whereas *magical* is often used in writing
> about Arthurian romances (A. Wilson 25).

5. Two or more authors

For a work with two authors, name both, either in a signal phrase or in parentheses.

> Carlson and Ventura's stated goal is to introduce Julio
> Cortázar, Marjorie Agosín, and other Latin American writers
> to an audience of English-speaking adolescents (v).

For a work by three or more authors, name the first author followed by *et al.*

> One popular survey of American literature breaks the contents
> into sixteen thematic groupings (Anderson et al. A19-24).

6. Organization or government as author
Acknowledge the organization either in a signal phrase or in parentheses. It's acceptable to shorten long names.

> The US government warns, "If you are overpaid, we
> will recover any payments not due you" (Social Security
> Administration 12).

7. Author unknown
If you don't know the author, use the work's title or a shortened version of the title in the parenthetical reference.

> A powerful editorial in last week's paper asserts that healthy
> liver donor Mike Hurewitz died because of "frightening" faulty
> postoperative care ("Every Patient's Nightmare").

8. Literary works
When referring to literary works that are available in many different editions, give the page numbers from the edition you are using, followed by information that will let readers of any edition locate the text you are citing.

Novels. Give the page and chapter number, separated by a semicolon.

> In *Pride and Prejudice*, Mrs. Bennet shows no warmth toward
> Jane and Elizabeth when they return from Netherfield
> (105; ch. 12).

Verse plays. Give act, scene, and line numbers, separated by periods.

> Macbeth continues the vision theme when he says, "Thou
> hast no speculation in those eyes / Which thou dost glare
> with" (3.3.96-97).

Poems. Give the part and the line numbers (separated by periods). If a poem has only line numbers, use the word *line(s)* only in the first reference.

> Whitman sets up not only opposing adjectives but also opposing nouns in "Song of Myself" when he says, "I am of old and young, of the foolish as much as the wise, / . . . a child as well as a man" (16.330-32).

> One description of the mere in *Beowulf* is "not a pleasant place" (line 1372). Later, it is labeled "the awful place" (1378).

9. Work in an anthology

Name the author(s) of the work, not the editor of the anthology—either in a signal phrase or in parentheses.

> "It is the teapots that truly shock," according to Cynthia Ozick in her essay on teapots as metaphor (70).

> In *In Short: A Collection of Creative Nonfiction*, readers will find both an essay on Scottish tea (Hiestand) and a piece on teapots as metaphors (Ozick).

10. Encyclopedia or dictionary

For an entry in an encyclopedia or dictionary, give the author's name, if available. For an entry without an author, give the entry's title in parentheses. If entries are arranged alphabetically, no page number is needed.

> According to *Funk & Wagnall's New World Encyclopedia*, early in his career Kubrick's main source of income came from "hustling chess games in Washington Square Park" ("Kubrick, Stanley").

11. Legal and historical documents

For legal cases and acts of law, name the case or act in a signal phrase or in parentheses. Italicize the name of a legal case.

> In 2005, the Supreme Court confirmed in *MGM Studios, Inc. v. Grokster, Ltd.* that peer-to-peer file sharing is copyright infringement.

Do not italicize the titles of laws, acts, or well-known historical documents such as the Declaration of Independence. Give the title and any relevant articles and sections in parentheses. It's fine to use common abbreviations such as *art.* or *sec.* and to abbreviate well-known titles.

> The president is also granted the right to make recess appointments (US Const., art. 2, sec. 2).

12. Sacred text

When citing a sacred text such as the Bible or the Qur'an for the first time, give the title of the edition, and in parentheses give the book, chapter, and verse (or their equivalent), separated by periods. MLA recommends abbreviating the names of the books of the Bible in parenthetical references. Later citations from the same edition do not have to repeat its title.

> The wording from *The New English Bible* follows: "In the beginning of creation, when God made heaven and earth, the earth was without form and void, with darkness over the face of the abyss, and a mighty wind that swept over the surface of the waters" (Gen. 1.1-2).

13. Multivolume work

If you cite more than one volume of a multivolume work, each time you cite one of the volumes, give the volume *and* the page number(s) in parentheses, separated by a colon and a space.

> Sandburg concludes with the following sentence about those paying last respects to Lincoln: "All day long and through the night the unbroken line moved, the home town having its farewell" (4: 413).

If your works cited list includes only a single volume of a multivolume work, give just the page number in parentheses.

14. Two or more works cited together
If you're citing two or more works closely together, you will sometimes need to provide a parenthetical reference for each one.

> Tanner (7) and Smith (viii) have looked at works from a cultural perspective.

If you include both in the same parentheses, separate the references with a semicolon.

> Critics have looked at both *Pride and Prejudice* and *Frankenstein* from a cultural perspective (Tanner 7; Smith viii).

15. Source quoted in another source
When you are quoting text that you found quoted in another source, use the abbreviation *qtd. in* in the parenthetical reference.

> Charlotte Brontë wrote to G. H. Lewes: "Why do you like Miss Austen so very much? I am puzzled on that point" (qtd. in Tanner 7).

16. Work without page numbers
For works without page numbers, including many online sources, identify the source using the author or other information either in a signal phrase or in parentheses.

> Studies show that music training helps children to be better at multitasking later in life ("Hearing the Music").

If the source has chapter, paragraph, or section numbers, use them with the abbreviations *ch., par.,* or *sec.* ("Hearing the Music," par. 2). Alternatively, you can refer to a heading on a screen to help readers locate text.

> Under the heading "The Impact of the Railroad," Rawls notes
> that the transcontinental railroad was called an iron horse and
> a greedy octopus.

For an audio or a video recording, give the hours, minutes, and seconds (separated by colons) as shown on the player: (00:05-08:30).

17. An entire work or a one-page article
If you cite an entire work rather than a part of it, or if you cite a single-page article, there's no need to include page numbers.

> Throughout life, John Adams strove to succeed (McCullough).

NOTES

Sometimes you may need to give information that doesn't fit into the text itself — to thank people who helped you, to provide additional details, to refer readers to other sources, or to add comments about sources. Such information can be given in a *footnote* (at the bottom of the page) or an *endnote* (on a separate page with the heading *Notes* just before your works cited list). Put a superscript number at the appropriate point in your text, signaling to readers to look for the note with the corresponding number. If you have multiple notes, number them consecutively throughout your paper.

> **Text**
> This essay will argue that small liberal arts colleges should not
> recruit athletes and, more specifically, that giving student athletes
> preferential treatment undermines the larger educational goals.[1]

Note

    I. I want to thank all those who have contributed to my thinking on this topic, especially my classmates and my teacher Marian Johnson.

LIST OF WORKS CITED

A works cited list provides full bibliographic information for every source cited in your text.

Core Elements

The new MLA style provides a list of "core elements" for documenting sources, advising writers to list as many of them as possible in the order that MLA specifies. We've used these general principles to provide templates and examples for documenting 53 kinds of sources college writers most often need to cite. The following general guidelines explain how to treat each of the core elements.

Authors and Other Contributors

- If there is one author, list the last name first: Morrison, Toni.

- If there are two authors, list the first author last name first and the second one first name first: Lunsford, Andrea, and Lisa Ede. Put their names in the order given in the work.

- If there are three or more authors, give the first author's name followed by *et al.*: Rose, Mike, et al.

- Include any middle names or initials: Heath, Shirley Brice; Toklas, Alice B.

- If you're citing an editor, translator, or others who are not authors, specify their role. For works with multiple contributors, put the one whose work you wish to highlight before the title, and list any others you want to mention after the title. For contributors named before the title, put the label after the name: Fincher, David, director. For those named after the title, specify their role first: directed by David Fincher.

Titles

- Include any subtitles and capitalize all the words in titles and subtitles except for articles (*a, an, the*), prepositions (*to, at, from,* and so on), and coordinating conjunctions (*and, but, for, or, nor, yet*) — unless they are the first or last word of a title or subtitle.

- Italicize the titles of books, periodicals, and other long whole works (*Pride and Prejudice, Wired*), even if they are part of a larger work.

- Enclose in quotation marks the titles of short works and sources that are part of larger works: "Letter from Birmingham Jail."

- To document a source that has no title, describe it without italics or quotation marks: Letter to the author, Review of doo wop concert.

Publisher

- Write most publishers' names in full, but omit words like *Company* or *Inc.*

- For university presses, use *U* for "University" and *P* for "Press": Princeton UP, U of California P.

Dates

- Whether to give just the year or to include the month and day depends on the source. Give the full date that you find there.

- For books, give the year of publication: 1948. If a book lists more than one date, use the most recent one.

- Periodicals may be published annually, monthly, seasonally, weekly, or daily. Give the full date that you find in the periodical: 2011, Apr. 2011, Spring 2011, 16 Apr. 2011.

- Abbreviate the months except for May, June, and July: Jan., Feb., Mar., Apr., Aug., Sept., Oct., Nov., Dec.

- Because online sources often change or even disappear, provide the date on which you accessed them: Accessed 6 June 2015.

- If an online source includes the time when it was posted or modified, include the time along with the date: 18 Oct. 2005, 9:20 a.m.

Location

- For most print articles and other short works, give a page number or range of pages: p. 24, pp. 24-35. For those that are not on consecutive pages, give the first page number with a plus sign: pp. 24+.

- For online sources, give the URL, omitting *http://* or *https://*. If a source has a permalink, give that.

- For sources found in a database, give the DOI for any source that has one. Otherwise, give the URL.

- For physical objects that you find in a museum, archive, or some other place, give the name of the place and its city: Menil

Collection, Houston. Omit the city if it's part of the place's name: Boston Public Library.

- For performances or other live presentations, name the venue and its city: Mark Taper Forum, Los Angeles. Omit the city if it's part of the venue's name: Berkeley Repertory Theatre.

Punctuation

- Use a period after the author name(s) that start an entry (Morrison, Toni.) and the title of the source you're documenting (*Beloved*.).

- Use a comma between the author's last and first names: Morrison, Toni.

- Sometimes you'll need to provide information about more than one work for a single source — for instance, when you cite an article from a periodical that you access through a database. MLA refers to the periodical and database (or any other entity that holds a source) as "containers." Use commas between elements within each container and put a period at the end of each container. For example:

Semuels, Alana. "The Future Will Be Quiet." *The Atlantic*, Apr. 2016, pp. 19-20. *ProQuest*, search.proquest.com/docview/ 1777443553?accountid+42654. Accessed 5 Apr. 2016.

The guidelines below should help you document kinds of sources you're likely to use. The first section shows how to acknowledge authors and other contributors and applies to all kinds of sources — print, online, or others. Later sections show how to treat titles, publication information, location, and access information for many specific kinds of sources. In general, provide as much information as possible for each source — enough to tell readers how to find a source if they wish to access it themselves.

Authors and Other Contributors

When you name authors and other contributors in your citations, you are crediting them for their work and letting readers know who's in on the conversation. The following guidelines for citing authors and other contributors apply to all sources you cite: in print, online, or in some other medium.

1. One author

Author's Last Name, First Name. *Title*. Publisher, Date.

Anderson, Curtis. *The Long Tail: Why the Future of Business Is Selling Less of More*. Hyperion, 2006.

2. Two authors

1st Author's Last Name, First Name, and 2nd Author's First and Last Names. *Title*. Publisher, Date.

Lunsford, Andrea, and Lisa Ede. *Singular Texts/Plural Authors: Perspectives on Collaborative Writing*. Southern Illinois UP, 1990.

3. Three or more authors

1st Author's Last Name, First Name, et al. *Title*. Publisher, Date.

Sebranek, Patrick, et al. *Writers INC: A Guide to Writing, Thinking, and Learning*. Write Source, 1990.

4. Two or more works by the same author

Give the author's name in the first entry, and then use three hyphens in the author slot for each of the subsequent works, listing them alphabetically by the first important word of each title.

Author's Last Name, First Name. *Title That Comes First
Alphabetically.* Publisher, Date.

---. *Title That Comes Next Alphabetically.* Publisher, Date.

Kaplan, Robert D. *The Coming Anarchy: Shattering the Dreams of
the Post Cold War.* Random House, 2000.

---. *Eastward to Tartary: Travels in the Balkans, the Middle East,
and the Caucasus.* Random House, 2000.

5. Author and editor or translator

Author's Last Name, First Name. *Title.* Role by First and Last
Names, Publisher, Date.

Austen, Jane. *Emma.* Edited by Stephen M. Parrish, W. W.
Norton, 2000.

Dostoevsky, Fyodor. *Crime and Punishment.* Translated by
Richard Pevear and Larissa Volokhonsky, Vintage Books,
1993.

Start with the editor or translator if you are focusing on their contri-
bution rather than the author's.

Pevear, Richard, and Larissa Volokhonsky, translators. *Crime
and Punishment.* By Fyodor Dostoevsky, Vintage Books,
1993.

6. No author or editor

When there's no known author or editor, start with the title.

The Turner Collection in the Clore Gallery. Tate Publications, 1987.

"Being Invisible Closer to Reality." *The Atlanta Journal-
Constitution,* 11 Aug. 2008, p. A3.

7. Organization or government as author

Organization Name. *Title.* Publisher, Date.

Diagram Group. *The Macmillan Visual Desk Reference.*
    Macmillan, 1993.

For a government publication, give the name of the government
first, followed by the names of any department and agency.

United States, Department of Health and Human Services,
    National Institute of Mental Health. *Autism Spectrum
    Disorders.* Government Printing Office, 2004.

When the organization is both author and publisher, start with the
title and list the organization only as the publisher.

Stylebook on Religion 2000: A Reference Guide and Usage Manual.
    Catholic News Service, 2002.

Articles and Other Short Works

Articles, essays, reviews, and other shorts works are found in journals, magazines, newspapers, other periodicals, and books — all of
which you may find in print, online, or in a database. For most short
works, you'll need to provide information about the author, the titles of both the short work and the longer work, any page numbers,
and various kinds of publication information, all explained below.

8. Article in a journal

Print

Author's Last Name, First Name. "Title of Article." *Name of
    Journal,* Volume, Issue, Date, Pages.

Cooney, Brian C. "Considering *Robinson Crusoe*'s 'Liberty of
    Conscience' in an Age of Terror." *College English,* vol. 69,
    no. 3, Jan. 2007, pp. 197-215.

Online

Author's Last Name, First Name. "Title of Article." *Name of Journal,* Volume, Issue, Date, Pages (if any), URL. Accessed Day Month Year.

Gleckman, Jason. "Shakespeare as Poet or Playwright? The Player's Speech in *Hamlet.*" *Early Modern Literary Studies,* vol. 11, no. 3, Jan. 2006, purl.oclc.org/emls/11-3/glechaml. htm. Accessed 31 Mar. 2015.

9. Article in a magazine

Print

Author's Last Name, First Name. "Title of Article." *Name of Magazine,* Date, Pages.

Neyfakh, Leon. "The Future of Getting Arrested." *The Atlantic,* Jan.-Feb. 2015, pp. 26+.

Online

Author's Last Name, First Name. "Title of Article." *Name of Magazine,* Date on web, Pages (if any), URL. Accessed Day Month Year.

Khazan, Olga. "Forgetting and Remembering Your First Language." *The Atlantic,* 24 July 2014, www.theatlantic. com/international/archive/2014/07/learning-forgetting-and-remembering-your-first-language/374906/. Accessed 2 Apr. 2015.

Documentation Map (MLA) / Article in a Print Journal

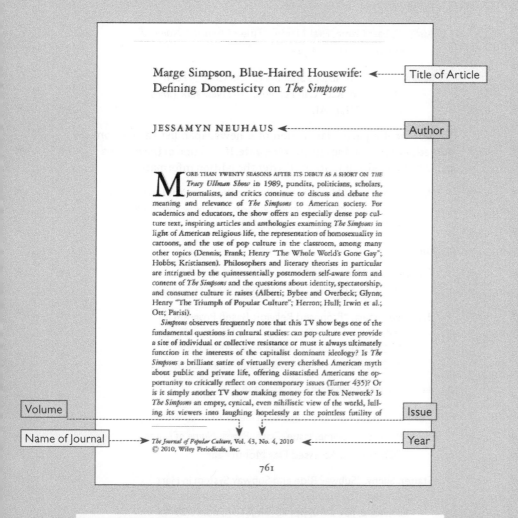

Marge Simpson, Blue-Haired Housewife: <------- Title of Article
Defining Domesticity on *The Simpsons*

JESSAMYN NEUHAUS <------------------------ Author

More than twenty seasons after its debut as a short on *The Tracy Ullman Show* in 1989, pundits, politicians, scholars, journalists, and critics continue to discuss and debate the meaning and relevance of *The Simpsons* to American society. For academics and educators, the show offers an especially dense pop culture text, inspiring articles and anthologies examining *The Simpsons* in light of American religious life, the representation of homosexuality in cartoons, and the use of pop culture in the classroom, among many other topics (Dennis; Frank; Henry "The Whole World's Gone Gay"; Hobbs; Kristiansen). Philosophers and literary theorists in particular are intrigued by the quintessentially postmodern self-aware form and content of *The Simpsons* and the questions about identity, spectatorship, and consumer culture it raises (Alberti; Bybee and Overbeck; Glynn; Henry "The Triumph of Popular Culture"; Herron; Hull; Irwin et al.; Ott; Parisi).

Simpsons observers frequently note that this TV show begs one of the fundamental questions in cultural studies: can pop culture ever provide a site of individual or collective resistance or must it always ultimately function in the interests of the capitalist dominant ideology? Is *The Simpsons* a brilliant satire of virtually every cherished American myth about public and private life, offering dissatisfied Americans the opportunity to critically reflect on contemporary issues (Turner 435)? Or is it simply another TV show making money for the Fox Network? Is *The Simpsons* an empty, cynical, even nihilistic view of the world, lulling its viewers into laughing hopelessly at the pointless futility of

Volume

Name of Journal -------> *The Journal of Popular Culture*, Vol. 43, No. 4, 2010 <------------ Year
© 2010, Wiley Periodicals, Inc.

Issue

761

Neuhaus, Jessamyn. "Marge Simpson, Blue-Haired Housewife:
Defining Domesticity on *The Simpsons*." *The Journal of
Popular Culture*, vol. 43, no. 4, 2010, pp. 761-81.

[211]

10. Article in a newspaper

Print

Author's Last Name, First Name. "Title of Article." *Name of Newspaper,* Date, Pages.

Saulny, Susan, and Jacques Steinberg. "On College Forms, a Question of Race Can Perplex." *The New York Times,* 14 June 2011, p. A1.

To document a particular edition of a newspaper, list the edition (*late ed., natl. ed.,* and so on) after the date. If a section of the newspaper is numbered, put that detail after the edition information.

Burns, John F., and Miguel Helft. "Under Pressure, YouTube Withdraws Muslim Cleric's Videos." *The New York Times,* 4 Nov. 2010, late ed., sec. 1, p. 13.

Online

Author's Last Name, First Name. "Title of Article." *Name of Newspaper,* Date on web, URL. Accessed Day Month Year.

Banerjee, Neela. "Proposed Religion-Based Program for Federal Inmates Is Canceled." *The New York Times,* 28 Oct. 2006, www.nytimes.com/2006/10/28/us/28prison.html?_r=0. Accessed 4 Apr. 2015.

11. Article accessed through a database

Author's Last Name, First Name. "Title of Article." *Name of Periodical,* Volume, Issue, Date, Pages. *Name of Database,* DOI or URL. Accessed Day Month Year.

Stalter, Sunny. "Subway Ride and Subway System in Hart Crane's 'The Tunnel.'" *Journal of Modern Literature,* vol. 33, no. 2, Jan. 2010, pp. 70-91. *JSTOR,* doi:10.2979/jml.2010.33.2.70. Accessed 30 Mar. 2015.

author   title   publication

Documentation Map (MLA) /
Article in an Online Magazine

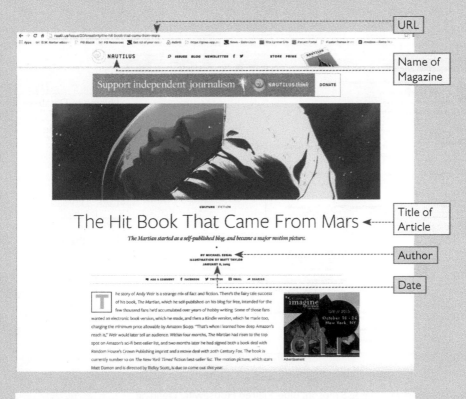

URL

Name of Magazine

Title of Article

Author

Date

Segal, Michael. "The Hit Book That Came From Mars." *Nautilus*. 8 Jan. 2015, nautil.us/issue/20/creativity/the-hit-book-that-came-from -mars. Accessed 10 Oct. 2016.

Documentation Map (MLA) /
Article Accessed through a Database

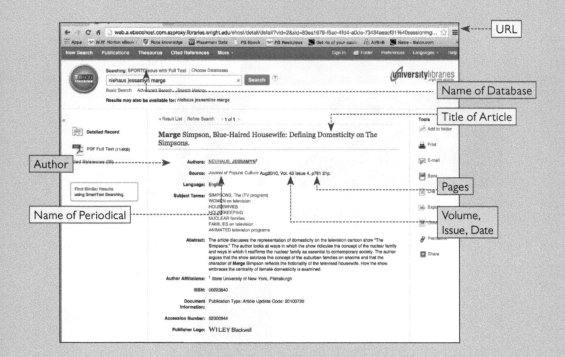

URL

Name of Database

Title of Article

Author

Pages

Name of Periodical

Volume, Issue, Date

Neuhaus, Jessamyn. "Marge Simpson, Blue-Haired Housewife: Defining
Domesticity on *The Simpsons*." *Journal of Popular Culture*, vol. 43,
no. 4, Aug. 2010, pp. 761-81. *SportsDiscus with Full Text*, ezproxy.
libraries.wright.edu/login?url=http://search.ebscohost.com/login
.aspx?direct=true&db=a9h&AN=52300944&site=ehost-live.
Accessed 24 Mar. 2016.

12. Entry in a reference work

Print

Author's Last Name, First Name (if any). "Title of Entry." *Title of Reference Book*, edited by Editor's First and Last Names (if any), Edition number, Publisher, Date, Pages.

"California." *The New Columbia Encyclopedia*, edited by William H. Harris and Judith S. Levey, 4th ed., Columbia UP, 1975, pp. 423-24.

"Feminism." *Longman Dictionary of American English*, Longman, 1983, p. 252.

Online

Document online reference works the same as print ones, adding the URL and access date after the date of publication.

"Baseball." *The Columbia Electronic Encyclopedia*, edited by Paul Lagassé, 6th ed., Columbia UP, 2012, www.infoplease. com/encyclopedia.Accessed 25 May 2016.

13. Editorial

Print

"Title of Editorial." Editorial. *Name of Periodical*, Date, Page.

"Gas, Cigarettes Are Safe to Tax." Editorial. *The Lakeville Journal*, 17 Feb. 2005, p. A10.

Online

"Title of Editorial." Editorial. *Name of Periodical*, Date on web, URL. Accessed Day Month Year.

"Keep the Drinking Age at 21." Editorial. *Chicago Tribune*, 28 Aug. 2008, articles.chicagotribune.com/2008-08-26/ news/0808250487_1_binge-drinking-drinking-age-alcohol-related-crashes. Accessed 26 Apr. 2015.

14. Letter to the editor

Author's Last Name, First Name. "Title of Letter (if any)."
Letter. *Name of Periodical,* Date on web, URL. Accessed
Day Month Year.

Pinker, Steven. "Language Arts." Letter. *The New Yorker,* 4 June
2012, www.newyorker.com/magazine/2012/06/04/
language-arts-2. Accessed 6 Apr. 2015.

15. Review

Print

Reviewer's Last Name, First Name. "Title of Review." Review
of *Title,* by Author's First and Last Names. *Name of
Periodical,* Date, Pages.

Frank, Jeffrey. "Body Count." Review of *The Exception,* by
Christian Jungersen. *The New Yorker,* 30 July 2007,
pp. 86-87.

If a review has no author or title, start with what's being reviewed:

Review of *Ways to Disappear,* by Idra Novey. *The New Yorker,*
28 Mar. 2016, p. 79.

Online

Reviewer's Last Name, First Name. "Title of Review." Review
of *Title,* by Author's First and Last Names. *Name of
Periodical,* Date, URL. Accessed Day Month Year.

Donadio, Rachel. "Italy's Great, Mysterious Storyteller." Review
of *My Brilliant Friend,* by Elena Ferrante. *The New York Review
of Books,* 18 Dec. 2014, www.nybooks.com/articles/2014/
12/18/italys-great-mysterious-storyteller. Accessed
28 Sept. 2015.

16. Comment on an online article

Commenter. Comment on "Title of Article." *Name of Periodical*, Date posted, Time posted, URL. Accessed Day Month Year.

Nick. Comment on "The Case for Reparations." *The Atlantic*, 22 May 2014, 3:04 p.m., www.theatlantic.com/ business/archive/2014/05/how-to-comment-on-reparations/371422/#article-comments. Accessed 8 May 2015.

Books and Parts of Books

For most books, you'll need to provide information about the author, the title, the publisher, and the year of publication. If you found the book inside a larger volume, a database, or some other work, be sure to specify that as well.

17. Basic entries for a book

Print

Author's Last Name, First Name. *Title*. Publisher, Year of publication.

Watson, Brad. *Miss Jane*. W. W. Norton, 2016

Ebook

Document an ebook as you would a print book, but add information about the ebook—or the type of ebook if you know it.

Watson, Brad. *Miss Jane*. Ebook, W. W. Norton, 2016.

Watson, Brad. *Miss Jane*. Kindle ed., W. W. Norton, 2016.

In a database

Author's Last Name, First Name. *Title*. Publisher, Year of publication. *Name of Database*, DOI or URL. Accessed Day Month Year.

Anderson, Sherwood. *Winesburg, Ohio.* B. W. Huebsch, 1919. *Bartleby.com,* www.bartleby.com/156/. Accessed 8 Apr. 2015.

18. Anthology

Last Name, First Name, editor. *Title.* Publisher, Year of publication.

Hall, Donald, editor. *The Oxford Book of Children's Verse in America.* Oxford UP, 1985.

Kitchen, Judith, and Mary Paumier Jones, editors. *In Short: A Collection of Brief Creative Nonfiction.* W. W. Norton, 1996.

19. Work in an anthology

Author's Last Name, First Name. "Title of Work." *Title of Anthology,* edited by First and Last Names, Publisher, Year of publication, Pages.

Achebe, Chinua. "Uncle Ben's Choice." *The Seagull Reader: Literature,* edited by Joseph Kelly, W. W. Norton, 2005, pp. 23-27.

Documentation Map (MLA) / Print Book

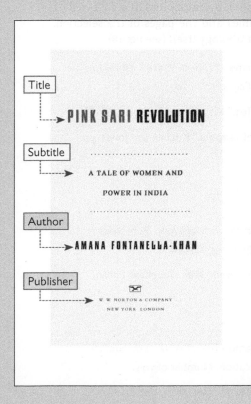

Title

PINK SARI REVOLUTION

Subtitle

A TALE OF WOMEN AND

POWER IN INDIA

Author

AMANA FONTANELLA-KHAN

Publisher

W. W. NORTON & COMPANY
NEW YORK · LONDON

Year of Publication

For my parents and James, naturally

Copyright © 2013 by Amana Fontanella-Khan

All rights reserved
Printed in the United States of America
First published as a Norton paperback 2014

For information about permission to reproduce selections from this book,
write to Permissions, W. W. Norton & Company, Inc.,
500 Fifth Avenue, New York, N.Y. 10110

For information about special discounts for bulk purchases, please contact
W. W. Norton Special Sales at specialsales@wwnorton.com or 800-233-4830

Manufacturing by Courier Westford
Book design by Barbara M. Bachman
Production manager: Anna Oler

Library of Congress Cataloging-in-Publication Data

Fontanella-Khan, Amana.
Pink sari revolution : a tale of women and power in India / Amana Fontanella-Khan.
—First Edition.
pages cm
Includes bibliographical references and index.
ISBN 978-0-393-06297-7 (hardcover)
1. Women—India—Social conditions. 2. Women's rights—India. 3. Feminism—India.
4. Pal, Sampat, 1963- I. Title.
HQ1743.F66 2013
305.4200954—dc23
2013018948

ISBN 978-0-393-34947-4 pbk.

W. W. Norton & Company, Inc.
500 Fifth Avenue, New York, N.Y. 10110
www.wwnorton.com

W. W. Norton & Company Ltd.
Castle House, 75/76 Wells Street, London W1T 3QT

1 2 3 4 5 6 7 8 9 0

Fontanella-Khan, Amana. *Pink Sari Revolution: A Tale of Women and Power in India.* W. W. Norton, 2013.

Two or more works from one anthology

Prepare an entry for each selection by author and title, followed by the anthology editors' last names and the pages of the selection. Then include an entry for the anthology itself (see no. 18).

Author's Last Name, First Name. "Title of Work." Anthology
    Editors' Last Names, Pages.

Hiestand, Emily. "Afternoon Tea." Kitchen and Jones, pp. 65-67.

Ozick, Cynthia. "The Shock of Teapots." Kitchen and Jones, pp.
    68-71.

20. Multivolume work

All volumes

Author's Last Name, First Name. *Title of Work*. Publisher,
    Year(s) of publication. Number of vols.

Churchill, Winston. *The Second World War*. Houghton Mifflin,
    1948-53. 6 vols.

Single volume

Author's Last Name, First Name. *Title of Work*. Vol. number,
    Publisher, Year of publication. Number of vols.

Sandburg, Carl. *Abraham Lincoln: The War Years*. Vol. 2,
    Harcourt, Brace & World, 1939. 4 vols.

21. Book in a series

Author's Last Name, First Name. *Title of Book*. Edited by First
    and Last Names, Publisher, Year of publication. Series Title.

Walker, Alice. *Everyday Use*. Edited by Barbara T. Christian,
    Rutgers UP, 1994. Women Writers: Texts and Contexts.

22. Graphic narrative

Author's Last Name, First Name. *Title*. Publisher, Year of publication.

Bechdel, Alison. *Fun Home: A Family Tragicomedy*. Houghton Mifflin, 2006.

If the work has both an author and an illustrator, start with the one whose work is more relevant to your research, and label the role of anyone who's not an author.

Pekar, Harvey. *Bob & Harv's Comics*. Illustrated by R. Crumb, Running Press, 1996.

Crumb, R., illustrator. *Bob & Harv's Comics*. By Harvey Pekar, Running Press, 1996.

23. Sacred text

If you cite a specific edition of a religious text, you need to include it in your works cited list.

The New English Bible with the Apocrypha. Oxford UP, 1971.

The Torah: A Modern Commentary. Edited by W. Gunther Plaut, Union of American Hebrew Congregations, 1981.

24. Edition other than the first

Author's Last Name, First Name. *Title*. Name or number of edition, Publisher, Year of publication.

Fowler, H. W. *A Dictionary of Modern English*. 2nd ed., Oxford UP, 1965.

25. Republished work

Author's Last Name, First Name. *Title*. Year of original publication. Current publisher, Year of republication.

Bierce, Ambrose. *Civil War Stories*. 1909. Dover, 1994.

26. Foreword, introduction, preface, or afterword

Part Author's Last Name, First Name. Name of Part. *Title of Book,* by Author's First and Last Names, Publisher, Year of publication, Pages.

Tanner, Tony. Introduction. *Pride and Prejudice*, by Jane Austen, Penguin, 1972, pp. 7-46.

27. Published letter

Letter Writer's Last Name, First Name. Letter to First and Last Names. Day Month Year. *Title of Book,* edited by First and Last Names, Publisher, Year of publication, Pages.

White, E. B. Letter to Carol Angell. 28 May 1970. *Letters of E. B. White*, edited by Dorothy Lobarno Guth, Harper & Row, 1976, p. 600.

28. Paper at a conference

Paper published in conference proceedings

Author's Last Name, First Name. "Title of Paper." *Title of Published Conference Proceedings,* edited by First and Last Names, Publisher, Year of publication, Pages.

Flower, Linda. "Literate Action." *Composition in the Twenty-first Century: Crisis and Change*, edited by Lynn Z. Bloom, et al., Southern Illinois UP, 1996, pp. 249-60.

Paper heard at a conference

Author's Last Name, First Name. "Title of Paper." Title of Conference, Day Month Year, Venue, City.

Hern, Katie. "Inside an Accelerated Reading and Writing Classroom." Conference on Acceleration in Developmental Education, 15 June 2016, Sheraton Inner Harbor Hotel, Baltimore.

29. Dissertation

> Author's Last Name, First Name. *Title.* Diss. Institution, Year, Publisher, Year of publication.

> Goggin, Peter N. *A New Literacy Map of Research and Scholarship in Computers and Writing.* Diss. Indiana U of Pennsylvania, 2000, University Microfilms International, 2001.

For an unpublished dissertation, put the title in quotation marks, and end with the institution and the year.

> Kim, Loel. "Students Respond to Teacher Comments: A Comparison of Online Written and Voice Modalities." Diss. Carnegie Mellon U, 1998.

Websites

Many sources are available in multiple media — for example, a print periodical that is also on the web and contained in digital databases — but some are published only on websites. This section covers the latter.

30. Entire website

> Last Name, First Name, role. *Title of Site.* Publisher, Date, URL. Accessed Day Month Year.

> Zalta, Edward N., principal editor. *Stanford Encyclopedia of Philosophy.* Metaphysics Research Lab, Center for the Study of Language, Stanford U, 1995-2015, plato.stanford. edu/index.html. Accessed 21 Apr. 2015.

Personal website

> Author's Last Name, First Name. *Title of Site.* Date, URL. Accessed Day Month Year.

> Heath, Shirley Brice. *Shirley Brice Heath.* 2015, shirleybriceheath. net. Accessed 6 June 2015.

Documentation Map (MLA) / Work on a Website

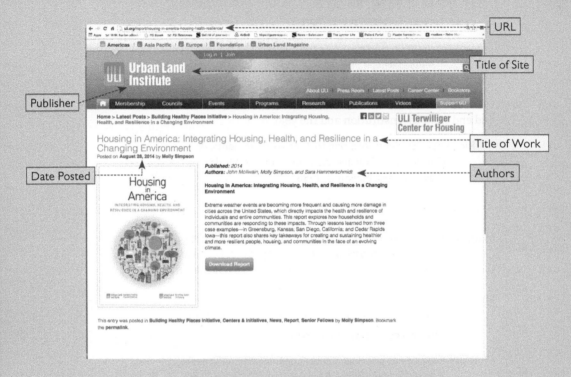

McIlwain, John, et al. "Housing in America: Integrating Housing, Health,
and Resilience in a Changing Environment." *Urban Land Institute*,
28 Aug. 2014, uli.org/report/housing-in-america-housing-health-
resilience. Accessed 17 Sept. 2015.

31. Work on a website

Author's Last Name, First Name (if any). "Title of Work." *Title of Site,* Publisher, Date, URL. Accessed Day Month Year.

"Global Minnesota: Immigrants Past and Present." *Immigration History Research Center,* U of Minnesota, 2015, cla.umn. edu.ihrc. Accessed 25 May 2016.

32. Blog entry

Author's Last Name, First Name. "Title of Blog Entry." *Title of Blog,* Date, URL. Accessed Day Month Year.

Hollmichel, Stefanie. "Bringing Up the Bodies." *So Many Books,* 10 Feb. 2014, somanybooksblog.com/2014/02/10/bring-up-the-bodies/. Accessed 12 Feb. 2014.

Document a whole blog as you would an entire website (no. 30) and a comment on a blog as you would a comment on an online article (no. 16).

33. Wiki

"Title of Entry." *Title of Wiki,* Publisher, Date, URL. Accessed Day Month Year.

"Pi." *Wikipedia,* Wikimedia Foundation, 28 Aug. 2013, en.wikipedia.org/wiki/Pi. Accessed 25 Oct. 2013.

Personal Communication and Social Media

34. Personal letter

Sender's Last Name, First Name. Letter to the author. Day Month Year.

Quindlen, Anna. Letter to the author. 11 Apr. 2013.

35. Email

Sender's Last Name, First Name. "Subject Line." Received by First and Last Names, Day Month Year.

Smith, William. "Teaching Grammar—Some Thoughts." Received by Richard Bullock, 19 Nov. 2013.

36. Text message

Sender's Last Name, First Name. Text message. Received by First and Last Names, Day Month Year.

Douglass, Joanne. Text message. Received by Kim Yi, 4 June 2015.

37. Post to an online forum

Author. "Subject line" or "Full text of short untitled post." *Name of Forum*, Day Month Year, URL.

@somekiryu. "What's the hardest part about writing for you?" *Reddit*, 22 Apr. 2016, redd.it/4fyni0.

38. Post to *Twitter, Facebook*, or other social media

Author. "Full text of short untitled post" or "Title" or Descriptive label. *Name of Site*, Day Month Year, Time, URL.

@POTUS (Barack Obama). "I'm proud of the @NBA for taking a stand against gun violence. Sympathy for victims isn't enough—change requires all of us speaking up." *Twitter*, 23 Dec. 2015, 1:21 p.m., twitter.com/POTUS/status/679773729749078016.

Black Lives Matter. "Rise and Grind! Did you sign this petition
yet? We now have a sign on for ORGANIZATIONS to
lend their support." *Facebook,* 23 Oct. 2015, 11:30 a.m.,
www.facebook.com/BlackLivesMatter/photos/a.294807
204023865.1073741829.180212755483311/504711973033
386/?type=3&theater.

@quarterlifepoetry. Illustrated poem about girl at Target.
Instagram, 22 Jan. 2015, www.instagram.com/p/
yLO6fSurRH/.

Audio, Visual, and Other Sources

39. Advertisement

Print

Name of Product or Company. Advertisement or Description
of it. *Name of Periodical,* Date, Page.

Cal Alumni Association. Sports merchandise ad. *California,* Spring
2016, p. 3.

Audio or video

Name of Product or Company. Advertisement or Description
of it. Date. *Name of Host Site,* URL. Accessed Day Month
Year.

Chrysler. Super Bowl commercial. 6 Feb. 2011. *YouTube,*
www.youtube.com/watch?v=SKLZ254Y_jtc. Accessed
1 May 2015.

40. Art

Original

Artist's Last Name, First Name. *Title of Art.* Year created,
Venue, City.

Van Gogh, Vincent. *The Potato Eaters.* 1885, Van Gogh Museum, Amsterdam.

Reproduction

Artist's Last Name, First Name. *Title of Art.* Year created. *Title of Book,* by First and Last Names, Publisher, Year of publication, Page.

Van Gogh, Vincent. *The Potato Eaters.* 1885. *History of Art: A Survey of the Major Visual Arts from the Dawn of History to the Present Day,* by H. W. Janson, Prentice-Hall/Harry N. Abrams, 1969, p. 508.

Online

Artist's Last Name, First Name. *Title of Art.* Year created. *Name of Site,* URL. Accessed Day Month Year.

Warhol, Andy. *Self-portrait.* 1979. *J. Paul Getty Museum,* www .getty.edu/art/collection/objects/106971/andy-warhol-self-portrait-american-1979/. Accessed 20 Jan. 2015.

41. Cartoon

Print

Author's Last Name, First Name. "Title of Cartoon." *Name of Periodical,* Date, Page.

Chast, Roz. "The Three Wise Men of Thanksgiving." *The New Yorker,* 1 Dec. 2003, p. 174.

Online

Author's Last Name, First Name. "Title of Cartoon." *Title of Site,* Date, URL. Accessed Day Month Year.

Munroe, Randall. "Up Goer Five." *xkcd,* 12 Nov. 2012, xkcd. com/1133/. Accessed 22 Apr. 2015.

42. Supreme Court case

First Plaintiff v. First Defendant. *United States Reports*
citation. Name of Court, Year of decision, URL.
Accessed Day Month Year.

District of Columbia v. Heller. 554 US 570. Supreme Court of
the US, 2008,www.lawcornell.edu/supct/html/07-290.
ZS.html. Accessed 3 June 2016.

43. Film

Name individuals based on the focus of your project — the director,
the screenwriter, the cinematographer, or someone else.

Title of Film. Role by First and Last Names, Production Studio,
Date.

Breakfast at Tiffany's. Directed by Blake Edwards, Paramount,
1961.

Streaming

Title of Film. Role by First and Last Names, Production Studio,
Date. *Streaming Service,* URL. Accessed Day Month Year.

Interstellar. Directed by Christopher Nolan, Paramount, 2014.
Amazon Prime Video, www.amazon.com/Interstellar-
Matthew-McConaughey/dp/B00TU9UFTS. Accessed
2 May 2015.

44. Interview

If the interview has a title, put it in quotation marks following the subject's name.

Broadcast

Subject's Last Name, First Name. Interview or "Title of
     Interview." *Title of Program,* Network, Day Month Year.

Gates, Henry Louis, Jr. Interview. *Fresh Air,* NPR, 9 Apr. 2002.

Published

Subject's Last Name, First Name. Interview or "Title of
     Interview." *Name of Publication,* Date, Pages.

Stone, Oliver. Interview. *Esquire,* Nov. 2004, pp. 170-71.

Personal

Subject's Last Name, First Name. Personal interview. Day
     Month Year.

Roddick, Andy. Personal interview. 17 Aug. 2013.

45. Map

"Title of Map." Publisher, URL. Accessed Day Month Year.

"National Highway System." US Department of Transportation
     Federal Highway Administration, www.fhwa.dot.gov/
     planning/images/nhs.pdf. Accessed 10 May 2015.

46. Musical score

Composer's Last Name, First Name. *Title of Composition.* Year
     of composition. Publisher, Year of publication.

Stravinsky, Igor. *Petrushka.* 1911. W. W. Norton, 1967.

47. Online video

> Author's Last Name, First Name. *Title. Name of Host Site,* Date, URL. Accessed Day Month Year.

Westbrook, Adam. *Cause/Effect: The Unexpected Origins of Terrible Things. Vimeo,* 9 Sept. 2014, vimeo.com/105681474. Accessed 20 Dec. 2015.

48. Oral presentation

> Presenter's Last Name, First Name. "Title of Presentation." Sponsoring Institution, Date, Location.

Cassin, Michael. "Nature in the Raw — The Art of Landscape Painting." Berkshire Institute for Lifelong Learning, 24 Mar. 2005, Clark Art Institute, Williamstown.

49. Podcast

If you accessed a podcast online, give the URL and date of access; if you accessed it through a service such as *iTunes* or *Spotify*, indicate that instead.

> Last Name, First Name, role. "Title of Episode." *Title of Program,* season, episode, Sponsor, Date, URL. Accessed Day Month Year.

Koenig, Sarah, host. "DUSTWUN." *Serial,* season 2, episode 1, WBEZ, 10 Dec. 2015, serialpodcast.org/season-two/1/ dustwun. Accessed 23 Apr. 2016.

Foss, Gilad, writer and performer. "Aquaman's Brother-in-Law." *Superhero Temp Agency,* season 1, episode 1, 16 Apr. 2015. *iTunes.*

50. **Radio program**

Last Name, First Name, role. "Title of Episode." *Title of Program*, Station, Day Month Year of broadcast, URL. Accessed Day Month Year.

Glass, Ira, host. "In Defense of Ignorance." *This American Life*, WBEZ, 22 Apr. 2016, thisamericanlife.org/radio-archives/episode/585/in-defense-of-ignorance. Accessed 2 May 2016.

51. **Sound recording**

Online

Last Name, First Name. "Title of Work." *Title of Album*, Distributor, Date. *Name of Audio Service*.

Simone, Nina. "To Be Young, Gifted and Black." *Black Gold*, RCA Records, 1969. *Spotify*.

CD

Last Name, First Name. "Title of Work." *Title of Album*, Distributor, Date.

Brown, Greg. "Canned Goods." *The Live One*, Red House, 1995.

52. **TV show**

Original Broadcast

"Title of Episode." *Title of Show*, role by First and Last Names, season, episode, Network, Day Month Year.

"The Silencer." *Criminal Minds*, written by Erica Messer, season 8, episode 1, NBC, 26 Sept. 2012.

DVD

"Title of Episode." Broadcast Year. *Title of DVD,* role by First and
    Last Names, season, episode, Production Studio, Release
    Year, disc number.

"The Pants Tent." 2003. *Curb Your Enthusiasm: Season One,*
    performance by Larry David, season 1, episode 1, HBO
    Video, 2006, disc 1.

Online

"Title of Episode." *Title of Show,* role by First and Last Names
    (if any), season, episode, Production Studio, Day Month
    Year. *Name of Host Site,* URL. Accessed Day Month Year.

"Shadows in the Glass." *Marvel's Daredevil,* season 1, episode 8,
    Netflix, 10 Apr. 2015. *Netflix,* www.netflix.com/watch/8
    0018198?trackId=13752289&tctx=0%2C7%2Cbcfd6259-
    6e64-4d51-95ab-2a9f747eabf0-158552415. Accessed 3
    Nov. 2015.

53. Video game

Last name, First name, role. *Title of Game.* Distributor, Date of
    release. Gaming System or Platform.

Metzen, Chris, and James Waugh, writers. *StarCraft II: Legacy of
    the Void.* Blizzard Entertainment, 2015. OS X.

FORMATTING A RESEARCH PAPER

Name, course, title. MLA does not require a separate title page. In
the upper left-hand corner of your first page, include your name,
your professor's name, the name of the course, and the date. Center
the title of your paper on the line after the date; capitalize it as you
would a book title.

Page numbers. In the upper right-hand corner of each page, one-half inch below the top of the page, include your last name and the page number. Number pages consecutively throughout your paper.

Font, spacing, margins, and indents. Choose a font that is easy to read (such as Times New Roman) and that provides a clear contrast between regular and italic text. Double-space the entire paper, including your works cited list. Set one-inch margins at the top, bottom, and sides of your text; do not justify your text. The first line of each paragraph should be indented one-half inch from the left margin.

Long quotations. When quoting more than three lines of poetry, more than four lines of prose, or dialogue between characters in a drama, set off the quotation from the rest of your text, indenting it one-half inch (or five spaces) from the left margin. Do not use quotation marks, and put any parenthetical documentation *after* the final punctuation.

> In *Eastward to Tartary*, Kaplan captures ancient and contemporary Antioch for us:
>
> > At the height of its glory in the Roman-Byzantine age, when it had an amphitheater, public baths, aqueducts, and sewage pipes, half a million people lived in Antioch. Today the population is only 125,000. With sour relations between Turkey and Syria, and unstable politics throughout the Middle East, Antioch is now a backwater—seedy and tumbledown, with relatively few tourists. I found it altogether charming. (123)

> In the first stanza of Arnold's "Dover Beach," the exclamations make clear that the speaker is addressing someone who is also present in the scene:
>
> > Come to the window, sweet is the night air!
> > Only, from the long line of spray

> Where the sea meets the moon-blanched land,
>
> Listen! You hear the grating roar
>
> Of pebbles which the waves draw back, and fling. (6-10)

Be careful to maintain the poet's line breaks. If a line does not fit on one line of your paper, put the extra words on the next line. Indent that line an additional quarter inch (or two spaces).

Illustrations. Insert illustrations close to the text that discusses them. For tables, provide a number (*Table 1*) and a title on separate lines above the table. Below the table, provide a caption and information about the source. For graphs, photos, and other figures, provide a figure number (*Fig. 1*),caption, and source information below the figure. If you give only brief source information (such as a parenthetical note), or if the source is cited elsewhere in your text, include it in your list of works cited. Be sure to make clear how any illustrations relate to your point.

List of Works Cited. Start your list on a new page, following any notes. Center the title and double-space the entire list. Begin each entry at the left margin, and indent subsequent lines one-half inch (or five spaces). Alphabetize the list by authors' last names (or by editors' or translators' names, if appropriate). Alphabetize works with no author or editor by title, disregarding *A*, *An*, and *The*. To cite more than one work by a single author, list them as in no. 4 on 548.

SAMPLE RESEARCH PAPER

Walter Przybylowski wrote the following analysis, "Holding Up the Hollywood Stagecoach: The European Take on the Western," for a first-year writing course. It is formatted according to the guidelines of the MLA (style.mla.org).

½"

Przybylowski   1

Walter Przybylowski

Professor Matin

English 102, Section 3

4 May 2009

Put your last name and the page num-ber in the upper-right corner of each page.

Center the title.

Holding Up the Hollywood Stagecoach:

The European Take on the Western

Double-space throughout.

The Western film has long been considered by film scholars and enthusiasts to be a distinctly American genre. Not only its subject matter but its characteristic themes originate in America's own violent and exciting past. For many years, Hollywood sold images of hard men fighting savages on the plains to the worldwide public; by ignoring the more complicated aspects of "how the West was won" and the true nature of relations between Native Americans and whites, filmmakers were able to reap great financial and professional rewards. In particular, the huge success of John Ford's 1939 film *Stagecoach* brought about countless imitations that led over the next few decades to American Westerns playing in a sort of loop, which reinforced the same ideas and myths in film after film.

Indent paragraphs 5 spaces or ½".

After the success of German-made Westerns in the 1950s, though, a new take on Westerns was ushered in by other European countries. Leading the Euro-Western charge, so to speak, were the Italians, whose cynical, often politically pointed Westerns left a permanent impact on an American-based genre. Europeans, particularly the Italians, challenged the dominant conventions of the American Western by complicating the morality of the characters, blurring the lines between good and evil, and also by complicating the traditional narrative, visual, and aural structures of Westerns. In this way, the genre motifs that *Stagecoach* initiated are explored in the European Westerns of the 1950s, 1960s, and early 1970s, yet with a striking difference in style. Specifically, Sergio Leone's 1968 film *Once Upon a Time in the West* broke many of the rules set by the Hollywood Western and in the process created a new visual language for the Western. Deconstructing key scenes from this film reveals the demythologization at work in many of the Euro-Westerns, which led to a genre enriched by its presentation of a more complicated American West.

 Stagecoach is a perfect example of almost all the visual, sound, and plot motifs that would populate "classic" Hollywood Westerns for the next few decades. The story concerns a group of people, confined for most of the movie inside a stagecoach, who are attempting to cross a stretch of land made dangerous by Apache Indians on the warpath. Little effort is made to develop the characters of the Indians, who appear mainly as a narrative device, adversaries that the heroes must overcome in order to maintain their peaceful existence. This plot, with minor changes, could be used as a general description for countless Westerns. In his book *Crowded Prairie: American National Identity in the Hollywood Western*, Michael Coyne explains the significance of *Stagecoach* to the Western genre and its influence in solidifying the genre's archetypes:

> [I]t was *Stagecoach* which . . . redefined the contours of the myth. The good outlaw, the whore with a heart of gold, the Madonna/Magdalene dichotomy between opposing female

Quotations of more than 4 lines are indented ½" (5 spaces) and double-spaced.

leads, the drunken philosopher, the last-minute cavalry rescue, the lonely walk down Main Street—all became stereotypes from *Stagecoach*'s archetypes. *Stagecoach* quickly became the model against which other "A" Westerns would be measured. (18-19)

For a set-off quotation, the parenthetical reference follows the closing punctuation.

Coyne is not exaggerating when he calls it "the model": in fact, all of these stereotypes became a sort of checklist of things that audiences expected to see. The reliance on a preconceived way to sell Western films to the public—where you could always tell the good characters from the bad and knew before the film ended how each character would end up—led to certain genre expectations that the directors of the Euro-Westerns would later knowingly reconfigure. As the influential critic Pauline Kael wrote in her 1965 book *Kiss Kiss Bang Bang*, "The original *Stagecoach* had a mixture of reverie and reverence about the American past that made the picture seem almost folk art; we wanted to believe in it even if we didn't" (52).

Verb in signal phrase is past tense because date of source is mentioned.

Parenthetical reference following a quotation within the main text goes before the closing punctuation of the sentence.

There seemed to be a need not just in Americans but in moviegoers around the world to believe that there was (or had been) a great untamed land out there just waiting to be cultivated. More important, as Kael pointed out, Americans wanted to believe that the building of America was a wholly righteous endeavor wherein the land was free for the taking—the very myth that Europeans later debunked through parody and subversive filmmaking techniques. According to Theresa Harlan, author of works on Native American art, the myth was based on the need of early white settlers to make their elimination of American Indians more palatable in light of the settlers' professed Christian beliefs. In her article "Adjusting the Focus for an Indigenous Presence," Harlan writes that

> Eurocentric frontier ideology and the representations of indigenous people it produced were used to convince many American settlers that indigenous people were incapable of discerning the difference between a presumed civilized existence and their own "primitive" state. (6)

Although this myth had its genesis long before the advent of motion pictures, the Hollywood Western drew inspiration from it and continued to legitimize and reinforce its message. *Stagecoach*, with its high level of technical skill and artistry, redefined the contours of the myth, and a close look at the elements that made the film the "classic" model of the Western is imperative in order to truly understand its influence.

The musical themes that underscore the actions of the characters are especially powerful in this regard and can be as powerful as the characters' visual representation on screen. In *Stagecoach*, an Apache does not appear until more than halfway through the movie, but whenever one is mentioned, the soundtrack fills with sinister and foreboding drumbeats. The first appearance of Indians is a scene without dialogue, in which the camera pans between the stagecoach crossing through the land and Apaches watching from afar. The music that accompanies this scene is particularly telling, since as the camera pans between stagecoach and Apaches, the music shifts in tone dramatically from a pleasant melody to a score filled with dread. When the heroes shoot and kill the Apaches, then, the viewer has already been subjected to specific film techniques to give the stagecoach riders moral certitude in their annihilation of the alien menace. To emphasize this point, the music swells victoriously every time an Apache is shown falling from a horse. This kind of score is powerful stuff to accompany an image and does its best to tell the viewers how they should react. When Europeans start to make Westerns, the line of moral certitude will become less distinct.

In her essay "Of Mother Nature and Marlboro Men: An Inquiry into the Cultural Meanings of Landscape Photography," Deborah Bright argues that landscape photography has reinforced certain formulaic myths about landscape, and the same can be said of the Hollywood Western during the 1940s and 1950s. For example, in *Stagecoach*, when the stagecoach finally sets out for its journey through Apache territory, a fence is juxtaposed against the vast wide-open country in the foreground. The meaning is clear--the stagecoach is leaving civilized society to venture into the wilds of the West, and music swells as the coach crosses into that vast landscape (Fig. 1). Ford uses landscape in this way to engender in the audience the desired response of longing for a time gone past, where there was land free for the taking and plenty to go around. Yet Bright suggests that "[i]f we are to redeem landscape photography from its narrow self-reflexive project, why not openly question the assumptions about nature and culture that it has traditionally served and use our practice instead to criticize them?" (141).

Figure number calls readers' attention to Illustration.

Brackets show that the writer has changed a capital letter to lowercase to make the quotation fit smoothly into his own sentence.

Fig. 1. In *Stagecoach*, swelling music signals the coach's passage through the western landscape. Photograph from *Internet Movie Database*, www.imdb.com.

Documentation of image source given after the caption.

This is exactly what Europeans, and Italians in particular, seem to have done with the Western. When Europeans started to make their own Westerns, they took advantage of their outsider status in relation to an American genre by openly questioning the myths that have been established by *Stagecoach* and its cinematic brethren.

Sergio Leone's *Once Upon a Time in the West* is a superior example of a European artist's take on the art form of the American Western. The title alone signals the element of storytelling: in a sublime stroke of titling, Leone makes the connection between Western films and fairy tales and announces that the genre myths that *Stagecoach* presented for audiences to revel in will now be questioned. In his book *Spaghetti Westerns*, Christopher Frayling observes that *"Once Upon a Time* is concerned with the 'language' and 'syntax' of the Western . . . an unmasking or 'display' of the terminology of the genre" (213). The "plot" of the film is flimsy, driven by the efforts of a mysterious character played by Charles Bronson to avenge himself against Henry Fonda's character, a lowdown gunfighter trying to become a legitimate businessman. Claudia Cardinale plays a prostitute who is trying to put her past behind her. All of these classic types from countless American Westerns are integrated into the "Iron Horse" plotline, wherein the coming of the railroad signifies great changes in the West. The similarities to American Westerns, on paper at least, seem to be so great as to make *Once Upon a Time* almost a copy of what had long been done in Hollywood, but a closer look at European Westerns and at this film in particular shows that Leone is consciously sending up the stereotypes. After all, he needs to work within the genre's language if he is to adequately challenge it.

The opening scene of *Once Upon a Time* runs roughly ten minutes and provides an introduction to many of the aesthetic and ideological changes made by the European Western to the American model. The viewer quickly notices how little dialogue is spoken during the whole ten minutes, since the requirements of post-synchronization (the

rerecording of the movie's dialogue after filming in order to produce
a clearer soundtrack) and country-specific dubbing into multiple
languages resulted in a reliance on strong visual storytelling. Financial
reasons made English the default language for most Euro-Westerns since
it produced the largest market and, consequently, the greatest monetary
rewards. Even cast members who could not speak it would sometimes
mouth the words in English. However, the use of post-synchronization
has an unsettling effect on any viewer, even an English-speaking one,
who is used to the polished soundtracks of a Hollywood film. When
viewers experience a post-synchronized film, the result is a distancing
from the material; certain characters match the words coming out of
their mouths better than others, so the movie takes on a surreal edge.
This visual touch perfectly complements Leone's goal—to divorce the
reality of the West from the myths encouraged by American Westerns.

During the opening of *Once Upon a Time in the West*, the viewer
is given a kind of audio and visual tour of Euro-Western aesthetics.
Leone introduces three gunmen in typical Italian Western style, with
the first presented by a cut to a dusty boot heel from which the camera
slowly pans up until it reaches the top of the character's cowboy hat.
During this pan, the gunman's gear and its authenticity—a major aspect
of the Italian Western—can be taken in by the audience. A broader
examination of the genre would show that many Euro-Westerns use this
tactic of hyperrealistic attention to costuming and weaponry, which
Ignacio Ramonet argues is intended to distract the viewer from the
unreality of the landscape:

Extreme realism of bodies (hairy, greasy, foul-smelling), clothes or objects (including mania for weapons) in Italian films is above all intended to compensate for the complete fraud of the space and origins. The green pastures, farms and cattle of American Westerns are replaced by large, deserted canyons. (32)

In the opening scene, the other two gunfighters are introduced by a camera panning across the room, allowing characters to materialize seemingly out of nowhere. Roger Ebert notes that Leone

> established a rule that he follows throughout . . . that the ability
> to see is limited by the sides of the frame. At important moments
> in the film, what the camera cannot see, the characters cannot
> see, and that gives Leone the freedom to surprise us with
> entrances that cannot be explained by the practical geography of
> his shots.

No page number given for online source.

It is these aesthetic touches created to compensate for a fraudulent landscape that ushered in a new visual language for the Western. The opening of *Once Upon a Time in the West* undercuts any preconceived notion of how a Western should be filmed, and this is exactly Leone's intention: "The director had obviously enjoyed dilating the audience's sense of time, exploiting, in his ostentatious way, the rhetoric of the Western, and dwelling on the tiniest details to fulfill his intention" (Frayling 197). By using jarring edits with amplified sounds, Leone informs the audience not only that he has seen all the popular Hollywood Westerns, but that he is purposely not going to give them that kind of movie. The opening ten-minute scene would be considered

When no signal phrase is used to introduce a quotation, the author's name is included in the parenthetical citation.

needlessly long in a typical Hollywood Western, but Leone is not making a copy of a Hollywood Western, and the length of such scenes allows for more meditation on the styling of the genre. In fact, it is this reliance on the audience's previously established knowledge of Westerns that allows Euro-Westerns to subvert the genre. Barry Langford, writing for *Film History*, claims that

> *Once Upon a Time* strips bare the form's claims on historical verisimilitude and pushes its innately ritualized and stylized aspects to near-parodic extremes that evacuate the film of narrative credibility and psychological realism alike. (31)

Leone and other directors of Euro-Westerns are asking the public to open their eyes, to not believe what is shown; they are attempting to take the camera's power away by parodying its effect. When Leone has characters magically appear in the frame, or amplifies the squeaking of a door hinge on a soundtrack, he is ridiculing the basic laws that govern American Westerns. The opening of *Once Upon a Time* can be read as a sort of primer for what is about to come for the rest of the film, and its power leaves viewers more attuned to what they are watching.

Leone's casting also works to heighten the film's subversive effect. Henry Fonda, the quintessential good guy in classic Hollywood Westerns like *My Darling Clementine*, is cast as the ruthless Frank, a gunman shown murdering a small child early in the film. In a 1966 article on Italian Westerns in the *Saturday Evening Post*, Italian director Maurizio Lucidi gave some insight into the European perspective that lay behind such choices:

We're adding the Italian concept of realism to an old American
myth, and it's working. Look at Jesse James. In your country he's
a saint. Over here we play him as a gangster. That's what he was.
Europeans today are too sophisticated to believe in the honest
gunman movie anymore. They want the truth and that's what we're
giving them. (qtd. in Fox 55)

A citation of a source the writer found quoted in another source.

Leone knew exactly what he was doing, and his casting of Fonda went a
long way toward confusing the audience's sympathies and complicating
the simple good guy versus bad guy model of Hollywood films. For this
reason, Fonda's entrance in the film is worth noting. The scene begins
with a close-up of a shotgun barrel, which quickly explodes in a series
of (gun)shots that establish a scene of a father and son out hunting near
their homestead. Here, Leone starts to move the camera more, with pans
from father to son and a crane shot of their house as they return home
to a picnic table with an abundance of food: the family is apparently
about to celebrate something. Throughout this scene, crickets chirp on the
soundtrack—until Leone abruptly cuts them off, the sudden silence quickly
followed by close-ups of the uneasy faces of three family members. Leone
is teasing the audience: he puts the crickets back on the soundtrack until
out of nowhere we hear a gunshot. Instead of then focusing on the source
or the target of the gunshot, the camera pans off to the sky, and for a
moment the viewer thinks the shot is from a hunter. We next see a close-up
of the father's face as he looks off into the distance, then is rattled when he
sees his daughter grasping the air, obviously shot. As he runs toward her,
tracked by the camera in a startling way, he is quickly shot down himself.

The family has been attacked seemingly out of nowhere, with only a young boy still alive. During the massacre, there is no musical score, just the abstract brutality of the slayings. Then Leone gives us a long camera shot of men appearing out of dust-blown winds, from nearby brush. It is obvious to the viewer that these men are the killers, but there is no clear sight of their faces: Leone uses long camera shots of their backs and an overhead shot as they converge on the young boy. This is the moment when Leone introduces Henry Fonda; he starts with the camera on the back of Fonda's head and then does a slow track around until his face is visible. At this point, audience members around the world would still have a hard time believing Fonda was a killer of these innocent people. Through crosscutting between the young boy's confused face and Fonda's smiling eyes, Leone builds a doubt in the audience—maybe he will not kill the boy. Then the crosscutting is interrupted with a close-up of Fonda's large Colt coming out of its holster, and Ennio Morricone's score, full of sadness, becomes audible. The audience's fears are realized: Fonda is indeed the killer. This scene is a clear parody of Hollywood casting stereotypes, and Leone toys with audience expectations by turning upside down the myth of the noble outlaw as portrayed by John Wayne in *Stagecoach*.

During the late 1960s and the early 1970s, Europeans were at odds with many of the foreign policies of the United States, a hostility expressed in Ramonet's characterization of this period as one "when American imperialism in Latin America and Southeast Asia was showing itself to be particularly brutal" (33). Morton, the railroad baron who is Frank's unscrupulous employer in *Once Upon a Time in the West*, can easily be read as a critique of the sometimes misguided ways Americans went about bringing their way of life to other countries. Morton represents the bringer of civilization, usually a good thing in the classic Western genre, where civilization meant doctors, schools, homes for everyone. But the Europeans question how this civilization was built. Leone, in a telling quotation, gives his perspective: "I see the history of the West as really the reign of violence by violence" (qtd. in Frayling 134).

Leone's critique of the "civilizing" of the American West becomes apparent in his depiction of Morton's demise at the hands of a bandit gang that Frank has tried to frame for the murder of the family. As Frank returns to Morton's train, wheezing and gasping resonates from the track. In a long, one-take shot, the camera follows Frank as he looks for Morton, and in the process dead and dying bodies in various poses are revealed strewn about the ground. Many people have died for the dream of "civilizing" the West, and there is nothing noble in their deaths. Frank finally finds Morton crawling along outside the train in mud, striving to reach a puddle; as he dies, the lapping waves of the Pacific Ocean—the goal toward which the civilizing of the West always pushes—can be heard.

Instead of the civilizing myth and its representations, the concern of *Once Upon a Time*—and the Euro-Western in general—is to give voice to the perspective of the marginal characters: the Native Americans, Mexicans, and Chinese who rarely rated a position of significance in a Hollywood Western. In *Once Upon a Time*, Bronson's character, Harmonica, pushes the plot forward with his need to avenge. Harmonica can be

seen as either Mexican or Native American, though it matters little
since his character stands in for all the racial stereotypes that populated
the American Western genre. When he and Frank meet in the movie's
climactic duel, Frank is clearly perplexed about why this man wants
to fight him, but his ego makes it impossible for him to refuse. They
meet in an abandoned yard, with Frank in the extreme foreground
and Harmonica in the extreme background (Fig. 2). The difference

Fig. 2. The climactic duel in *Once Upon a Time in the West* challenges
the casting and costuming stereotypes of the Hollywood Western.
Photograph from *Internet Movie Database*, www.imdb.com.

between the two is thus presented from both physical and ideological standpoints: Frank guns down settlers to make way for the railroad (and its owner), whereas Harmonica helps people to fend for themselves. Morricone's score dominates the soundtrack during this final scene, with a harmonica blaring away throughout. The costuming of Frank in black and Harmonica in white is an ironic throwback to classic Hollywood costuming and one that suggests Harmonica is prevailing over the racial stereotypes of American Westerns. Leone milks the scene for all it's worth, with the camera circling Harmonica as Frank looks for a perfect point to start the duel. Harmonica never moves, his face steadily framed in a close-up. Meanwhile, Frank is shown in mostly long shots; his body language shows that he is uncertain about the outcome of the duel, while Harmonica knows the ending.

As the two seem about to draw, the camera pushes into Harmonica's eyes, and there is a flashback to a younger Frank walking toward the camera, putting a harmonica into the mouth of a boy (the young Harmonica), and forcing him to participate in Frank's hanging of the boy's older brother. This brutal scene, in which Frank unknowingly seals his own destiny, is set in actual American locations and is taken directly from John Ford Westerns; Leone is literally bringing home the violence dealt to minorities in America's past. As soon as the brother is hanged, the scene returns to the present, and Frank is shot through the heart. As he lies dying, we see a look of utter disbelief on his face as he asks Harmonica, "Who are you?" At this moment, a harmonica is shoved into his mouth. Only then does recognition play over Frank's face; as he falls to the ground, his face in close-up is a grotesque death-mask not unlike the massacred victims of Morton's train. The idea of past misdeeds coming back to haunt characters in the present is a clear attempt to challenge the idea that the settlers had a moral right to conquer and destroy indigenous people in order to "win" the West.

The tremendous success of *Stagecoach* was both a blessing and curse for the Western genre. Without it, the genre would surely never have gained the success it did, but this success came with ideological and creative limitations. Both the popularity and the limitations of the American Western may have inspired European directors to attempt something new with the genre, and unlike American filmmakers, they could look more objectively at our history and our myths. Leone's demythologization of the American Western has proved a valuable addition to the Western genre. The effect of the Euro-Western can be seen in American cinema as early as *The Wild Bunch* in 1969—and as recently as the attention in *Brokeback Mountain* to types of Western characters usually marginalized. In this way, Italian Westerns forced a new level of viewing of the Western tradition that made it impossible to ever return to the previous Hollywood model.

List of works cited
begins on a new
page. Heading is
centered.

Works Cited

Each entry begins
at the left margin,
with subsequent
lines indented.

List is alphabet-
ized by authors'
last names or by
title for works with
no author.

Bright, Deborah. "Of Mother Nature and Marlboro Men: An Inquiry into the Cultural Meanings of Landscape Photography." *The Contest of Meaning: Critical Histories of Photography*, edited by Richard Bolton, MIT P, 1993, pp. 125-43.

Coyne, Michael. *The Crowded Prairie: American National Identity in the Hollywood Western*. I. B.Tauris, 1997.

Ebert, Roger. "The Good, the Bad and the Ugly." *Chicago Sun-Times*, 3 Aug. 2003, www.rogerebert.com/reviews/great-movie-the-good-the-bad-and-the-ugly-1968. Accessed 25 Jan. 2012.

Fox, William. "Wild Westerns, Italian Style." *The Saturday Evening Post*, 6 Apr. 1968, pp. 50-55.

Frayling, Christopher. *Spaghetti Westerns: Cowboys and Europeans from Karl May to Sergio Leone*. St. Martin's Press, 1981.

Harlan, Theresa. "Adjusting the Focus for an Indigenous Presence." *Overexposed: Essays on Contemporary Photography*, edited by Carol Squiers, New Press, 1999.

Kael, Pauline. *Kiss Kiss Bang Bang*. Bantam Books, 1965.

Langford, Barry. "Revisiting the 'Revisionist' Western." *Film & History*, vol. 33, no. 2, 2003, pp. 26-35. *Project Muse*, muse.jhu.edu/article/396082/pdf. Accessed 2 Feb. 2012.

Once Upon a Time in the West. Directed by Sergio Leone, performances by Henry Fonda and Charles Bronson. Paramount, 1968.

Ramonet, Ignacio. "Italian Westerns as Political Parables." *Cineaste*, vol. 15, no. 1, 1986, pp. 30-35. *JSTOR*, www.jstor.org/stable/41686858. Accessed 2 Feb. 2012.

Stagecoach. Directed by John Ford. United Artists, 1939.

EIGHTEEN

APA Style

AMERICAN PSYCHOLOGICAL ASSOCIATION (APA) style calls for (1) brief documentation in parentheses near each in-text citation and (2) complete documentation in a list of references at the end of your text. The models in this chapter draw on the *Publication Manual of the American Psychological Association*, 6th edition (2010). Additional information is available at www.apastyle.org.

A DIRECTORY TO APA STYLE

In-Text Documentation   256

1. Author named in a signal phrase 256
2. Author named in parentheses 257
3. Authors with the same last name 257
4. Two authors 257
5. Three or more authors 258
6. Organization or government as author 258
7. Author unknown 258
8. Two or more works cited together 259
9. Two or more works by one author in the same year 259
10. Source quoted in another source 259
11. Work without page numbers 259
12. An entire work 260
13. Personal communication 260

Notes   260

Reference List   261

Print Books   261

Documentation Map: Print Book 264

1. One author 262
2. Two or more works by the same author 262
3. Two or more authors 262
4. Organization or government as author 263
5. Author and editor 263
6. Edited collection 263
7. Work in an edited collection 265
8. Unknown author 265
9. Edition other than the first 265
10. Translation 265
11. Multivolume work 266
12. Article in a reference book 266

Print Periodicals   267

13. Article in a journal paginated by volume 267
14. Article in a journal paginated by issue 267
15. Article in a magazine 268
16. Article in a newspaper 268
17. Article by an unknown author 268
18. Book review 268
19. Letter to the editor 269

Online Sources   269

Documentation Map: Work from a Website 271
Documentation Map: Article in a Journal with DOI 273
Documentation Map: Article Accessed through a Database with DOI 274

20. Work from a nonperiodical website 270
21. Article in an online periodical 270
22. Article available only through a database 272
23. Article or chapter in a web-document or online reference work 272
24. Electronic book 275
25. Wiki entry 275
26. Online discussion source 275
27. Blog entry 276
28. Online video 276
29. Podcast 276

Other Kinds of Sources   276

30. Film, video, or DVD 276
31. Music recording 277
32. Proceedings of a conference 277
33. Television program 277
34. Software or computer program 277

35. Government document 278
36. Dissertation 278
37. Technical or research report 278

Sources Not Covered by APA   279

Formatting a Research Essay   279

Sample Research Essay   281

Throughout this chapter, you'll find models and examples that are color-coded to help you see how writers include source information in their texts and reference lists: brown for author or editor, yellow for title, gray for publication information—place of publication, publisher, date of publication, page number(s), and so on.

IN-TEXT DOCUMENTATION

Brief documentation in your text makes clear to your reader precisely what you took from a source and, in the case of a quotation, precisely where (usually, on which page) in the source you found the material you are quoting.

PARAPHRASES and SUMMARIES are more common than QUOTATIONS in APA-style projects. See Chapter 25 for more on all three kinds of citation. As you cite each source, you will need to decide whether to name the author in a signal phrase—"as McCullough (2001) wrote"—or in parentheses— "(McCullough, 2001)." Note that APA requires you to use the past tense or present perfect tense for verbs in SIGNAL PHRASES: "Moss (2003) argued," "Moss (2003) has argued."

1. Author named in a signal phrase

If you are quoting, you must give the page number(s). You are not required to give the page number(s) with a paraphrase or a summary, but APA encourages you to do so, especially if you are citing a long or complex work; most of the models in this chapter do include page numbers.

Author quoted

Put the date in parentheses right after the author's name; put the page in parentheses as close to the quotation as possible.

> McCullough (2001) described John Adams as having "the hands of a man accustomed to pruning his own trees, cutting his own hay, and splitting his own firewood" (p. 18).

Notice that in this example, the parenthetical reference with the page number comes *after* the closing quotation marks but *before* the period at the end of the sentence.

Author paraphrased or summarized

Put the date in parentheses right after the author's name; follow the date with the page.

> John Adams' hands were those of a laborer, according to McCullough (2001, p. 18).

2. Author named in parentheses

If you do not mention an author in a signal phrase, put his or her name, a comma, and the year of publication in parentheses as close as possible to the quotation, paraphrase, or summary.

Author quoted

Give the author, date, and page in one set of parentheses, or split the information between two sets of parentheses.

> One biographer (McCullough, 2001) has said John Adams had "the hands of a man accustomed to pruning his own trees, cutting his own hay, and splitting his own firewood" (p. 18).

Author paraphrased or summarized

Give the author, date, and page in parentheses toward the beginning or end of the paraphrase or summary.

> John Adams' hands were those of a laborer (McCullough, 2001, p. 18).

3. Authors with the same last name

If your reference list includes more than one person with the same last name, include initials in all documentation to distinguish the authors from one another.

> Eclecticism is common in modern criticism (J. M. Smith, 1992, p. vii).

4. Two authors

Always mention both authors. Use *and* in a signal phrase, but use an ampersand (&) in parentheses.

> Carlson and Ventura (1990) wanted to introduce Julio Cortázar, Marjorie Agosín, and other Latin American writers to an audience of English-speaking adolescents (p. v).

> According to the Peter Principle, "In a hierarchy, every employee tends to rise to his level of incompetence" (Peter & Hull, 1969, p. 26).

5. Three or more authors

In the first reference to a work by three to five persons, name all contributors. In subsequent references, name the first author followed by *et al.*, Latin for "and others." Whenever you refer to a work by six or more contributors, name only the first author, followed by *et al.* Use *and* in a signal phrase, but use an ampersand (&) in parentheses.

> Faigley, George, Palchik, and Selfe (2004) have argued that where there used to be a concept called *literacy*, today's multitude of new kinds of texts has given us *literacies* (p. xii).

> Peilen et al. (1990) supported their claims about corporate corruption with startling anecdotal evidence (p. 75).

6. Organization or government as author

If an organization name is recognizable by its abbreviation, give the full name and the abbreviation the first time you cite the source. In subsequent references, use only the abbreviation. If the organization does not have a familiar abbreviation, always use its full name.

First reference

(American Psychological Association [APA], 2008)

Subsequent references

(APA, 2008)

7. Author unknown

Use the complete title if it is short; if it is long, use the first few words of the title under which the work appears in the reference list.

> *Webster's New Biographical Dictionary* (1988) identifies William James as "American psychologist and philosopher" (p. 520).

> A powerful editorial asserted that healthy liver donor Mike Hurewitz died because of "frightening" faulty postoperative care ("Every Patient's Nightmare," 2007).

8. Two or more works cited together

If you cite multiple works in the same parentheses, place them in the order that they appear in your reference list, separated by semicolons.

> Many researchers have argued that what counts as "literacy" is not necessarily learned at school (Heath, 1983; Moss, 2003).

9. Two or more works by one author in the same year

If your list of references includes more than one work by the same author published in the same year, order them alphabetically by title, adding lowercase letters ("a," "b," and so on) to the year.

> Kaplan (2000a) described orderly shantytowns in Turkey that did not resemble the other slums he visited.

10. Source quoted in another source

When you cite a source that was quoted in another source, let the reader know that you used a secondary source by adding the words *as cited in.*

> During the meeting with the psychologist, the patient stated repeatedly that he "didn't want to be too paranoid" (as cited in Oberfield & Yasik, 2004, p. 294).

11. Work without page numbers

Instead of page numbers, some electronic works have paragraph numbers, which you should include (preceded by the abbreviation *para.)* if you are referring to a specific part of such a source. In sources with neither page nor paragraph numbers, refer readers to a particular part of the source if possible, perhaps indicating a heading and the paragraph under the heading.

> Russell's dismissals from Trinity College at Cambridge and from City College in New York City have been seen as examples of the controversy that marked his life (Irvine, 2006, para. 2).

12. An entire work

You do not need to give a page number if you are directing readers' attention to an entire work.

> Kaplan (2000) considered Turkey and Central Asia explosive.

When you are citing an entire website, give the URL in the text. You do not need to include the website in your reference list. To cite part of a website, see no. 20 on p. 481.

> Beyond providing diagnostic information, the website for the
> Alzheimer's Association includes a variety of resources for family and
> community support of patients suffering from Alzheimer's disease
> (http://www.alz.org).

13. Personal communication

Document email, telephone conversations, interviews, personal letters, messages from nonarchived electronic discussion sources, and other personal texts as *personal communication,* along with the person's initial(s), last name, and the date. You do not need to include such personal communications in your reference list.

> L. Strauss (personal communication, December 6, 2013) told about
> visiting Yogi Berra when they both lived in Montclair, New Jersey.

NOTES

You may need to use *content notes* to give an explanation or information that doesn't fit into your text. To signal a content note, place a superscript numeral at the appropriate point in your text. Include this information as a footnote, and put the notes on a separate page with the heading *Notes,* after your reference list. If you have multiple notes, number them consecutively throughout your text. Here is an example from *In Search of Solutions: A New Direction in Psychotherapy* (2003).

Text with superscript

An important part of working with teams and one-way mirrors is taking the consultation break, as at Milan, BFTC, and MRI.[1]

Content note

[1] It is crucial to note here that while working within a team is fun, stimulating, and revitalizing, it is not necessary for successful outcomes. Solution-oriented therapy works equally well when working solo.

REFERENCE LIST

A reference list provides full bibliographic information for every source cited in your text with the exception of entire websites and personal communications. See page 618 for guidelines on preparing such a list; for a sample reference list, see page 634.

Print Books

For most books, you'll need to provide the author, the publication date, the title and any subtitle, and the place of publication and publisher.

Important Details for Documenting Print Books

- **AUTHORS:** Use the author's last name, but replace the first and middle names with initials (D. Kinder for Donald Kinder).
- **DATES:** If more than one year is given, use the most recent one.
- **TITLES:** Capitalize only the first word and proper nouns and proper adjectives in titles and subtitles.
- **PUBLICATION PLACE:** Give city followed by state (abbreviated) or country, if outside the United States (for example, Boston, MA; London, England; Toronto, Ontario, Canada). If more than one city is given, use the first. Do not include the state or country if the publisher is a university whose name includes that information.

- **PUBLISHER:** Use a shortened form of the publisher's name (Little, Brown for Little, Brown and Company), but retain *Association, Books,* and *Press* (American Psychological Association, Princeton University Press).

1. One author

Author's Last Name, Initials. (Year of publication). *Title.* Publication City, State or Country: Publisher.

Lewis, M. (2003). *Moneyball: The art of winning an unfair game.* New York, NY: Norton.

2. Two or more works by the same author

If the works were published in different years, list them chronologically.

Lewis, B. (1995). *The Middle East: A brief history of the last 2,000 years.* New York, NY: Scribner.
Lewis, B. (2003). *The crisis of Islam: Holy war and unholy terror.* New York, NY: Modern Library.

If the works were published in the same year, list them alphabetically by title, adding "a," "b," and so on to the year.

Kaplan, R. D. (2000a). *The coming anarchy: Shattering the dreams of the post cold war.* New York, NY: Random House.
Kaplan, R. D. (2000b). *Eastward to Tartary: Travels in the Balkans, the Middle East, and the Caucasus.* New York, NY: Random House.

3. Two or more authors

For two to seven authors, include all names.

First Author's Last Name, Initials, Next Author's Last Name, Initials, & Final Author's Last Name, Initials. (Year of publication). *Title.* Publication City, State or Country: Publisher.

author   title   publication

Levitt, S. D., & Dubner, S. J. (2005). *Freakonomics: A rogue economist
explores the hidden side of everything.* New York, NY: Morrow.

For a work by eight or more authors, name just the first six authors, followed
by three ellipsis points, and end with the final author (see no. 21 for an example from a magazine article).

4. Organization or government as author

Sometimes an organization or a government agency is both author and publisher. If so, use the word *Author* as the publisher.

Organization Name or Government Agency. (Year of publication). *Title.*
Publication City, State or Country: Publisher.

Catholic News Service. (2002). *Stylebook on religion 2000: A reference
guide and usage manual.* Washington, DC: Author.

5. Author and editor

Author's Last Name, Initials. (Year of edited edition). *Title.* (Editor's
Initials Last Name, Ed.). Publication City, State or Country:
Publisher. (Original work[s] published year[s])

Dick, P. F. (2008). *Five novels of the 1960s and 70s.* (J. Lethem, Ed.).
New York, NY: Library of America. (Original works published
1964-1977)

6. Edited collection

First Editor's Last Name, Initials, Next Editor's Last Name, Initials, &
Final Editor's Last Name, Initials. (Eds.). (Year of edited edition).
Title. Publication City, State or Country: Publisher.

Raviv, A., Oppenheimer, L., & Bar-Tal, D. (Eds.). (1999). *How children
understand war and peace: A call for international peace education.*
San Francisco, CA: Jossey-Bass.

Documentation Map (APA) / Print Book

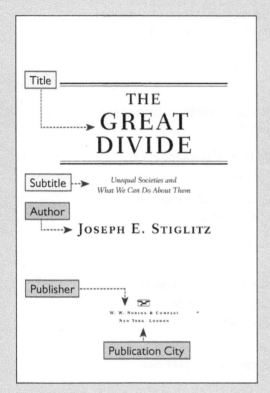

Stiglitz, J. E. (2015). *The great divide: Unequal societies and what we can do about them.* New York, NY: Norton.

7. Work in an edited collection

Author's Last Name, Initials. (Year of publication). Title of article or chapter. In Initials Last Name (Ed.), *Title* (pp. pages). Publication City, State or Country: Publisher.

Harris, I. M. (1999). Types of peace education. In A. Raviv, L. Oppenheimer, & D. Bar-Tal (Eds.), *How children understand war and peace: A call for international peace education* (pp. 46-70). San Francisco, CA: Jossey-Bass.

8. Unknown author

Title. (Year of publication). Publication City, State or Country: Publisher.

Webster's new biographical dictionary. (1988). Springfield, MA: Merriam-Webster.

If the title page of a work lists the author as *Anonymous,* treat the reference list entry as if the author's name were Anonymous, and alphabetize it accordingly.

9. Edition other than the first

Author's Last Name, Initials. (Year). *Title* (name or number ed.). Publication City, State or Country: Publisher.

Burch, D. (2008). *Emergency navigation: Find your position and shape your course at sea even if your instruments fail* (2nd ed.). Camden, ME: International Marine/McGraw-Hill.

10. Translation

Author's Last Name, Initials. (Year of publication). *Title* (Translator's Initials Last Name, Trans.). Publication City, State or Country: Publisher. (Original work published Year)

Hugo, V. (2008). *Les misérables* (J. Rose, Trans.). New York, NY: Modern Library. (Original work published 1862)

11. Multivolume work

Author's Last Name, Initials. (Year). *Title* (Vols. numbers). Publication City, State or Country: Publisher.

Nastali, D. P. & Boardman, P. C. (2004). *The Arthurian annals: The tradition in English from 1250 to 2000* (Vols. 1-2). New York, NY: Oxford University Press USA.

One volume of a multivolume work

Author's Last Name, Initials. (Year). *Title of whole work* (Vol. number). Publication City, State or Country: Publisher.

Spiegelman, A. (1986). *Maus* (Vol. 1). New York, NY: Random House.

12. Article in a reference book

Unsigned

Title of entry. (Year). In *Title of reference book* (Name or number ed., Vol. number, pp. pages). Publication City, State or Country: Publisher.

Macrophage. (2003). In *Merriam-Webster's collegiate dictionary* (11th ed., p. 745). Springfield, MA: Merriam-Webster.

Signed

Author's Last Name, Initials. (Year). Title of entry. In *Title of reference book* (Vol. numher, pp. pages). Publication City, State or Country: Publisher.

Wasserman, D. E. (2006). Human exposure to vibration. In *International encyclopedia of ergonomics and human factors* (Vol. 2, pp. 1800-1801). Boca Raton, FL: CRC.

author   title   publication

Print Periodicals

For most articles, you'll need to provide information about the author; the date; the article title and any subtitle; the periodical title; and any volume or issue number and inclusive page numbers.

Important Details for Documenting Print Periodicals

- **AUTHORS:** List authors as you would for a book (see p. 600).
- **DATES:** For journals, give year only. For magazines and newspapers, give year followed by a comma and then month or month and day.
- **TITLES:** Capitalize article titles as you would for a book. Capitalize the first and last words and all principal words of periodical titles. Do not capitalize *a, an, the,* or any prepositions or coordinating conjunctions unless they begin the title of the periodical.
- **VOLUME AND ISSUE:** For journals and magazines, give volume or volume and issue, depending on the journal's pagination method. For newspapers, do not give volume or issue.
- **PAGES:** Use *p.* or *pp.* for a newspaper article but not for a journal or magazine article. If an article does not fall on consecutive pages, give all the page numbers (for example, 45, 75-77 for a journal or magazine; pp. C1, C3, C5-C7 for a newspaper).

13. Article in a journal paginated by volume

Author's Last Name, Initials. (Year). Title of article. *Title of Journal,
    volume,* pages.

Gremer, J. R., Sala, A., & Crone, E. E. (2010). Disappearing plants: Why
    they hide and how they return. *Ecology, 91,* 3407-3413.

14. Article in a journal paginated by issue

Author's Last Name, Initials. (Year). Title of article. *Title of Journal,
    volume*(issue), pages.

Weaver, C., McNally, C., & Moerman, S. (2001). To grammar or not to
    grammar: That is not the question! *Voices from the Middle, 8*(3),
    17-33.

15. Article in a magazine

If a magazine is published weekly, include the day and the month. If there are a volume number and an issue number, include them after the magazine title.

Author's Last Name, Initials. (Year, Month Day). *Title of article. Title of Magazine, volume*(issue), page(s).

Gregory, S. (2008, June 30). Crash course: Why golf carts are more hazardous than they look. *Time, 171*(26), 53.

If a magazine is published monthly, include the month(s) only.

16. Article in a newspaper

If page numbers are consecutive, separate them with a hyphen. If not, separate them with a comma.

Author's Last Name, Initials. (Year, Month Day). Title of article. *Title of Newspaper,* p(p). page(s).

Schneider, G. (2005, March 13). Fashion sense on wheels. *The Washington Post*, pp. F1, F6.

17. Article by an unknown author

Title of article. (Year, Month Day). *Title of Periodical, volume*(issue), pages *or* p(p). page(s).

Hot property: From carriage house to family compound. (2004, December). *Berkshire Living, 1*(1), 99.

Clues in salmonella outbreak. (2008, June 21). *New York Times*, p. A13.

18. Book review

Reviewer's Last Name, Initials. (Date of publication). Title of review [Review of the book *Title of Work*, by Author's Initials Last Name]. *Title of Periodical, volume*(issue), page(s).

author   title   publication

Brandt, A. (2003, October). Animal planet [Review of the book
    Intelligence of apes and other rational beings, by D. R. Rumb &
    D. A. Washburn]. *National Geographic Adventure, 5*(10), 47.

If the review does not have a title, include the bracketed information about
the work being reviewed immediately after the date of publication.

19. Letter to the editor

Author's Last Name, Initials. (Date of publication). Title of letter [Letter
    to the editor]. *Title of Periodical, volume*(issue), *or* p(p). page(s).

Hitchcock, G. (2008, August 3). Save our species [Letter to the editor].
    San Francisco Chronicle, p. P-3.

Online Sources

Not every online source gives you all the data that APA would like to see in
a reference entry. Ideally, you will be able to list author's or editor's name;
date of first electronic publication or most recent revision; title of document;
information about print publication if any; and retrieval information: DOI
(digital object identifier, a string of letters and numbers that identifies an
online document) or URL. In some cases, additional information about electronic publication may be required (title of site, retrieval date, name of sponsoring institution).

Important Details for Documenting Online Sources

- **AUTHORS:** List authors as you would for a print book or periodical.
- **TITLES:** For websites and electronic documents, articles, or books, capitalize title and subtitles as you would for a book; capitalize periodical
  titles as you would for a print periodical.
- **DATES:** After the author, give the year of the document's original publication on the web or of its most recent revision. If neither of those years
  is clear, use *n.d.* to mean "no date." For undated content or content that
  may change (for example, a wiki entry), include the month, day, and
  year that you retrieved the document. You don't need to include the retrieval date for content that's unlikely to change.

- **DOI OR URL:** Include the DOI instead of the URL in the reference whenever one is available. If no DOI is available, provide the URL of the home page or menu page. If you do not identify the sponsoring institution, you do not need a colon before the URL or DOI. When a URL won't fit on the line, break the URL before most punctuation, but do not break *http://.*

20. Work from a nonperiodical website

Author's Last Name, Initials. (Date of publication). Title of work. *Title of site.* DOI or Retrieved Month Day, Year [if necessary], from URL

Cruikshank, D. (2009, June 15). Unlocking the secrets and powers of the brain. *National Science Foundation.* Retrieved from http://www.nsf .gov/discoveries/disc_summ.jsp?cntn_id=114979&org=NSF

When citing an entire website, include the URL in parentheses within the text. Do not include the website in your list of references.

21. Article in an online periodical

When available, include the volume number and issue number as you would for a print source. If no DOI has been assigned, provide the URL of the homepage or menu page of the journal or magazine, even for articles that you access through a database.

Article in an online journal

Author's Last Name, Initials. (Year). Title of article. *Title of Journal, volume*(issue), pages. DOI or Retrieved from URL

Corbett, C. (2007). Vehicle-related crime and the gender gap. *Psychology, Crime & Law, 13,* 245-263. doi:10.1080/10683160600822022

Article in an online magazine

Author's Last Name, Initials. (Year, Month Day). Title of article. *Title of Magazine, volume*(issue). DOI or Retrieved from URL

Documentation Map (APA) / Work from a Website

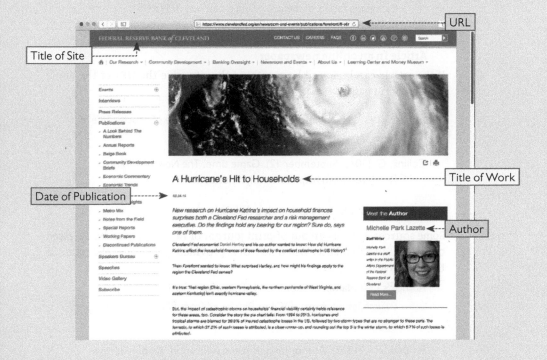

URL

Title of Site

Title of Work

Date of Publication

Author

Lazette, M. P. (2015, February 25). A hurricane's hit to households.
Federal Reserve Bank of Cleveland. Retrieved from https://www
.clevelandfed.org/enNewsroom%20and%20Events/Publications/
Forefront/Katrina.aspx

Barreda, V. D., Palazzesi, L., Tellería, M. C., Katinas, L., Crisci, J. N., Bromer, K., . . . Bechis, F. (2010, September 24). Eocene Patagonia fossils of the daisy family. *Science, 329*(5949). doi:10.1126=sciences.1193108

Article in an online newspaper

If the article can be found by searching the site, give the URL of the home page or menu page.

> Author's Last Name, Initials. (Year, Month Day). Title of article. *Title of Newspaper.* Retrieved from URL

> Collins, G. (2012, September 12). Game time. *The New York Times.* Retrieved from http://www.nytimes.com

22. Article available only through a database

Some sources, such as an out-of-print journal or rare book, can be accessed only through a database. When no DOI is provided, give either the name of the database or its URL.

> Author's Last Name, Initials. (Year). Title of article. *Title of Journal, volume*(issue), pages. DOI or Retrieved from Name of database or URL

> Simpson, M. (1972). Authoritarianism and education: A comparative approach. *Sociometry, 35*(2), 223-234. Retrieved from http://www.jstor.org/stable/2786619

23. Article or chapter in a web document or online reference work

For a chapter in a web document or an article in an online reference work, give the URL of the chapter or entry if no DOI is provided.

> Author's Last Name, Initials. (Year). Title of entry. In Initials Last Name (Ed.), *Title of reference work.* DOI or Retrieved from URL

> Korfmacher, C. (2006). Personal identity. In J. Fieser & B. Dowden (Eds.), *Internet encyclopedia of philosophy.* Retrieved from http://www.iep.utm.edu/person-i/

Documentation Map (APA) / Article in a Journal with DOI

Title of Journal

Publication Year

DOI

Author

Volume

Pages

Title of Article

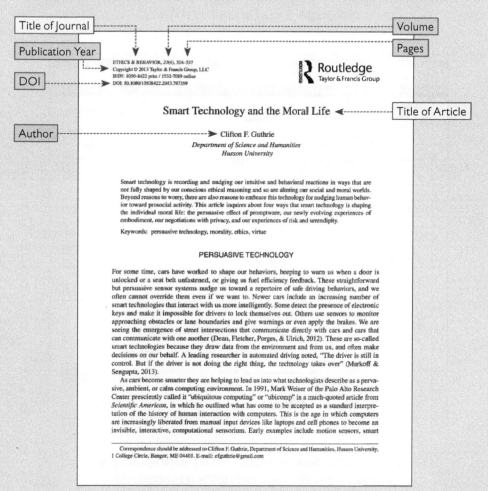

ETHICS & BEHAVIOR, 23(4), 324–337
Copyright © 2013 Taylor & Francis Group, LLC
ISSN: 1056-8422 print / 1532-7019 online
DOI: 10.1080/10508422.2013.787359

Routledge
Taylor & Francis Group

Smart Technology and the Moral Life

Clifton F. Guthrie

Department of Science and Humanities
Husson University

Smart technology is recording and nudging our intuitive and behavioral reactions in ways that are not fully shaped by our conscious ethical reasoning and so are altering our social and moral worlds. Beyond reasons to worry, there are also reasons to embrace this technology for nudging human behavior toward prosocial activity. This article inquires about four ways that smart technology is shaping the individual moral life: the persuasive effect of promptware, our newly evolving experiences of embodiment, our negotiations with privacy, and our experiences of risk and serendipity.

Keywords: persuasive technology, morality, ethics, virtue

PERSUASIVE TECHNOLOGY

For some time, cars have worked to shape our behaviors, beeping to warn us when a door is unlocked or a seat belt unfastened, or giving us fuel efficiency feedback. These straightforward but persuasive sensor systems nudge us toward a repertoire of safe driving behaviors, and we often cannot override them even if we want to. Newer cars include an increasing number of smart technologies that interact with us more intelligently. Some detect the presence of electronic keys and make it impossible for drivers to lock themselves out. Others use sensors to monitor approaching obstacles or lane boundaries and give warnings or even apply the brakes. We are seeing the emergence of street intersections that communicate directly with cars and cars that can communicate with one another (Dean, Fletcher, Porges, & Ulrich, 2012). These are so-called smart technologies because they draw data from the environment and from us, and often make decisions on our behalf. A leading researcher in automated driving noted, "The driver is still in control. But if the driver is not doing the right thing, the technology takes over" (Markoff & Sengupta, 2013).

As cars become smarter they are helping to lead us into what technologists describe as a pervasive, ambient, or calm computing environment. In 1991, Mark Weiser of the Palo Alto Research Center presciently called it "ubiquitous computing" or "ubicomp" in a much-quoted article from *Scientific American*, in which he outlined what has come to be accepted as a standard interpretation of the history of human interaction with computers. This is the age in which computers are increasingly liberated from manual input devices like laptops and cell phones to become an invisible, interactive, computational sensorium. Early examples include motion sensors, smart

Correspondence should be addressed to Clifton F. Guthrie, Department of Science and Humanities, Husson University, 1 College Circle, Bangor, ME 04401. E-mail: cfguthrie@gmail.com

Guthrie, C. F. (2013). Smart technology and the moral life. *Ethics & Behavior, 23,* 324–337. doi:10.1080/10508422.2013.787359

Documentation Map (APA) / Article Accessed through a Database with DOI

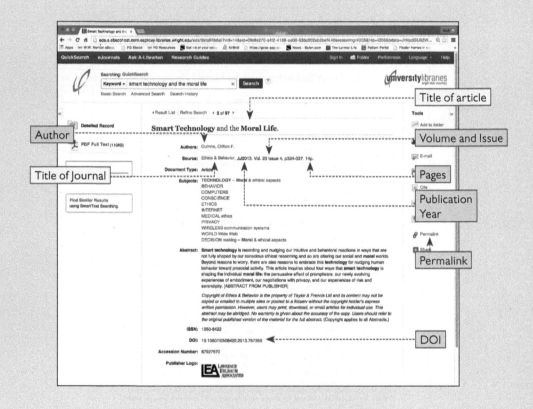

Title of article

Author

Title of Journal

Volume and Issue

Pages

Publication Year

Permalink

DOI

Guthrie, C. F. (2013). Smart technology and the moral life. *Ethics & Behavior*, 23, 324–337. doi:10.1080/10508422.2013.787359

24. Electronic book

Author's Last Name, Initials. (Year). *Title of book.* DOI or Retrieved from
 URL

TenDam, H. (n.d.). *Politics, civilization & humanity.* Retrieved from http://
 onlineoriginals.com/showitem.asp?itemID=46&page=2

For an ebook based on a **print version**, include a description of the digital
format in brackets after the **book title.**

Blain, M. (2009). *The sociology of terror: Studies in power, subjection, and
 victimage ritual* [Adobe Digital Editions version]. Retrieved from
 http://www.powells.com/sub/AdobeDigitalEditionsPolitics
 .html?sec_big_link=1

25. Wiki entry

Give the entry title and the date of posting, or *n.d.* if there is no date. Then
include the retrieval date, the name of the wiki, and the URL for the entry.

Title of entry. (Year, Month Day). Retrieved Month Day, Year, from Title
 of wiki: URL

Discourse. (n.d.). Retrieved November 8, 2013, from Psychology Wiki:
 http://psychology.wikia.com/wiki/Discourse

26. Online discussion source

If the name of the list to which the message was posted is not part of the
URL, include it after *Retrieved from.* The URL you provide should be for the
archived version of the message or post.

Author's Last Name, Initials. (Year, Month Day). Subject line of message
 [Descriptive label]. Retrieved from URL

Baker, J. (2005, February 15). Re: Huffing and puffing [Electronic
 mailing list message]. Retrieved from American Dialect Society
 electronic mailing list: http://listserv.linguistlist.org/cgi-bin
 /wa?A2=ind0502C&L=ADS-L&P=R44

Do not include email or other nonarchived discussions in your list of references. Simply give the sender's name in your text. See no. 13 on page 598 for guidelines on identifying such sources in your text.

27. Blog entry

Author's Last Name, Initials. (Year, Month Day). Title of post [Blog post]. Retrieved from URL

Collins, C. (2009, August 19). Butterfly benefits from warmer springs? [Blog post]. Retrieved from http://www.intute.ac.uk/blog/2009/08/19/butterfly-benefits-from-warmer-springs/

28. Online video

Last Name, Initials (Writer), & Last Name, Initials (Producer). (Year, Month Day posted). *Title* [Descriptive label]. Retrieved from URL

Coulter, J. (Songwriter & Performer), & Booth, M. S. (Producer). (2006, September 23). *Code monkey* [Video file]. Retrieved from http://www.youtube.com/watch?v=v4Wy7gRGgeA

29. Podcast

Writer's Last Name, Initials. (Writer), & Producer's Last Name, Initials. (Producer). (Year, Month Day). Title of podcast. *Title of site or program* [Audio podcast]. Retrieved from URL

Britt, M. A. (Writer & Producer). (2009, June 7). Episode 97: Stanley Milgram study finally replicated. *The Psych Files Podcast* [Audio podcast]. Retrieved from http://www.thepsychfiles.com/

Other Kinds of Sources

30. Film, video, or DVD

Last Name, Initials (Producer), & Last Name, Initials (Director). (Year). *Title* [Motion picture]. Country: Studio.

Wallis, H. B. (Producer), & Curtiz, M. (Director). (1942). *Casablanca* [Motion picture]. United States: Warner.

31. Music recording

Composer's Last Name, Initials. (Year of copyright). Title of song. On *Title of album* [Medium]. City, State or Country: Label.

Veloso, C. (1997). Na baixado sapateiro. On *Livros* [CD]. Los Angeles, CA: Nonesuch.

32. Proceedings of a conference

Author's Last Name, Initials. (Year of publication). Title of paper. In *Proceedings Title* (pp. pages). Publication City, State or Country: Publisher.

Heath, S. B. (1997). Talking work: Language among teens. In *Symposium about Language and Society—Austin* (pp. 27-45). Austin: Department of Linguistics at the University of Texas.

33. Television program

Last Name, Initials (Writer), & Last Name, Initials (Director). (Year). Title of episode [Descriptive label]. In Initials Last Name (Producer), *Series title*. City, State or Country: Network.

Dunkle, R. (Writer), & Lange, M. (Director). (2012). Hit [Television series episode]. In E. A. Bernero (Executive Producer), *Criminal minds*. New York, NY: NBC.

34. Software or computer program

Title and version number [Computer software]. (Year). Publication City, State or Country: Publisher.

Elder Scrolls V: Skyrim [Computer software]. (2012). Rockwood, MD: Bethesda.

35. Government document

Government Agency. (Year of publication). *Title*. Publication City, State or Country: Publisher.

U.S. Department of Health and Human Services, Centers for Disease Control and Prevention. (2009). *Fourth national report on human exposure to environmental chemicals.* Washington, DC: Government Printing Office.

Online government document

Government Agency. (Year of publication). *Title* (Publication No. [if any]). Retrieved from URL

U.S. Department of Health and Human Services, National Institutes of Health, National Institute of Mental Health. (2006). *Bipolar disorder* (NIH Publication No. 06-3679). Retrieved from http://www.nimh.nih .gov/health/publications/bipolar-disorder/nimh-bipolar-adults.pdf

36. Dissertation

Include the database name and accession number for dissertations that you retrieve from a database.

Author's Last Name, Initials. (Year). *Title of dissertation* (Doctoral dissertation). Retrieved from Name of database. (accession number)

Knapik, M. (2008). *Adolescent online trouble-talk: Help-seeking in cyberspace* (Doctoral dissertation). Retrieved from ProQuest Dissertation and Theses database. (AAT NR38024)

For a dissertation that you access on the web, include the name of the institution after *Doctoral dissertation*. For example: (Doctoral dissertation, University of North Carolina). End your documentation with *Retrieved from* and the URL.

37. Technical or research report

Author's Last Name, Initials. (Year). *Title of report* (Report number). Publication City, State or Country: Publisher.

Elsayed, T., Namata, G., Getoor, L., & Oard., D. W. (2008). *Personal name resolution in email: A heuristic approach* (Report No. LAMP-TR-150). College Park: University of Maryland.

Sources Not Covered by APA

To document a source for which APA does not provide guidelines, look at models similar to the source you have cited. Give any information readers will need in order to find it themselves—author; date of publication; title; publisher; information about electronic retrieval (DOI or URL); and any other pertinent information. You might want to test your reference note to be sure it will lead others to your source.

FORMATTING A RESEARCH ESSAY

Title page. APA generally requires a title page. At the upper left-hand corner of the page, include "Running head:" and a shortened version of your title in capital letters. The page number (1) should go in the upper right-hand corner. Center the full title of the paper, your name, and the name of your school on separate lines about halfway down the page. You may add an "Author Note" at the bottom of the page to provide course information, acknowledgments, or contact information.

Page numbers. Use a shortened title in capital letters in the upper left-hand corner of each page; place the page number in the upper right-hand corner. Number pages consecutively throughout.

Fonts, spacing, margins, and indents. Use a serif font (such as Times New Roman or **Bookman**) for the text, and a sans serif font (such as Calibri or **Verdana**) for figure labels. Double-space the entire paper, including any notes and your list of references. Leave one-inch margins at the top, bottom, and sides of your text; do not justify the text. The first line of each paragraph should be indented one-half inch (or five to seven spaces) from the left margin. APA recommends using two spaces after end-of-sentence punctuation.

Headings. Though they are not required in APA style, headings can help readers follow your text. The first level of heading should be bold, centered, and capitalized as you would any other title; the second level of heading should be bold and flush with the left margin; the third level should be bold and indented, with only the first letter and proper nouns capitalized and with a period at the end of the heading, with the text following on the same line.

First Level Heading

Second Level Heading

Third level heading. Text follows on the same line.

Abstract. An abstract is a concise summary of your paper that introduces readers to your topic and main points. Most scholarly journals require an abstract; check with your instructor about his or her preference. Put your abstract on the second page, with the word *Abstract* centered at the top. Unless your instructor specifies a length, limit your abstract to 250 words or fewer.

Long quotations. Indent quotations of more than forty words one-half inch (or five to seven spaces) from the left margin. Do not use quotation marks, and place the page number(s) in parentheses *after* the end punctuation.

> Kaplan (2000) captured ancient and contemporary Antioch for us:
>> At the height of its glory in the Roman-Byzantine age, when it had an amphitheater, public baths, aqueducts, and sewage pipes, half a million people lived in Antioch. Today the population is only 125,000. With sour relations between Turkey and Syria, and unstable politics throughout the Middle East, Antioch is now a backwater—seedy and tumbledown, with relatively few tourists. (p. 123)
>
> Antioch's decline serves as a reminder that the fortunes of cities can change drastically over time.

Reference list. Start your list on a new page after the text but before any endnotes. Center the title, and double-space the entire list. Each entry should begin at the left margin, and subsequent lines should be indented one-half inch (or five to seven spaces). Alphabetize the list by authors' last names (or by editors' names, if appropriate). Alphabetize works that have no author or editor by title, disregarding *A, An,* and *The.* Be sure every source listed is cited in the text; do not include sources that you consulted but did not cite.

Illustrations. For each table, provide a number (*Table 1*) and a descriptive title on separate lines above the table; below the table, include a note with information about the source. For figures—charts, diagrams, graphs, photos, and so on—include a figure number (*Figure 1*) and information about the source in a note below the figure. Number tables and figures separately, and be sure to discuss any illustrations so that readers know how they relate to the rest of your text.

Table 1
Hours of Instruction Delivered per Week

	American classrooms	Japanese classrooms	Chinese classrooms
First grade			
Language arts	10.5	8.7	10.4
Mathematics	2.7	5.8	4.0
Fifth grade			
Language arts	7.9	8.0	11.1
Mathematics	3.4	7.8	11.7

Note. Adapted from "Peeking Out from Under the Blinders: Some Factors We Shouldn't Forget in Studying Writing," by J. R. Hayes, 1991, National Center for the Study of Writing and Literacy (Occasional Paper No. 25). Retrieved from National Writing Project website: http://www.nwp.org/

SAMPLE RESEARCH ESSAY

Katryn Sheppard wrote the following paper, "Early Word Production: A Study of One Child's Word Productions," for a psychology course. It is formatted according to the guidelines of the *Publication Manual of the American Psychological Association,* 6th edition (2010).

A shortened title in all capital letters is used as a running head in the upper left corner of each page; on the title page, it is preceded by the label "Running head" and a colon. Page numbers appear in the upper right corner.

Running head: EARLY WORD PRODUCTION   1

The title is centered on the page, with your name and the school name below.

Early Word Production: A Study of One Child's Word Productions

Katryn Sheppard

Portland State University

EARLY WORD PRODUCTION 2

Abstract

Early word production, one of the initial stages of language development in children, plays an important role in the development of later language skills. This study identifies the word classes and number of words spoken in a recorded interaction (Bloom, 1973) by one normally developing child of sixteen months and analyzes aspects of the child's speech, with the goal of noting if the characteristics observed were supported by the existing research on early word production or if they deviated from those findings. The words that I analyzed fell into six categories: nouns, spatial terms, adjectives, negatives, social phrases, and verbs. Although the frequency with which the child used words from some of these categories reflected the expectations established by previous research, her use of words in other categories was less predictable. Noting word usage in the six categories led to an analysis of the functions that those categories served in the child's semantic communication at this early stage of language development.

Abstract begins on a new page. Heading is centered.

Abstract text does not need a paragraph indent.

Use two letter spaces after each sentence.

250 words or fewer.

Early Word Production: A Study of One Child's Word Productions

Introduction

Each step in the course of language development and acquisition in children provides a foundation for later skills and eventual mastery of the language. Early word production, a stage of language development in which children have only a few words in their vocabularies, provides the foundation for later vocabulary building and language production and has been shown to be closely linked to later language performance skills (Walker, Greenwood, Hart, & Carta, 1994). The early word production stage is therefore worthy of examination, as it "signals that children have a new tool that will enable them to learn about and participate more fully in their society" (Uccelli & Pan, 2013, p. 95).

Because so few words are produced by children in this early stage, the analysis of their word production focuses on the particular word classes and how frequently each class of words appears in speech. When examining typically developing English-speaking children who have few words in their productive vocabulary, Bates et al. (1994) found that the words produced were most often nouns, while other categories more seldom appeared. These less frequent categories included verbs and closed-class words. *Closed-class* words are function words, which include the categories of articles, conjunctions, numbers, pronouns, and prepositions; they are called closed-class words because new members cannot be added to these categories.

Reporting on the most common kinds of the nouns uttered in early vocabularies, Nelson (1973) found that children "began by naming

---

Title is centered.

First-level headings are centered, bold, and capitalized.

Essay is double-spaced.

Because this source has fewer than six authors, all authors are included in its first citation; subsequent references name only the first author, followed by et al. The year of publication is included in the reference.

Because this source has more than six authors, the signal phrase gives the first author's name followed by et al. The signal phrase uses past tense, and the year of publication is given in parentheses.

Indent each paragraph ½" (5-7 spaces).

objects exhibiting salient properties of change whether as the result
of the child's own action . . . or independent of it" (p. 1). In other words,
nouns that point to consistent, concrete objects are most prevalent in
early speech, because "children learn to name and understand categories
that are functionally relevant to them" (Anglin, 1995, p. 165)—they learn
to name the objects they see and interact with day to day.

The author, year, and page number are given in parentheses right after a quotation.

Although nouns make up the largest percentage of the words
produced by children in the earlier stages of language acquisition, other
word classes like verbs and adjectives also appear. While they do occur
in children's first fifty words, "verbs, adjectives, and function words each
account for less than 10 percent" of total utterances (Uccelli & Pan, 2013,
p. 96). Infrequent use of these categories supports the idea that, while
all word classes are represented, nouns are still expected to occur most
often.

Because the authors are not named in a signal phrase, their names are given in parentheses, with an ampersand rather than and between them. A page number is provided for a direct quotation.

Other lexical items that can be found in the speech of children
with limited vocabulary are words indicating spatial relationships, how
things relate to one another in physical space. According to Bowerman
(2007), "children's earliest spatial words are topological forms like 'in'
and 'on'" (p. 177). This observation supports the hypothesis that those
prepositions are among the first lexical items children acquire (Brown,
1973; Zukowski, 2013).

The page number is provided in parentheses for a direct quotation when the author and year of the work are given earlier in the signal phrase.

Multiple sources cited in the same parentheses are ordered alphabetically and separated by a semicolon.

Overall, the research on early word production in children who are
just beginning to acquire their first language has found that the majority
of words produced will be nouns that refer to concrete objects. According
to Pine (1992), children frequently use their early words to describe or

label, or to do both. Pine concluded that "children are making referential statements about the world with the kind of vocabulary items which they happen to have available to them" (p. 53). That is, children try to comment on referents (the things that words stand for) in various ways using just the limited language skills that they possess in their early stage of development.

Taking into account prior research on the early words children produce, I analyzed the classes and categories of words that appear in a transcript of a young child speaking. I wanted to compare this particular child's speech with what is expected during this early stage of language development, knowing that research predicts a higher number of nouns than other word classes in the data. I was interested to know whether nouns would occur as frequently as the literature would have me believe, and whether or not spatial terms would appear in such early speech. Furthermore, I wanted to note whether verbs occur as infrequently as expected and, if so, what words the child used instead of verbs to convey action.

Method

The transcript that I chose to analyze is one sample from a series of six recordings by Bloom (1973) of her daughter, Allison, a normally developing, English-speaking child. Allison's age in the samples ranged from 1 year 4 months and 21 days to 2 years and 10 months. The transcript that I analyzed was the earliest of these. Information about the socioeconomic status of Allison and her family was not available in the transcript or the North American English manual of the CHILDES

EARLY WORD PRODUCTION   6

database (MacWhinney, 2000), from which the transcript came.
However, we can assume the family was from the professional class, as
Bloom was a professor at Columbia University.

 According to information in the CHILDES manual, the recordings
took place in the Audio-Visual Studio at Teachers College, Columbia
University, in a room that contained some furniture and toys. The
sessions were conducted with audio-recording devices alone; as a result,
no videos were available through the CHILDES database. Each recording
session lasted 40 minutes, for a total of four hours of recording. Bloom
(1973) describes her role in the interaction as "more investigator than
mother" (p. 11), but the interactions seem to have been more relaxed
than one associates with investigators and not structured according to
a test or other prearranged activity. Rather, the interactions were led by
the child's actions in relation to her mother and objects in the room.

 The data are organized in six separate transcripts, arranged
chronologically. They contain the actual utterances and morphological
notation indicating the parts of speech being used. Bloom initially
transcribed the recordings, and later Lois Hood, a fellow researcher,
revised the transcript, which was revised again by a larger group of
researchers that also included Hood. Each time, the researchers added
notes to provide situational context. Each line of the transcript is
numbered, and there was an attempt to divide the data in a way that
reflected where there was "a shift in topic or focus" (Bloom, 1973,
p. 11).

> *The date is placed right after the author's name; the page number in parentheses is as close to the quotation as possible.*

Results

During the 40-minute exchange between Bloom and Allison, Allison produced a total of 362 occurrences of identifiable words. I did not distinguish between single- and multi-word utterances because that distinction was not relevant to the purpose of this study. Not all of Allison's turns in the conversation were intelligible; only intelligible words were included in my analysis. Altogether, I identified 27 different words (types) used by the subject, although there were many repetitions (tokens) of words. I assigned the 27 words to six categories: nouns, spatial terms, adjectives, negatives, social phrases, and verbs.

The category of nouns contained the largest number of distinct words or types as well as the largest number of instances or tokens, as shown in Figure 1. Allison used a total of 12 nouns, and all reflected concrete concepts. These included household objects, nouns that referenced people, and the names of animals referring to toys present at the time of recording. The most frequently used noun was "baby" (n=25); "chair" was second (n= 24). The total number of nouns represented 122 occurrences, or 34% of the total words uttered.

The second most frequent category of words found in Allison's utterances was spatial terms. Five different spatial terms, or types, occurred, with "up" being the most common (n= 48). All of the spatial terms Allison used referred to her immediate surroundings—for example, the chair that she wanted to climb "up" or "down" from. Altogether, 120 of Allison's words were spatial words, accounting for 33% of her speech by word count.

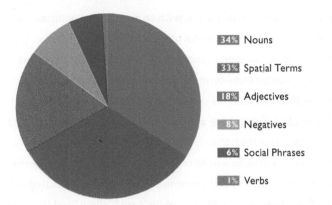

34% Nouns

33% Spatial Terms

18% Adjectives

8% Negatives

6% Social Phrases

1% Verbs

Figure 1. Words uttered by the subject, by word category (n=362). Data recorded in transcripts by L. Bloom (1973), accessed through the CHILDES database (MacWhinney, 2000).

Figure is numbered, and a description and source information are given.

The third most frequently used category of words in the data was adjectives, of which there were three types. Although "more" was the most frequently occurring adjective, "gone" was also often repeated. I will elaborate on the special role that adjectives played in Allison's speech in the discussion and conclusion section.

Negatives also appeared with some frequency in Allison's speech, although the category comprised only one type: "no." The word occurred 28 times (n=28), sometimes referring back to and negating other words that she had previously spoken, at other times negating the word or words that followed. The level of emphasis Allison placed on the word varied: sometimes her utterance was transcribed as "no"; other times, it was transcribed more emphatically, with an exclamation point, as "no!" This negative term accounted for 8% of her total words.

The remaining categories, social phrases and verbs, occurred less frequently. Social phrases—terms or utterances that are appropriately used in specific social contexts—were present in the transcript in two different words: "uhoh" (n= 20), and "oh" (n= 3). Together, these add up to a total of 23 words in the transcript that were social phrases.

The category of verbs was by far the least common in the subject's production. Four different verbs were used, three of which occurred only a single time. "Stop" was used twice, while "turn," "climb," and "sit" were each used once. A total of five words (n=5) were identified as verbs.

Discussion and Conclusion

Allison's single-word utterances fell into six identifiable categories, the frequency of which varied considerably. Some categories contained only a few items that were not repeated often, while other words and categories of words showed up repeatedly. Allison's tendency to use words in certain categories matches the findings of the existing research literature on child language production. In other instances, Allison's use of words differed slightly from what might be expected.

As predicted, nouns made up a large portion of Allison's speech. Since researchers have found the majority of early words to be nouns, it was not surprising that Allison used the greatest number of different words within the noun category and likewise showed the greatest number of repeated tokens in this category. Furthermore, the kinds of nouns Allison used are also in line with the finding that children in the early stages of language acquisition focus on concrete concepts. All of the nouns that Allison used referred to things in the room where the recording took place, mostly common objects that she could draw attention to. For instance, Allison used the noun "baby" when she wanted to communicate something to her mother about a baby doll she wanted to play with.

The category of spatial terms also accounted for a large percentage of the words Allison produced. The most frequent utterance of any word in any category in the transcript was of the word "up." That word, like other spatial terms, was often repeated and sometimes took the place of a more complex construction, as when the subject said "up" as she was struggling to get up onto the chair and "down" when she wished to get back down. Allison's choice of words fits with Bowerman's (2007) descriptions of children's first spatial terms: "early acquired spatial words revolve around relationships of . . . verticality (up, down)" (p. 180). This use of spatial terms contrasts with more complex spatial terms that appear in later development. However, the fact that Allison used five different words within the spatial word category could suggest that those terms play several important roles in her communication at this early stage.

As previously noted, adjectives like "gone" and "more" were words that played important roles in Allison's speech when she wanted to convey something to her mother, as when she finished eating a cookie and repeatedly told her mother "more." This single word seemed to stand in for a more elaborate question or request Allison could not produce at this stage, such as "Give me more." "Gone" was also used repeatedly in the same context to refer to the cookie. The use of "gone" to describe what had happened to the cookie might be seen as evidence of Pine's (1992) observation that children's early words are used to label and describe objects around them.

While the category of adjectives did not form as large a portion of Allison's speech as either nouns or spatial words, it was somewhat surprising that adjectives composed 18% of total words in this transcript. Generally, adjectives and other word classes that are not nouns are expected to account for a much smaller percentage of words spoken in early word production (Bates et al., 1994).

One feature of Allison's utterances that did adhere to what is expected for a typical child at this age was her use of negatives. Although she used only one negative word—"no"—the word was repeated frequently enough to be the fourth most common category in the transcript. Her use of "no" rather than any other negative conformed to Brown's (1973) finding that other forms of negation like "not" and "don't" appear only in later stages of linguistic development. In this very early stage, Allison's reliance on "no" alone seems typical.

There were varied contexts in which Allison used "no." In some cases, the word seemed to convey a lack of something, as when she uttered "cookie," looked around for the cookies, and then said "no." This sequence of events might indicate that Allison was conveying the lack of cookies to her mother. A similar exchange revolved around a picture of a girl, when Allison turned the picture over and, upon finding the

EARLY WORD PRODUCTION   12

other side was blank, said "no," evidently trying to convey that there was nothing on that side of the picture. On other occasions, "no" was produced as an answer to a question. In one example, Bloom asked Allison if the cup was for her (i.e., Bloom), to which the girl replied "no" and took the cup back from her mother. While adhering to the use of the single, simple form of negation that might be expected, Allison's utterances of "no" were varied in purpose and effective in communicating a range of ideas.

The remaining categories, social phrases and verbs, made up only a small percentage of Allison's words. Social words appeared infrequently and sometimes were attached to other words, as when the subject said "uhoh there." The infrequency of social phrases in Allison's early speech reflects typical aspects of early vocabulary development. As Santelmann (2014) explained, at this stage in a child's linguistic development, nearly all lexical items will be nouns and adjectives, with a limited number of social phrases.

True to previous research findings, verbs formed the least frequently used category in Allison's speech. Allison used the four different verbs to describe what something was in the act of doing or what she intended to do. For example, she used "stop" to describe a toy car coming to a stop. The remaining three verbs were produced when Allison was performing an action herself, as when she said "turn" when she was turning the pages of a book, "climb" when she was trying to climb up onto the chair, and "sit" when she was going to sit on the chair. Although four different verbs showed up in Allison's speech, the total number of tokens from the verb category was significantly lower than for any of the other word categories. This follows what researchers generally expect of children's early speech, which includes only a small percentage of verbs (Uccelli & Pan, 2013).

While Allison used these four verbs to communicate action, she often used other words to convey the same meaning. For example, Allison used "up" in two different contexts. The first was in narrating an action she was performing, as when she said "up" while attempting to get up onto the chair. The second was as a request to Bloom to help her up. Allison also used the spatial term "down" to indicate similar intentions.

When not using spatial terms in place of more specific verbs, Allison used nouns to communicate intention and action. For example, one instance of her uttering the word "cookie" was to tell to her mother that she wanted a cookie, indicating this intention without using any verb. This pattern occurred in other contexts, as when she used the concrete noun "chair" but not the verb "sit" to indicate that she wanted to get onto the chair. The use of nouns instead of verbs when communicating certain concepts is perhaps expected, given the established preponderance of nouns in early word production. It also supports the idea that children communicate using the tools at hand (Pine, 1992): since Allison frequently employed nouns and spatial terms, it would seem that those are the tools that she had to rely on to convey whole hosts of meaning.

The results of my analysis of the transcript of Allison interacting

EARLY WORD PRODUCTION 14

with Bloom revealed aspects of the child's speech that were mostly in line with the established features of early word production. The frequency of the use of different word classes conformed to previous findings that concrete nouns are most common, but other categories varied from the expected patterns. Her choice of the spatial terms "up" and "down" and the simple negative "no" is typical of children at this age. However, the uncommon frequency of adjectives in her speech indicates that they are important to how she communicated certain meanings; like spatial terms, they often filled in for verbs in cases where the actual verb was beyond her vocabulary. Her use of verbs, while predictably limited, showed how she employed the few verbs that she had and how she conveyed meaning when she did not have the precise verbs available to her. Overall, Allison used a somewhat varied set of words to communicate a wide range of meanings even though she had only a limited vocabulary to work with.

EARLY WORD PRODUCTION   15

List of references begins on a new page. Heading is centered.

References

Entries are arranged alphabetically.

Anglin, J. M. (1995). Classifying the world through language: Functional relevance, cultural significance, and category name learning. *International Journal of Intercultural Relations, 19*(2), 161-181. Retrieved from http://www.sciencedirect.com/science/journal/01471767

All lines except the first are indented ½" (5-7 spaces).

Bates, E., Marchman, V., Thal, D., Fenson, L., Dale, P., Reznick, J. S., & Hartung, J. (1994). Developmental and stylistic variation in the composition of early vocabulary. *Journal of Child Language, 21*(1), 85-123. Retrieved from http://search.proquest.com/docview/58280873?accountid=13265

URL given for an article accessed through a database. Do not add a period at the end of a URL.

Bloom, L. (1973). *One word at a time: The use of single-word utterances before syntax.* The Hague, Netherlands: Mouton.

Bowerman, M. (2007). Containment, support, and beyond: Constructing topological spatial categories in first language acquisition. In M. Aurnague, M. Hickmann, & L. Vieu (Eds.), *The categorization of spatial entities in language and cognition* (pp. 177-203). Amsterdam, Netherlands: John Benjamins.

Entries for a work found in an edited collection includes the editors' names, first initial followed by last name.

Brown, R. (1973). *A first language: The early stages.* Cambridge, MA: Harvard University Press.

MacWhinney, B. (2000). *The CHILDES Project: Tools for analyzing talk.* (3rd ed.). Mahwah, NJ: Lawrence Erlbaum.

EARLY WORD PRODUCTION        16

Nelson, K. (1973). Structure and strategy in learning to talk. *Monographs of the Society for Research in Child Development, 38*(1), 1-135. Retrieved from http://onlinelibrary.wiley.com/journal/10.1111/%2 8ISSN%291540-5834

Pine, J. M. (1992). The functional basis of referentiality: Evidence from children's spontaneous speech. *First Language, 12*(1), 39-55. Retrieved from http://fla.sagepub.com/proxy.lib.pdx.edu/content/12/34/39.full.pdf+html

Santelmann, L. (2014). *Development of morphology and syntax* [PowerPoint slides]. Retrieved from https://d2l.pdx.edu/d2l/le/content/450980/viewContent/1515576/View

Uccelli, P., & Pan, B. A. (2013). Semantic development. In J. Berko Gleason & N. Bernstein Ratner (Eds.), *The development of language* (pp. 89-112). Boston, MA: Pearson.

Walker, D., Greenwood, C., Hart, B., & Carta, J. (1994). Prediction of school outcomes based on early language production and socioeconomic factors. *Child Development, 65*(2), 606-621. Retrieved from http://onlinelibrary.wiley.com/journal/10.1111/%28ISSN%291467-8624

Zukowski, A. (2013). Putting words together. In J. Berko Gleason & N. Bernstein Ratner (Eds.), *The development of language* (pp. 120-156). Boston, MA: Pearson.

When the source type is unconventional, unclear, or important to point out, indicate the medium in brackets.

Readings

JUANA MORA { *Acculturation Is Bad for Our Health: Less Fast Food, More Nopalitos¹*

JUANA MORA (b. 1953) emigrated from Mexico to the United States with her parents and seven siblings in 1960. She received her BA in linguistics from the University of California, Santa Cruz, and her PhD from Stanford University. Mora is a national expert on Latina-focused substance-abuse treatment and prevention, and she works with community-based nonprofit organizations. Currently she is a professor of Chicana/o Studies at California State University, Northridge. Her books include *Handbook for Conducting Drug Abuse Research with Hispanic Populations* (2002) and *Latino Social Policy: A Participatory Research Model* (2004).

In the following essay, Mora looks at the health status of Latinos living in the United States, particularly those who are recent immigrants. Much of what she finds is disturbing: for many Latinos, acculturation, health-care inequalities, and environmental conditions combine to endanger their health. Immigrants would do well, she counsels, to look to their cultural traditions to protect them from common health problems.

WHAT IS THE HEALTH STATUS OF LATINOS IN THE UNITED STATES?

IT IS DIFFICULT TO ANSWER this question because (1) Latinos are a diverse population of cultural groups with different histories and cultural

¹Literally, "little cactus" (Spanish); the edible pads of young prickly pear cactus with the spines removed.

"Acculturation Is Bad for Our Health: Eat More Nopalitos" by Juana M. Mora, from CHICANOS IN THE CONVERSATION. Copy 2008 by Juana M. Mora. Reprinted by permission of the author.

practices that influence health, and (2) health researchers until recently did not include Latinos in their studies. However, new studies that have focused on the health of Latinos are giving us a new understanding of the health and health care needs of Latinos. Based on these studies, we can summarize the health status of Latinos as follows:

Good News

- Immigrant Latinas give birth to healthy babies;
- Latina mothers have relatively low infant mortality rates (children of Latinas are less likely to die at birth compared to whites);
- Latinos have lower rates of heart disease, cancer, and stroke compared to non-Latinos (Hayes-Bautista, 2002; Myers & Rodriguez, 2003).

Bad News

- Latinos have higher death rates related to diabetes, HIV-AIDS, alcohol-related cirrhosis of the liver, and homicide compared to whites;
- Latinos are more likely to receive health care in a hospital emergency room and are less likely than whites to have a regular health care provider;
- The longer Latino immigrants live in this country, the greater risk there is to their health due to increases in alcohol and other drug use, smoking, poor diets, and less physical activity (Hayes-Bautista, 2002; Vega et al., 1998; Myers & Rodriguez, 2003).

The last point is perhaps the most disturbing since we supposedly immigrate to the United States to better our lives and to create opportunities for our children. It seems, however, that from a health perspective, the health gains that are brought to the United States by immigrant populations are lost in the process of transitioning from the home culture to new cultural norms and environments. The gains in healthy births, for example, are at risk as U.S.-born or U.S.-raised Latinas increase their alcohol intake, other drug use, and smoking, and live more stressful lives. Zambrana et al. (1997), for example, found that women of Mexican origin who had higher levels of acculturation experienced more prenatal stress, which in turn was associated with preterm deliveries and lower-birth-weight babies. The impact of increased drug use and smoking may also lead to more instances of heart disease, cancers, and strokes. Some studies (Espino & Maldonado, 1990) have found an increase in hypertension among more acculturated, middle-aged Mexican Americans. And other studies (Vega et al., 1998) have found higher rates of psychiatric disorders, including major depression among U.S.-born or -raised Latinos. According to leading health experts, immigrants come to this country at some risk to their physical well-being and mental health. So what happens to an apparently healthy immigrant lifestyle after several years of residing and working in the United States?

WHY IS ACCULTURATION BAD FOR OUR HEALTH?

Part of the changes that occur as immigrants adapt to the United States are that their daily habits and environments change. For example, there is evidence that when immigrants, particularly immigrant children or the children of immigrants, grow up in the United States, they will be exposed to and eat more fast food, will not have access to home-grown foods that they may have had in their home countries, and are more likely to be raised in unsafe and unhealthy low-income neighborhoods where there is a disproportionate amount of fast food, alcohol, and tobacco advertising (Maxwell & Jacobson, 1989). These are not optimum conditions for healthy growth and prosperity. Apparently, upon arrival to the United States and for years after, there is a greater reliance on inexpensive fast food for survival. There is also less physical activity, particularly for immigrant children who remain indoors watching TV, often for many hours, because neighborhoods are unsafe or are not suitable for outdoor play. Scholars have for a long time described immigration as a dangerous, stressful journey with long-term effects on the family (Falicov, 1998; Igoa, 1995).

Our families bring us here to improve our educational opportunities and to live better lives. But they seldom know about the long-term effects of immigration such as the stress produced by learning a new language and culture, living in new and sometimes dangerous environments and having less time to raise and supervise children. In fact, experts have identified a series of disorders that can result from the immigration process alone. These include post-traumatic stress disorder, disturbed sleeping and eating patterns, depression, and so on. However, the long-term effects of immigration that include poorer diets, less physical activity, substance abuse, and unsafe neighborhoods are perhaps more disturbing and can have more of an effect on the long-term health of subsequent generations of Latinos. What else contributes to poor health outcomes for Latinos living in the United States?

Inequality in Health Care

Acculturation into U.S. health norms, including a greater reliance on fast food and poor environments, contribute to the poor health outcomes of Latinos, but the disparities in health between Latinos and whites can also be explained by a noted difference in the quality of health care. According to a report by the Institute of Medicine (2003), racial and ethnic minorities tend to receive lower-quality health care than whites do, even when insurance status, income, age, and severity of conditions are comparable. The findings of this study are as follows:

- Minorities and persons of lower socioeconomic status are less likely to receive cancer-screening services and are more likely to have late-stage cancer when the disease is diagnosed.

- Minorities and patients of lower socioeconomic status are less likely to receive recommended diabetic services and are more likely to be hospitalized for diabetes and its complications.

- When hospitalized for acute myocardial infarction, Latinos are less likely to receive optimal care.

- Racial and ethnic minorities and persons of lower socioeconomic status are more likely to die from HIV.

- Being a member of an ethnic or racial minority is also associated with receiving more amputations and treatment for late-stage cancer.

Thus, in addition to changes in daily habits, poor quality of health care, even for Latinos who are insured, adds to the increasing negative health outcomes for Latinos.

Poor, Unsafe Neighborhoods and Environments

The health status of Latinos is also affected by the environmental conditions of the places where they live, work, play, and raise their children. When immigrants arrive in this country, they most often are not able to afford homes in clean, safe neighborhoods or expensive, nutritious food. Studies (Igoa, 1995; Vega et al., 1998; Maugh & McConnell, 1998) have found that, because immigrant parents sometimes work more than one job, the care of the children is assigned to older siblings who resort to nearby, inexpensive fast food for themselves and the children in their care. The majority of Latino immigrants live in crowded urban environments associated with all the risks to health and safety that over-concentrations of liquor stores, air pollution from industrial facilities, and freeways bring to these environments. In Southern California, new studies (Morello-Frosch et al., 2002) examining the impact of environmental conditions on the health of Latino families and children are finding a disproportionate burden on the health of poor and ethnic minority communities that house more than their share of toxic waste, pesticide runoff, lead exposure from old housing, trash, graffiti, and air pollution. It has been estimated that environmental exposures contribute 10 to 20 percent to the causes of diseases, including respiratory illnesses such as asthma, developmental delays and learning disabilities, cancers, and birth defects. A report of the impact of power-plant pollution and the effects on Latino health issued by the League of United Latin American Citizens (LULAC) (Keating, 2004) reported that 71 percent of Latinos in the United States live in counties that violate federal air-pollution standards. Another study in New York found that children in low-income families are eight times more likely to be poisoned by lead exposure than children in high-income families (Cahn & Thompson, 2003). These environmental conditions are clearly hazardous to the health of Latino immigrant families and children. What can immigrant families do to prepare for the opportunities as well as the risks of immigration?

OUR CULTURE IS PROTECTIVE: LOOK FOR THE STRENGTHS

While the outlook for Latino health looks grim due to the triple threat of acculturation, lower-quality health care, and environmentally unhealthy living conditions in the United States, there are strengths within our culture that can be protective of health. We can maintain some of our traditions, including growing our own food even if there is only a small space in which to do so, we can listen to our *abuelos y abuelas*[2] to learn about how they lived and stayed healthy, and we can advocate for safer, cleaner neighborhoods. In San Diego, the residents of Barrio Logan have come together to advocate for cleaner air and safer neighborhoods. In Los Angeles, community residents in some of the poorest neighborhoods

---

[2]Grandfathers and grandmothers (Spanish).

organize community clean-up efforts. Families can grow their own food, even if they live in crowded spaces, by organizing community gardens. Even in crowded spaces, we must find the physical and spiritual space for maintaining and honoring those aspects of our culture and tradition that are protective and help us live better lives. I live in a suburb of Los Angeles. When I moved into my home, the first thing my mother did was to plant a *nopal*,[3] oregano, and *yerba buena* [4] in my small back yard. This was her way of giving me her strength and knowledge. We can utilize our space, as small as it might be, in ways that maintain the positive aspects of our *cultura*.[5] We no longer have to give up everything that is sacred and honored. And if maintaining a healthy diet that includes *frijoles y "nopales"*[6] in our diets is part of what we want, then we can do that. After all, acculturation does not mean complete assimilation and loss of your culture. It allows for individuals to keep the best from their original culture and learn to positively adapt to the new culture.

REFERENCES

Cahn, L., & Thompson, G. (2003). The Politics of poison. Retrieved from http://www.prattarea.org

Espino, D. V., & Maldonado, D. (1990). Hypertension and acculturation in elderly Mexican Americans: Results from 1982–1984 Hispanic HANES. *Journal of Gerontology, 45*, M209–M213.

Falicov, C. J. (1998). *Latino families in therapy: A guide to multicultural practice.* New York: Guilford Press.

Hayes-Bautista, D. (2002). "The Latino health research agenda for the twenty-first century." In M. Suarez-Orozco & M. Paez (eds.), *Latinos remaking america.* David Rockefeller Center for Latin American Studies, Harvard University. Berkeley: University of California Press.

[3]Cactus (Spanish, from Nahuatl).
[4]Mint; literally, "good herb" (Spanish).
[5]Culture (Spanish).
[6]Beans and cactus (Spanish).

Igoa, C. (1995). *The inner world of the immigrant child.* New Jersey: Lawrence Erlbaum.

Institute of Medicine (2003). *Unequal treatment: Confronting racial and ethnic disparities in healthcare.* Washington, DC: National Academies Press.

Keating, M. (2004). *Air of injustice: How air pollution affects the health of Hispanics and Latinos.* Washington, DC: League of United Latin American Citizens.

Maxwell, B., & Jacobson, M. (1989). *Marketing disease to Hispanics: The selling of alcohol, tobacco and junk foods.* Washington, DC: Center for Science in the Public Interest.

Maugh, T. H., & McConnell, P. J. (1998). Americanization a health risk, *Los Angeles Times,* p. A1.

Morello-Frosch, R., Pastor, M., Porras, C., & Sadd, J. (2002). "Environmental justice and regional inequality in southern California: Implications for research," *Environmental Health Perspectives Supplements, 110* (Supplement 2), 149–154.

Myers, H. F., & Rodriguez, N. (2003). "Acculturation and physical health in racial and ethnic minorities." In K. M. Chun, P. B. Organista, & G. Marin (eds), *Acculturation: Advances in theory, measurement and applied research.* Washington, DC: American Psychological Association.

Vega, W. A., Kolody, B., Aguilar-Gaxiola, S., Alderete, E., Catalano, R., & Caraveo-Anduaga, J. (1998). Lifetime prevalence of DSM-III-R psychiatric disorders among urban and rural Mexican Americans in California. *Archives of General Psychiatry, 55,* 771–782.

Zambrana, R. E., Scrimshaw, S. C. M., Collins, N., & Dunkel-Schetter, C. (1997). Prenatal health behaviors and psychosocial risk factors in pregnant women of Mexican origin: The role of acculturation. *American Journal of Public Health, 87,* 1022–1026.

OLGA KHAZAN { *Why Don't Convenience Stores*
                Sell Better Food?

OLGA KHAZAN is a writer for the *Atlantic*, where she covers health, gender, and science. She has also contributed to the *Washington Post, Los Angeles Times*, and *Forbes*. In 2014 Khazan was named one of the ten best science writers by *RealClearScience*, a website that aggregates and produces articles on "science stories from around the globe." In 2013 *Foreign Policy* magazine put her on its list of the top one hundred "Twitterati"; follow her @olgakhazan. This essay first appeared in the March 2, 2015, issue of the *Atlantic*.

New programs aim to put more produce in corner stores in order to improve the health of low-income communities. Will it work?
AT A SMALL CORNER STORE in northeast Washington, Nola Liu, a community-outreach officer with the D.C. Central Kitchen, whirled around a deli case with a clipboard in hand, passing out a recipe for cinnamon pear crisps to anyone who would take it.

She thrust a card at a man in a blue knit hat who was on his way out.

"Are you gonna make it for me?" he asked.
"No, you have to make it yourself," she responded.
"I'm not much of a baker," he said, and walked out.   5

Fresh pears are a relatively new arrival at this store, which is called Thomas & Sons. Just a few months ago, the extent of its produce selection was a small refrigerated case holding a few forlorn fruits and onions, all going at a premium. The owner, Jae Chung, was reluctant to stock things like tomatoes, which would often go bad while they lingered on the shelves.

"Why Don't Convenience Stores Sell Better Food?" from *The Atlantic*, March 2, 2015. Copyright © 2105 The Atlantic Media Co., as first published in The Atlantic Magazine. All rights reserved. Distributed by Tribune Content Agency, LLC.

Now, a brand-new refrigerated vegetable case sits front and center amid all the beer and bulletproof glass. ("I have some unruly customers," Chung explains.) Inside are apples, lemons, limes, and grapes packaged neatly in plastic containers. Additional baskets hold potatoes and bananas. The case was provided by the D.C. Central Kitchen as part of their Healthy Corners program, which seeks to expand the fruit and vegetable offerings in corner stores across the District.

Not only did the nonprofit give Chung the fridge for free, it will also replace any items that go bad at no extra cost. They sell the greens to him for cheap, too. Chung says before, he had to buy his fresh produce stock at Costco and pick it up himself. After he added in his markup, a tomato at Thomas & Sons would sell for about $2.50. Now, it's more like $1 to $1.50—on par with what someone might pay for a bag of chips or package of donuts. (At Walmart, a pack of four tomatoes goes for $2.48, or about 60 cents per tomato.)

Nearly every city has neighborhoods that suffer from a lack of access   10 to cheap, easy, and healthful options, and Washington, D.C. is no exception. Tiny, independent corner stores—the kind that have wall-to-wall

The Healthy Corners fridge at Thomas & Sons.

beverage cases, rows of brightly-packaged junk food, and just one or two cash registers—are crammed into every nook of the city. They're an essential part of the food landscape, providing everything from make-do lunch fare for construction workers to emergency beer for hipsters on their way to house parties. According to the D.C. Central Kitchen's calculations, 88 percent of food retailers in the District sell mostly junk food or processed food. Two hundred thousand of the District's residents live in an area where the closest grocery store is three times further away than the closest fast-food or convenience store.

One solution is to lure more large grocery stores to these so-called "food deserts." But it's often much easier, some advocates argue, to simply get the ubiquitous corner stores to start selling healthier food.

Size is the main reason most American corner and convenience stores don't stock very many fruits and vegetables. Many food distributors require a minimum order—say 250 apples—for a delivery. That's easy for places like Safeway or Giant, but it's harder for small shops that sell maybe two dozen apples each week. Corner-store owners who do opt to sell produce end up buying it at prices similar to those regular consumers pay. On top of that, produce requires refrigeration, which adds to the cost for store owners. And unlike Cheetos or Oreos, vegetables rot.

The Healthy Corners program has lowered most of these hurdles. The D.C. Central Kitchen already owned a fleet of trucks that it used for food deliveries to homeless shelters and transitional homes. In 2011, the organization realized it could use the same drivers to bring produce to local corner shops. Because it serves many different types of facilities, the Kitchen has substantial buying power: It's more akin to a large restaurant than a tiny retailer. That, combined with its strategy of buying from local farms and seeking philanthropic grants, helps drive down prices.

"We buy product that's aesthetically or geometrically challenged," says the organization's chief executive officer, Mike Curtin. Some of it is produce that's "the wrong shape or size to fit in the right box to fit in the right truck to fit in bins in the grocery store that are organized by size." But it's still perfectly good—and corner-store owners were happy to have it.

The Healthy Corners program targets areas where there is not a full-   15
service grocery store within a quarter-mile. In addition to promoting fruit
and veggie recipes in the stores, D.C. Central Kitchen staffers have also
held cooking demonstrations and doled out free samples. It's not enough,
store owners told me, to simply install a produce fridge and expect the
community to flock.

There are now 67 such Healthy Corners in D.C., most of which are
in lower-income neighborhoods. According to the nonprofit's own numbers, the corner stores in the program sold more than 140,000 pieces of
produce within the past 10 months, up from about 17,000 in the seven-
month period between September 2011 and April 2012.

The organization says it wants to help grow these types of programs in
other cities. It recently consulted on a similar project in Rochester, New
York. Separate initiatives focusing on corner stores have sprouted up in
Chicago, Manhattan, and Denver.

The idea that food deserts, or even insufficient produce intake, are a
cause of obesity has come under fire recently. One study in *Health Affairs*
last year found that when a new grocery store opened up in a food desert
in Philadelphia, neither locals' weight nor their diets changed. Roland
Sturm, an economist with the RAND Corporation, wrote a paper (which
I covered when it came out) about how people of all incomes now eat
about 30 pounds more vegetables and fruit annually than they did in
1970. Obesity rates have worsened all the while.

People still rely on corner shops primarily for household essentials, like
toilet paper, or for a filling meal they can eat on the run. Chung says that
occasionally parents thank him for providing fruit as an after-school snack
option. Still, "customers' behavior hasn't really changed at this point," he
says.

At Thomas & Sons, one man plopped a 12-pack of Yuengling on the   20
counter and announced to the cashier, "I ain't working today, so I'm going to drink." At Wheeler Market, another Healthy Corners store, some
customers eyed the fridge full of fruit before grabbing a package of donuts.

"This is not going to end obesity, or diabetes. It's naive to think that's the case," Curtin says. "People will avail themselves of this food, but are they still going to eat junk food? Sure."

But perhaps reducing obesity shouldn't be the goal, or at least not an immediate one. Other than weight loss, there are plenty of advantages of eating well, like preventing some forms of cancer. And even produce-heavy, organic grocery stores still sell brownies. (Curtin points out that no one would say, "Oh, we shouldn't open up a Whole Foods in McLean [a wealthy D.C. suburb], because people are still going to buy chips.")

The Healthy Corners do seem to resemble a European style of grocery shopping that some public-health advocates extoll. Rather than pack up the family and head to Kroger every Saturday, returning with a trunk full of Teddy Grahams and assorted meats, many Europeans buy their produce on the way home from work from the dozens of small green-grocers that dot their street corners. These independent merchants—many of them recent immigrants—wedge their stores into the bottom floors of larger buildings, their melons and squashes stacked neatly in blue bins on the sidewalk.

Jaap Seidell, an obesity expert at Vrije Universiteit Amsterdam, said these small vegetable shops, which have proliferated across both large and small towns in Europe, offer a great deal of variety at prices that are even lower than those of grocery stores. They don't seem to run into the same distribution and cost issues that their American counterparts struggle with. "It's in season, they don't have to store it for a long time, they don't have to cool it, and there's a lot of demand for it," Seidell says. "There's a lot less cost and waste involved."

Of course, the Dutch way of life makes on-the-fly veggie shopping eas-   25
ier. Big grocery-store runs aren't very practical anyway, Seidell notes, because almost everyone bikes or walks to work. Most Dutch women work
part-time, so they have ample time to procure and cook fresh food.

Woldeabzghi (in the white sweater) entertains customers at Wheeler Market.

In the Netherlands, he says, "It has always been like this: you have butchers, bakers, and the vegetable farmer."

Curtin says the success or failure of Healthy Corners will not hinge on whether "we put vegetables in 67 corner stores, and some people are still fat." It's about allowing people to decide what kind of diet they'd like to have.

Muller Woldeabzghi, the owner of Wheeler Market in southeast D.C., says he sells maybe 10 to 20 pieces of the Healthy Corners produce each day, accounting for about 10 percent of his sales. He said some customers come to Wheeler instead of the Giant, which is one and a half miles away, because they lack transportation, but others simply like the shop's community feel. It's "a neighborhood feeling," he says. "They want to support us, we want to support them."

When I asked one Wheeler shopper what he thought of the fridge, he seemed skeptical. "Why would someone go to the corner store for produce?" one man said on his way out. "Why wouldn't they go to the market?"

Several other customers I spoke with, though, seemed to take a more 30 Dutch view.

"It's convenient," said Laray Winn, who lives in the neighborhood. "You can make it here in an emergency and get whatever you need."

Demetrius Cain, who lives across the street, says his 6-year-old son is also a fan. Sometimes when he's bored, the boy runs over and comes home with a still-chilled apple. It's not exactly a revolution, but at least it's not a Twinkie.

SARA GOLDRICK-RAB { *Expanding the National School*
KATHARINE BROTON { *Lunch Program to Higher*
EMILY BRUNJES COLO { *Education*

SARA GOLDRICK-RAB, KATHARINE BROTON, and EMILY BRUNJES COLO wrote
this essay in April 2016 for the Wisconsin HOPE Lab, an institute based at the
University of Wisconsin at Madison that focuses on "research aimed at improving
equitable outcomes in postsecondary education" and works on translating scientific research into practice. Goldrick-Rab, the lab's founding director, is a professor
of higher education policy studies and sociology at Temple University. Broton,
a research assistant, is a doctoral candidate in sociology, and Colo is an assistant
researcher.

IN THE EARLY 20TH CENTURY, communities and philanthropists came
together to provide lunch to hungry school children. Some recognized
that children couldn't learn as well when they were hungry and others
felt a moral imperative to meet this basic need. Decades later, the federal
government joined in these efforts and launched the National School
Lunch Program (NSLP).[1] Since its inception, the NSLP has reduced the
incidence of malnutrition, boosted intake of protein, fiber, and other
nutrients for children, and increased educational attainment.[2] In 2015
more than 30 million children received lunch every day, in about
100,000 schools and other institutions across the country.[3]

In today's economy the continuation of education beyond high school
is common and increasingly necessary for a well-paying job. But many of
the nation's undergraduates are struggling to concentrate on their education due to hunger. Over 200 food pantries are operating on college
and university campuses, and staff and faculty are reaching into their own

"Expanding the National School Lunch Program to Higher Education," from The Wisconsin
Hope Lab, April 25, 2016. Reprinted by permission of the publisher.

pockets to provide lunch money to struggling students. Federal support to address this problem may improve academic achievement among undergraduates, as it has among schoolchildren, boosting degree completion rates.[4] We therefore propose expanding the NSLP to higher education.

THE NEW DEMOGRAPHICS OF AMERICAN HIGHER EDUCATION

Three in four undergraduates defy traditional stereotypes.[5] Just 13% live on college campuses, and nearly half attend community colleges. One in four students is a parent, juggling childcare responsibilities with class assignments. About 75% work for pay while in school, including a significant number of full-time workers. The number of students qualified for the federal Pell Grant—a proxy for low-income status—grew from about 6 million in 2007–2008 to about 8.5 million in 2013–14. This is unsurprising given that participation in the NSLP grew by 3.7 million students during that time.[6] With more than one in five children living in poverty, college-going rates at a national high, and the price of higher education continuing to rise, food insecurity among undergraduates is probably more common than ever.[7]

But eligibility for the federally funded food safety net on which many schoolchildren rely (including the Supplemental Nutrition Assistance Program or SNAP, the National School Lunch Program, and the School Breakfast Program), ends abruptly for most when they enter college. Though students' financial needs remain while pursuing a postsecondary education—which is increasingly a prerequisite for a basic standard of living—food assistance becomes very difficult to access. This may be why undergraduates are at greater risk of food insecurity compared to the general population.[8]

Insufficient attention to the nutritional needs of undergraduates could contribute to the inadequate production of college-educated labor. Over 60% of jobs now require some college education, but there are not enough people with college degrees to meet this growing demand. By 2018, the U.S. is predicted to need an additional 3 million individuals with an associate's degree or higher and another 4.7 million with postsecondary certificates.[9] This demand, along with a desire to have the highest proportion of college graduates in the world, led President Obama to encourage all Americans to "get more than a high school diploma" and focus the national education agenda on improving college completion rates.[10]

Enough students start college to meet these goals, but not enough finish. Among first-time, full-time students seeking a bachelor's degree, 59% graduate within six years while 29% of students seeking an associate's degree obtain one within three years. These completion rates mask significant variation by economic background. Just 14% of students from the lowest socioeconomic quartile had completed a bachelor's or higher degree within eight years of high school graduation compared to 29% of those from middle socioeconomic families and 60% of students from the highest socioeconomic quartile.[11] By one estimate, students from high-income families are six times more likely to graduate from college than those from low-income families.[12] Moreover, these gaps persist even after controlling for prior academic achievement.[13]

Lack of resources is at the root of this problem.[14] The price of college is rising faster than inflation, faster than healthcare costs, and faster than need-based financial aid.[15] The Pell Grant, the flagship federal program, does not buy what it used to. When it was created, the grant paid for roughly 80% of the total cost to attend a public four-year college or university, including tuition, fees, and living costs. Today it covers barely one-third.[16] As a result, students from low- and moderate-income families have a great deal of unmet financial need.

This means that after all grants and scholarships are accounted for, a dependent student from a family in the lowest income quartile (i.e., $21,000 median annual earnings) has to devote 59% of her family's total income to attend a public four-year college for one year, or 40% to attend a public two-year college. The situation for independent students is even worse.

On average, independent students over age 24 in the bottom income quartile must pay more than 100% of their annual income in order to attend a two- or four-year public college. Given these numbers, is it any surprise that so many people feel college is simply unaffordable?

FOOD INSECURITY IN HIGHER EDUCATION

Nationally, about half of all Pell recipients are from families living below the federal poverty line. Many of these students come to college to escape the material hardship they have long endured.[17] Yet food security is not examined on any national surveys of undergraduates—so there is limited information about the extent to which undergraduates struggle to find enough food to eat.[18]

In 2015, the Wisconsin HOPE Lab partnered with the Healthy Minds Study at the University of Michigan, the Association of Community College Trustees, and Single Stop to administer a survey at 10 community colleges in seven states. More than 4,000 students completed a standardized assessment of food security.[19] It revealed that half of all respondents (52%) were at least marginally food insecure over the past 30 days.[20] Specifically, 13% were marginally secure, indicating anxiety over their food supply, 19% had a low level of security marked by reductions in the quality or variety of their diet, and 21% indicated a very low level of food security—or hunger.[21] The most prevalent challenge facing community college students appears to be their ability to eat balanced meals, which research suggests may affect their cognitive functioning.[22] In addition, 39% of students said that the food they bought didn't last and they did not have sufficient money to purchase more. Twenty-eight percent cut the size of their meals or skipped meals at least once, and 22% did so on at least three days in the last 30 days. More than one in four respondents (26%) ate less than they felt they should, and 22% said that they had gone hungry due to lack of money.

This problem isn't limited to community colleges. In 2008 the HOPE Lab surveyed more than 2,000 Pell Grant recipients attending 42 public colleges and universities across Wisconsin, and found that during their first semester of college, 71% reported that they had changed their food shopping or eating habits due to a lack of funds. Twenty-seven percent of students indicated that in the past month, they did not have enough money to buy food, ate less then they felt they should, or cut the size of their meals because there was not enough money. When asked if they ever went without eating for an entire day because they lacked enough money for food, 7% of students said yes.[23] In 2015 the HOPE Lab went into the field again with a survey of about 1,100 low- and middle-income undergraduates at eight four-year and two two-year colleges in Wisconsin.[24] Most students—61%—experienced food insecurity at some point during the academic year. Forty-seven percent said that they were unable to afford a balanced diet. Almost as many students reported that the food they purchased didn't last or that they cut the size of meals or skipped meals altogether. Each of these experiences was reported by 42% of students surveyed. And 37% reported that because of financial constraints they ate less than they thought they should.

There are likely consequences to these circumstances. Several studies of elementary and secondary school students show an inverse relationship between food insecurity and academic achievement.[25] Similarly, a study using data from two community colleges in Maryland found that food insecure students were 22% less likely than food secure students to have high grades.[26]

As Madeline Pumariega, chancellor of the Florida University System, puts it, "When a student is hungry, he does not feel safe, and it is hard to help him synthesize class material. We have to meet students' basic needs in order for them to fully concentrate on assimilating the information in a class in a way that they can apply it, learn, and take it forward."[27]

BEYOND SNAP

When undergraduates need assistance affording food, colleges and universities often refer them to SNAP. While in theory SNAP could support them, in practice the help it provides is quite limited.[28] An analysis of the National Postsecondary Student Aid Survey of 2012 revealed that just 27% of undergraduates who are likely eligible for SNAP actually participate in the program.[29] Eligibility issues aside, SNAP take-up rates among undergraduates are quite low.

Further limiting the impact of SNAP, most low-income college students   15 are ineligible. In order to qualify, students must work at least 20 hours per week, take part in the Federal Work Study (FWS) program, have children, or participate in other safety net programs.[30] It can be very difficult for undergraduates, especially those without children, to meet these criteria. Consider the FWS program. It is underfunded and misallocated, such that only 1 in 10 Pell recipients at public colleges or universities receive any support. Moreover, apart from FWS, Pell recipients may struggle to secure and maintain 20 hours per week of employment due to increasingly common labor practices that require flexibility and availability incompatible with the demands of students' class schedules.[31]

Moreover, working long hours while in college is counterproductive, reducing academic achievement and inhibiting course completion.[32] Students working 20 or more hours per week are more likely to drop out of college. And among those who manage to graduate, working extends their time to degree and thus increases their college costs.[33]

Even so, students who are food insecure are more likely to work than their food secure peers. According to one study, the typical food insecure college student works 18 hours per week. Employed students are nearly twice as likely to report experiences with food insecurity, indicating that work and financial aid are not enough to meet the financial demands of attending college.[34]

SNAP also has limited utility for undergraduates because it is rarely accepted on college campuses where students spend their time. Qualified retailers must meet stringent requirements on the types and quantities of staple foods such as meats, dairy, and vegetables they sell, and also be equipped with challenging sales hardware. While Oregon State University just became one of the first universities in the country to accept SNAP, additional proposed changes to rules for retailers may make it very difficult for other schools to follow suit.[35]

In the meantime, campuses are opening food banks and food pantries. The College and University Food Bank Alliance, co-founded by student affairs professionals Clare Cady and Nate Smyth-Tyge, now supports over 200 food banks on college campuses across the nation.[36] Feeding America reports that one in ten of its 45.5 million clients are college students.[37] Organizations such as Single Stop and the Working Families Success Network are also expanding to help colleges develop these services to meet students' needs, in the absence of a clear and cohesive food safety net.

EXPAND THE NATIONAL SCHOOL LUNCH PROGRAM

Given the growing crisis of food insecurity in higher education, the National School Lunch Program should be expanded to include colleges and universities in order to promote college completion. This would require modifying the authorizing legislation to redefine "school" and extend program participation to include adults.[38]   20

Under current NSLP rules, students may receive free or reduced price lunches if their family income is below 185 percent of the annual income poverty level guideline established by the U.S. Department of Health and Human Services and updated annually by the Census Bureau (currently $21,756 for a family of four).[39] Pell Grant eligibility requirements map onto this standard. For example, the median adjusted gross income among Pell recipients in the public sector is just under $17,000 per year, and 85% have incomes below 200% of the poverty line.[40] Students already identified as qualified via the financial aid system (e.g., Pell Grant awardees) could be deemed eligible for the program to cut down on administrative costs. The NSLP provides precedent for this "direct certification" approach and research indicates that it increases participation, lowers administrative costs, and reduces error in who receives benefits.[41] It might also be wise to consider exercising the Community Eligibility Option, introduced in the Healthy, Hunger-Free Kids Act of 2010, at high-poverty community colleges....

Expanding the NSLP to all public and private not-for-profit colleges and universities, and students of all ages, would provide food assistance to approximately 7 million Pell recipients—increasing the NSLP total program size by about one-quarter (in 2015, there were 30.5 million children participating).[42] As in elementary and secondary schools, broad expansion might facilitate creative delivery models so that campuses can effectively serve both on and off-campus students while also reducing stigma.

Program expansion should build on existing efforts. Some colleges are already taking steps to implement a school lunch–type program on their campus. For example, Bunker Hill Community College is working with its cafeteria vendor to buy a basic lunch (sandwich, fruit, and milk) at wholesale rather than retail prices, and distributing those lunches to students in need. Other colleges provide a limited number of food vouchers (with a particular dollar value) to help hungry students get something to eat in the school cafeteria. More often faculty and staff members report taking it upon themselves to help students obtain food on an individual basis.

Program expansion could proceed in stages, perhaps starting with public two-year college students, in selected states, or with selected populations. A gradual rollout based on pilot or demonstration projects could be used to iron out implementation challenges and assess impacts. We recommended splitting pilot projects between two approaches to distribution. One approach ought to provide money for lunches directly to colleges and require that they provide free or reduced priced lunches to Pell recipients on their campuses, much as the existing NSLP program does. The other approach should provide a campus based food voucher directly to students. Vouchers could be distributed through existing campus ID or expense card systems. Under a lunch voucher system, monies could be distributed to students either in lump sums once per semester, or on a more periodic basis—perhaps once per month or biweekly. If vouchers are provided directly to students, requirements for institutions to provide low-cost healthy options would also be needed. Both efforts should be rigorously evaluated, with attention paid to impacts on nutritional outcomes as well as academic progress.

The U.S. Department of Agriculture should work with the U.S. Department of Education to plot the expansion. And any expansion must include provisions for state matching, to ensure that new federal money does not displace existing state level investments in public higher education. A rough estimate based on current program costs is that the costs of full program expansion would total around $4 billion per year.[43] 25

Investing in college students by offering them the food assistance they need to do well in school has immense long-term potential. It will likely improve college attainment and reduce future dependency on the social safety net.[44] Congress is currently considering legislation to reauthorize child nutrition programs, including the NSLP. This is an optimal time to reshape this program to include undergraduates. These students have proven to be good investments by surviving poverty and graduating high school. Additional support can help ensure that they successfully complete college and become competitive in today's labor market, improving their odds of economic stability for the long-term.

NOTES

1. Gunderson, G. W. (1971). The National School Lunch Program: Background and development. U.S. Department of Agriculture, Food and Nutrition Service. Available at http://www.fns.usda.gov/ sites/default/files/NSLP-Program%20History.pdf

2. Fox, M.K, W. Hamilton, & B.H. Lin. (2004). Effects of food assistance and nutrition programs on nutrition and health: Volume 3, literature review. USDA Economic Research Service Report (FANRR-19-3); Hinrichs, P. (2010). The effects of the National School Lunch Program on education and health. *Journal of Policy*

Analysis and Management, 29(3), 479–505; Rosenbaum, D. & Z. Neuberger. (2005). *Food and nutrition programs: Reducing hunger, bolstering nutrition.* Center on Budget and Policy Priorities, Washington, D.C.

3. Oliveira, V. (2016). The food assistance landscape: FY 2015 annual report. U.S. Department of Agriculture, Economic Information Bulletin Number 150.

4. Gassman-Pines, A. and L. E. Bellows. 2015. The timing of SNAP benefit receipt and children's academic achievement. Paper presented at the Association for Public Policy Analysis and Management annual meeting. Available at https://appam.confex.com/appam/2015/webprogram/Paper13559.html; Price, D., Long, M., Quast, S., McMaken, J., & Kioukis, G. (2014). Public benefits and community colleges: Lessons from the Benefits Access for College Completion Evaluation. OMG Center for Collaborative Learning, Philadelphia, PA. Available at http://www.equalmeasure.org/wp-content/uploads/2014/12/BACC-Final-Report-FINAL-111914.pdf

5. Casselman, B. (2013, July 6). Number of the week: 'Non-traditional' students are majority on College Campuses. *The Wall Street Journal.*

6. Kelchen, R. (2015). "Analyzing trends in Pell grant recipients and expenditures." Brookings Institution, Washington, DC. Available at http://www.brookings.edu/blogs/brown-center-chalkboard/posts/2015/07/28-pell-grant-trends-kelchen; Food Research and Action Center (2015). National School Lunch Program: Trends and factors affecting student participation. Available at http://frac.org/pdf/national_school_lunch_report_2015.pdf

7. Bartfeld, J. (2016.) SNAP and the school meal programs. In J. Bartfeld, C. Gundersen, T. Smeeding & J. Ziliak (Eds), *SNAP matters: How food stamps affect health and well-being.* Stanford University Press. Goldrick-Rab, S. (forthcoming). *Paying the price: College costs, financial aid, and the betrayal of the American dream.* University of Chicago Press.

8. Broton, K., Frank, V., & Goldrick-Rab, S. (2014). *Safety, security, and college attainment: An investigation of undergraduates' basic needs and institutional response.* Wisconsin HOPE Lab, Madison, WI.

9. Carnevale, A. P., Smith, N., & Strohl, J. (2010). *Help wanted: Projections of job and education requirements through 2018.* Georgetown University Center on Education and the Workforce.

10. Obama, B. (2009, February 24). Address to joint session of congress.

11. U.S. Department of Education. (2015). *The condition of education.*

12. Bailey, M. J., & Dynarski, S. M. (2011). *Gains and gaps: Changing inequality in US college entry and completion.* National Bureau of Economic Research, Cambridge, MA.

13. U.S. Department of Education. (2015). *The condition of education.*

14. Goldrick-Rab, S. (forthcoming). *Paying the price: College costs, financial aid, and the betrayal of the American dream.* University of Chicago Press.

15. Kurzleben, D. (2013, Oct. 23). "Just how fast has college tuition grown?" *U.S. News & World Report.*

16. Goldrick-Rab, S. (forthcoming). *Paying the price: College costs, financial aid, and the betrayal of the American dream.* University of Chicago Press.

17. Goldrick-Rab, S. (forthcoming). *Paying the price: College costs, financial aid, and the betrayal of the American dream.* University of Chicago Press.

18. The Wisconsin HOPE Lab has requested that the federal government add these items to data collection on undergraduates. Wisconsin HOPE Lab. (2015). Request to add measurement of food insecurity to the National Postsecondary Student Aid Study. Available at http://wihopelab.com/publications/NPSAS%20Brief%20 2015_WI%20HOPE%20Lab_ACE.pdf

19. U.S. Department of Agriculture, Economic Research Service. (2012). *U.S. Household Food Security Module: Six-Item Short Form.* Available at http://www.ers.usda.gov/datafiles/Food_Security_in_the_United_States/Food_Security_Survey_Modules/short2012.pdf.

20. Goldrick-Rab, S., K. Broton, & D. Eisenberg. (2015). *Hungry to learn: Addressing food & housing insecurity among undergraduates.* Wisconsin HOPE Lab, Madison, WI.

21. U.S. Department of Agriculture, Economic Research Service. (2012). *U.S. household food security module: Six-item short form.* Available at http://www.ers.usda.gov/datafiles/Food_Security_in_the_United_States/Food_Security_Survey_Modules/short2012.pdf.

22. Maroto, M. E., Snelling, A., & Linck, H. (2015). Food insecurity among community college students: Prevalence and association with grade point average. *Community College Journal of Research and Practice, 39*(6), 515–526.

23. Broton, K., Frank, V., & Goldrick-Rab, S. (2014). *Safety, security, and college attainment.* Wisconsin HOPE Lab, Madison, WI.

24. Wisconsin HOPE Lab. (2016). What we're learning: Food and housing insecurity among college students. Data Brief 16-01. Available at: http://wihopelab.com/publications/Wisconsin_HOPE_Lab_Data%20Brief%2016-01_Undergraduate_Housing%20and_Food_Insecurity.pdf

25. Cady, C. L. (2014). Food insecurity as a student issue. *Journal of College and Character, 15*(4), 265–272; Alaimo, K., Olson, C. M., & Frongillo, E. A. (2001). Food insufficiency and American school-aged children's cognitive, academic, and psychosocial development. *Pediatrics, 108*(1), 44–53; Alaimo, K. (2005). Food insecurity in the United States: An overview. *Topics in Clinical Nutrition, 20*(4), 281–298; Jyoti, D. F., Frongillo, E. A., & Jones, S. J. (2005). Food

insecurity affects school children's academic performance, weight gain, and social skills. *The Journal of Nutrition, 135*(12), 2831–2839; Winicki, J., & Jemison, K. (2003). Food insecurity and hunger in the kindergarten classroom: Its effect on learning and growth. *Contemporary Economic Policy, 21*(2), 145–157.

26. Maroto, M. E., Snelling, A., & Linck, H. (2015). Food insecurity among community college students: Prevalence and association with grade point average. *Community College Journal of Research and Practice, 39*(6).

27. Goldrick-Rab, S., Broton, K., & Gates. (2013). Clearing the path to a brighter future: Addressing barriers to community college access and success. Association of Community College Trustees, Washington, D.C., and Single Stop USA, New York, NY.

28. Duke-Benfield, A.E. (2015). Bolstering Non-Traditional Student Success: A Comprehensive Student Aid System Using Financial Aid, Public Benefits, and Refundable Tax Credits. Center for Postsecondary and Economic Success at the Center for Law and Social Policy, Washington, D.C. Available at http://www.clasp.org/resources-and-publications/publication-1/Bolstering-NonTraditional-Student-Success.pdf

29. "Likely eligible" means students with incomes under 130% of the federal poverty line who work at least 20 hours per week, take part in work-study, receive TANF or have a dependent child under age 6; Gault, B., J. Hayes, C. Williams, & M. Froehner. (2014.) Public benefit eligibility and receipt among low-income college students—Working draft. Institute for Women's Policy Research, Washington, D.C.

30. United States Department of Agriculture. Supplemental Nutrition Assistance Program (SNAP) website: http://www.fns.usda.gov/snap/students.

31. Goldrick-Rab, S. (forthcoming). *Paying the price: College costs, financial aid, and the betrayal of the American dream.* University of Chicago Press.

32. Dadgar, M. (2012). The academic consequences of employment for students enrolled in community college. CCRC working paper no. 46. New York, NY: Community College Research Center at Columbia University; Darolia, R. (2014). Working (and studying) day and night: Heterogeneous effects of working on the academic performance of full-time and part-time students. *Economics of Education Review, 38,* 38–50.; DeSimone, J. S. (2008). The impact of employment during school on college student academic performance. NBER working paper 14006. National Bureau of Economic Research, Cambridge, MA; Stinebrickner, R., & Stinebrickner, T. R. (2003). Working during school and academic performance. *Journal of Labor Economics, 21*(2), 473–491.

33. Bound, J., Lovenheim, M. F., & Turner, S. (2012). Increasing time to baccalaureate degree in the United States. *Education Finance and Policy, 7*(4), 375–424; Bozick, R. (2007). Making it through the first year of college: The role of students' economic resources, employment, and living arrangements. *Sociology of Education, 80*(3), 261–285; Ehrenberg, R. G., & Sherman, D. R. (1987). Employment while in college, academic achievement, and post-college outcomes: A summary of results. *The Journal of Human Resources, 22*(1), 1–23; Horn, L. J., & Malizio, A. G. (1998). *Undergraduates who work.* National Postsecondary Student Aid Study, 1996. Washington, D.C.: U.S. Department of Education.; Orszag, J. M., Orszag, P. R., & Whitmore, D. M. (2001). *Learning and earning: Working in college.* Newton, MA: Upromise, Inc.; Van Dyke, R., Little, B., & Callender, C. (2005). *Survey of higher education students' attitudes to debt and term-time working and their impact on attainment.* Higher Education Funding Council for England, Bristol, England.

34. Patton-López, M. M., López-Cevallos, D. F., Cancel-Tirado, D. I., & Vazquez, L. (2014). Prevalence and correlates of food insecurity among students attending a midsize rural university in Oregon. *Journal of Nutrition Education and Behavior, 46*(3), 209–214.

35. OSU participation in SNAP to help improve food access. (2016). Oregon State University. Available at http://oregonstate.edu/ua/ncs/archives/2016/jan/osu-participation-snap-help-improve-student-food-access; Enhancing retailer standards in the Supplemental Nutrition Assistance Program (SNAP). Proposed rule. *Federal Register: The Daily Journal of the United States Government.* Available at https://www.federalregister.gov/articles/2016/02/17/2016-03006/enhancing-retailer-standards-in-the-supplemental-nutrition-assistance-program-snap

36. College & University Food Bank Alliance webpage. Available at www.cufba.org.

37. Resnikoff, N. (2014, August 8). "The hunger crisis in America's universities." *MSNBC.*

38. Agriculture, Subchapter A—Child Nutrition Programs, 7CFR210 (2014). Available at http://www.fns.usda.gov/sites/default/files/7CFR210_2014.pdf

39. The poverty guidelines updated periodically in the Federal Register by the U.S. Department of Health and Human Services under the authority of 42 U.S.C. 9902(2). Available at http://aspe.hhs.gov/POVERTY/07poverty.shtml

40. Goldrick-Rab, S. (forthcoming). Paying the price: *College costs, financial aid, and the betrayal of the American dream.* University of Chicago Press.

41. Bartfeld, J. (2016). SNAP and the school meal programs. In J. Bartfeld, C. Gundersen, T. Smeeding & J. Ziliak (Eds), *SNAP matters: How food stamps affect health and well-being.* Stanford University

Press; Gleason, P. et al. (2003). Direct certification in the National School Lunch Program—Impacts on program access and integrity. Prepared by Mathematics Policy Research for U.S. Department of Agriculture; Cole, N. (2007). Data matching in the National School Lunch Program: 2005 final report. Prepared by Abt Associates for U.S. Department of Agriculture; Ponza, M., Gleason, P., Hulsey, L., and Moore, Q. (2007). NSLP/SBP access, participation, eligibility and certification study. Prepared by Mathematics Policy Research for U.S. Department of Agriculture.

42. According to Title IV program volume reports, 8.6 million students received Pell Grants in 2013–14. College Board did some calculations of the Pell volume at each institution type (see http://trends. collegeboard.org/student-aid/figures-tables/percentage-distribution-pell-grants-sector-over-time). According to their calculations, for-profits made up 20% of Pell recipients in 2013-14. We subtract these students for program estimates. For the current number in NSLP see http://www.fns.usda.gov/sites/default/files/pd/slsummar.pdf

43. Neuberger, Z. & Namian, T. (2016). Who benefits from federal subsidies for free and reduced price school meals? Center on Budget and Policy Priorities, Washington, D.C. Available at http://www. cbpp.org/research/who-benefits-from-federal-subsidies-for-free-and-reduced-price-school-meals; for reimbursement amounts per meal see http://www.fns.usda.gov/school-meals/rates-reimbursement; For the cost of meals in the NSLP see: http://www.fns.usda. gov/sites/default/files/MealCostStudy.pdf

44. Price, D., Long, M., Quast, S., McMaken, J., & Kioukis, G. (2014). Public benefits and community colleges: Lessons from the benefits access for college completion evaluation. OMG Center for Collaborative Learning, Philadelphia, PA. Available at http://www.equal-measure.org/wp-content/uploads/2014/12/BACC-Final-Report-FINAL-111914.pdf

RACHEL CARSON { *The Obligation to Endure*

RACHEL CARSON (1907–1964) was born in Springdale, Pennsylvania, graduated from Pennsylvania College for Women in 1929, and received her MA in zoology from Johns Hopkins University in 1932. After writing three books on oceanic topics, she refocused her attention to the effects of pesticides on humans and the environment. In 1962 she published *Silent Spring*, a work that explained the way chemicals affect the ecosystem and helped launch the modern environmentalism movement. Before her death from breast cancer she testified in congressional hearings and called for new policies to regulate chemicals in the environment and to protect human health.

In this chapter from *Silent Spring*, Carson translates her research into accessible prose. She begins by presenting information, but she gradually produces so much evidence to support her claims that her expository writing subtly takes on a persuasive tone, revealing the dangers that humanity both creates and experiences when using chemicals to control the environment.

THE HISTORY OF LIFE EARTH has been a history of interaction between living things and their surroundings. To a large extent, the physical form and the habits of the earth's vegetation and its animal life have been molded by the environment. Considering the whole span of earthly time, the opposite effect, in which life actually modifies its surroundings, has been relatively slight. Only within the moment of time represented by the present century has one species—man—acquired significant power to alter the nature of his world.

"The Obligation to Endure", from *Silent Spring* by Rachel Carson. Copyright © 1962 by Rachel Carson, renewed 1990 by Roger Christie. Reprinted by permission of Houghton Mifflin Harcourt Publishing Company. All rights reserved.

During the past quarter century this power has not only increased to one of disturbing magnitude but it has changed in character. The most alarming of all man's assaults upon the environment is the contamination of air, earth, rivers, and sea with dangerous and even lethal materials. This pollution is for the most part irrecoverable; the chain of evil it initiates not only in the world that must support life but in living tissues is for the most part irreversible. In this now universal contamination of the environment, chemicals are the sinister and littlerecognized partners of radiation in changing the very nature of the world—the very nature of its life. Strontium 90, released through nuclear explosions into the air, comes to earth in rain or drifts down as fallout, lodges in soil, enters into the grass or corn or wheat grown there, and in time takes up its abode in the bones of a human being, there to remain until his death. Similarly, chemicals sprayed on croplands or forests or gardens lie long in soil, entering into living organisms, passing from one to another in a chain of poisoning and death. Or they pass mysteriously by underground streams until they emerge and, through the alchemy of air and sunlight, combine into new forms that kill vegetation, sicken cattle, and work unknown harm on those who drink from once- pure wells. As Albert Schweitzer[1] has said, "Man can hardly even recognize the devils of his own creation."

It took hundreds of millions of years to produce the life that now inhabits the earth—eons of time in which that developing and evolving and diversifying life reached a state of adjustment and balance with its surroundings. The environment, rigorously shaping and directing the life it supported, contained elements that were hostile as well as supporting. Certain rocks gave out dangerous radiation; even within the light of the sun, from which all life draws its energy, there were short- wave radiations with power to injure. Given time—time not in years but in millennia—life adjusts, and a balance has been reached. For time is the essential ingredient; but in the modern world there is no time.

[1]French- German doctor (1875–1965) and philosopher.

The rapidity of change and the speed with which new situations are created follow the impetuous and the heedless pace of man rather than the deliberate pace of nature. Radiation is no longer merely the background radiation of rocks, the bombardment of cosmic rays, the ultraviolet of the sun that have existed before there was any life on earth; radiation is now the unnatural creation of man's tampering with the atom. The chemicals to which life is asked to make its adjustment are no longer merely the calcium and silica and copper and all the rest of the minerals washed out of the rocks and carried in rivers to the sea; they are the synthetic creations of man's inventive mind, brewed in his laboratories, and having no counterparts in nature.

To adjust to these chemicals would require time on the scale that is 5 nature's; it would require not merely the years of a man's life but the life of generations. And even this, were it by some miracle possible, would be futile, for the new chemicals come from our laboratories in an endless stream; almost 500 annually find their way into actual use in the United States alone. The figure is staggering and its implications are not easily grasped—500 new chemicals to which the bodies of men and animals are required somehow to adapt each year, chemicals to - tally outside the limits of biologic experience.

Among them are many that are used in man's war against nature. Since the mid- 1940's over 200 basic chemicals have been created for use in killing insects, weeds, rodents, and other organisms described in the modern vernacular as "pests"; and they are sold under several thousand different brand names.

These sprays, dusts, and aerosols are now applied almost universally to farms, gardens, forests, and homes—nonselective chemicals that have the power to kill every insect, the "good" and the "bad," to still the song of birds and the leaping of fish in the streams, to coat the leaves with a deadly film, and to linger on in soil—all this though the intended target may be only a few weeds or insects. Can anyone believe it is possible to lay down such a barrage of poisons on the surface of the earth without making it unfit for all life? They should not be called "insecticides," but "biocides."

The whole process of spraying seems caught up in an endless spiral. Since DDT[2] was released for civilian use, a process of escalation has been going on in which ever more toxic materials must be found. This has happened because insects, in a triumphant vindication of Darwin's principle of the survival of the fittest, have evolved super races immune to the particular insecticide used, hence a deadlier one has always to be developed—and then a deadlier one than that. It has happened also because, for reasons to be described later, destructive insects often undergo a "flareback," or resurgence, after spraying, in numbers greater than before. Thus the chemical war is never won, and all life is caught in its violent crossfire.

Along with the possibility of the extinction of mankind by nuclear war, the central problem of our age has therefore become the contamination of man's total environment with such substances of incredible potential for harm—substances that accumulate in the tissues of plants and animals and even penetrate the germ cells to shatter or alter the very material of heredity upon which the shape of the future depends.

Some would- be architects of our future look toward a time when it will 10 be possible to alter the human germ plasm by design. But we may easily be doing so now by inadvertence, for many chemicals, like radiation, bring about gene mutations. It is ironic to think that man might determine his own future by something so seemingly trivial as the choice of an insect spray.

All this has been risked—for what? Future historians may well be amazed by our distorted sense of proportion. How could intelligent beings seek to control a few unwanted species by a method that contaminated the entire environment and brought the threat of disease and death even to their own kind? Yet this is precisely what we have done. We have done it, moreover, for reasons that collapse the moment we examine them. We are told that the enormous and expanding use of pesticides is necessary to maintain farm production. Yet is our real problem not one of *overproduction?*

[2]Dichloro- Diphenyl- Trichloroethane, a synthetic pesticide banned in the United States in 1972.

Our farms, despite measures to remove acreages from production and to pay farmers *not* to produce, have yielded such a staggering excess of crops that the American taxpayer in 1962 is paying out more than one billion dollars a year as the total carrying cost of the surplus-food storage program. And is the situation helped when one branch of the Agriculture Department tries to reduce production while another states, as it did in 1958, "It is believed generally that reduction of crop acreages under provisions of the Soil Bank will stimulate interest in use of chemicals to obtain maximum production on the land retained in crops"?

All this is not to say there is no insect problem and no need of control. I am saying, rather, that control must be geared to realities, not to mythical situations, and that the methods employed must be such that they do not destroy us along with the insects.

The problem whose attempted solution has brought such a train of disaster in its wake is an accompaniment of our modern way of life. Long before the age of man, insects inhabited the earth—a group of extraordinarily varied and adaptable beings. Over the course of time since man's advent, a small percentage of the more than half a million species of insects have come into conflict with human welfare in two principal ways: as competitors for the food supply and as carriers of human disease.

Disease-carrying insects become important where human beings are crowded together, especially under conditions where sanitation is poor, as in time of natural disaster or war or in situations of extreme poverty and deprivation. Then control of some sort becomes necessary. It is a sobering fact, however, as we shall presently see, that the method of massive chemical control has had only limited success, and also threatens to worsen the very conditions it is intended to curb.

Under primitive agricultural conditions the farmer had few insect problems. These arose with the intensification of agriculture—the devotion of immense acreages to a single crop. Such a system set the stage for explosive increases in specific insect populations. Single-crop farming does not take advantage of the principles by which nature works; it is agriculture 15 as an engineer might conceive it to be. Nature has introduced great variety into the landscape, but man has displayed a passion for simplifying it. Thus he undoes the built-in checks and balances by which nature holds the species within bounds. One important natural check is a limit on the amount of suitable habitat for each species. Obviously then, an insect that lives on wheat can build up its population to much higher levels on a farm devoted to wheat than on one in which wheat is intermingled with other crops to which the insect is not adapted.

The same thing happens in other situations. A generation or more ago, the towns of large areas of the United States lined their streets with the noble elm tree. Now the beauty they hopefully created is threatened with complete destruction as disease sweeps through the elms, carried by a beetle that would have only limited chance to build up large populations and to spread from tree to tree if the elms were only occasional trees in a richly diversified planting.

Another factor in the modern insect problem is one that must be viewed against a background of geologic and human history: the spreading of thousands of different kinds of organisms from their native homes to invade new territories. This worldwide migration has been studied and graphically described by the British ecologist Charles Elton in his recent book *The Ecology of Invasions.* During the Cretaceous Period, some hundred million years ago, flooding seas cut many land bridges between continents and living things found themselves confined in what Elton calls "colossal separate nature reserves." There, isolated from others of their kind, they developed many new species. When some of the land masses were joined again, about 16 million years ago, these species began to move out into new territories—a movement that is not only still in progress but is now receiving considerable assistance from man.

The importation of plants is the primary agent in the modern spread of species, for animals have almost invariably gone along with the plants, quarantine being a comparatively recent and not completely effective innovation. The United States Office of Plant Introduction alone has introduced almost 200,000 species and varieties of plants from all over the world. Nearly half of the 180 or so major insect enemies of plants in the United States are accidental imports from abroad, and most of them have come as hitchhikers on plants. In new territory, out of reach of the restraining hand of the natural enemies that kept down its numbers in its native land, an invading plant or animal is able to become enormously abundant. Thus it is no accident that our most troublesome insects are introduced species.

These invasions, both the naturally occurring and those dependent on human assistance, are likely to continue indefinitely. Quarantine and massive chemical campaigns are only extremely expensive ways of buying time. We are faced, according to Dr. Elton, "with a life- anddeath need not just to find new technological means of suppressing this plant or that animal"; instead we need the basic knowledge of animal populations and their relations to their surroundings that will "promote an even balance and damp down the explosive power of outbreaks and new invasions." Much of the necessary knowledge is now available but we do not use it. We train ecologists in our universities and even employ them in our governmental agencies but we seldom take their advice. We allow the chemical death rain to fall as though there were no alternative, whereas in fact there are many, and our ingenuity could soon discover many more if given opportunity.

Have we fallen into a mesmerized state that makes us accept as inevi-   20
table that which is inferior or detrimental, as though having lost the will or the vision to demand that which is good? Such thinking, in the words of the ecologist Paul Shepard, "idealizes life with only its head out of water, inches above the limits of toleration of the corruption of its own environment. . . . Why should we tolerate a diet of weak poisons, a home in insipid surroundings, a circle of acquaintances who are not quite our enemies, the noise of motors with just enough relief to prevent insanity? Who would want to live in a world which is just not quite fatal?"

Yet such a world is pressed upon us. The crusade to create a chemically sterile, insect-free world seems to have engendered a fanatic zeal on the part of many specialists and most of the so-called control agencies.

On every hand there is evidence that those engaged in spraying operations exercise a ruthless power. "The regulatory entomologists . . . function as prosecutor, judge and jury, tax assessor and collector and sheriff to
enforce their own orders," said Connecticut entomologist Neely Turner.
The most flagrant abuses go unchecked in both state and federal agencies.

It is not my contention that chemical insecticides must never be used. I
do contend that we have put poisonous and biologically potent chemicals
indiscriminately into the hands of persons largely or wholly ignorant of
their potentials for harm. We have subjected enormous numbers of people
to contact with these poisons, without their consent and often without
their knowledge. If the Bill of Rights contains no guarantee that a citizen
shall be secure against lethal poisons distributed either by private individuals or by public officials, it is surely only because our forefathers, despite their considerable wisdom and foresight, could conveive of no such
problem.

I contend, furthermore, that we have allowed these chemicals to be used
with little or no advance investigation of their effect on soil, water, wildlife,
and man himself. Future generations are unlikely to condone our lack of
prudent concern for the integrity of the natural world that supports all life.

There is still very limited awareness of the nature of the threat. This is
an era of specialists, each of whom sees his own problem and is unaware
of or intolerant of the larger frame into which it fits. It is also an era dominated by industry, in which the right to make a dollar at whatever cost is
seldom challenged. When the public protests, confronted with some obvious evidence of damaging results of pesticide applications, it is fed little
tranquilizing pills of half- truth. We urgently need an end to these false
assurances, to the sugar coating of unpalatable facts. It is the public that is
being asked to assume the risks that the insect controllers calculate. The
public must decide whether it wishes to continue on the present road, and
it can do so only when in full possession of the facts. In the words of Jean
Rostand,[3] "The obligation to endure gives us the right to know."

[3]French biologist and philosopher (1894–1977).

CAROLE CADWALLADR

{ *Google, Democracy, and the*
Truth about Internet Search }

CAROLE CADWALLADR is a journalist who writes features articles for the *Guardian* and the *Observer*, two British newspapers. She is also the author of the novel *The Family Tree* (2006). This piece first appeared on the *Observer* website on December 4, 2016.

Tech-savvy right-wingers have been able to "game" the algorithms of internet giants and create a new reality where Hitler is a good guy, Jews are evil and... Donald Trump becomes president.

HERE'S WHAT YOU DON'T WANT TO DO late on a Sunday night. You do not want to type seven letters into Google. That's all I did. I typed: "a-r-e." And then "j-e-w-s." Since 2008, Google has attempted to predict what question you might be asking and offers you a choice. And this is what it did. It offered me a choice of potential questions it thought I might want to ask: "are jews a race?," "are jews white?," "are jews christians?," and finally, "are jews evil?"

Are Jews evil? It's not a question I've ever thought of asking. I hadn't gone looking for it. But there it was. I press enter. A page of results appears. This was Google's question. And this was Google's answer: Jews *are* evil. Because there, on my screen, was the proof: an entire page of results, nine out of 10 of which "confirm" this. The top result, from a site called Listovative, has the headline: "Top 10 Major Reasons Why People Hate Jews." I click on it: "Jews today have taken over marketing, militia, medicinal,

"Google, Democracy, and the Truth about Internet Search," by Carole Cadwalladr. The Guardian, December 4, 2016. Copyright © 2017 Guardian News & Media Ltd. Reprinted with permission.

technological, media, industrial, cinema challenges etc and continue to face the worlds [sic] envy through unexplained success stories given their inglorious past and vermin like repression all over Europe."

Google *is* search. It's the verb, to Google. It's what we all do, all the time, whenever we want to know anything. We Google it. The site handles at least 63,000 searches a second, 5.5 billion a day. Its mission as a company, the one-line overview that has informed the company since its foundation and is still the banner headline on its corporate website today, is to "organize the world's information and make it universally accessible and useful." It strives to give you the best, most relevant results. And in this instance the third-best, most relevant result to the search query "are Jews . . ." is a link to an article from stormfront.org, a neo-Nazi website. The fifth is a YouTube video: "Why the Jews are Evil. Why we are against them."

The sixth is from Yahoo Answers: "Why are Jews so evil?" The seventh result is: "Jews are demonic souls from a different world." And the 10th is from jesus-is-saviour.com: "Judaism is Satanic!"

There's one result in the 10 that offers a different point of view. It's a   5 link to a rather dense, scholarly book review from thetabletmag.com, a Jewish magazine, with the unfortunately misleading headline: "Why Literally Everybody In the World Hates Jews."

I feel like I've fallen down a wormhole, entered some parallel universe where black is white, and good is bad. Though later, I think that perhaps what I've actually done is scraped the topsoil off the surface of 2016 and found one of the underground springs that has been quietly nurturing it. It's been there all the time, of course. Just a few keystrokes away . . . on our laptops, our tablets, our phones. This isn't a secret Nazi cell lurking in the shadows. It's hiding in plain sight.

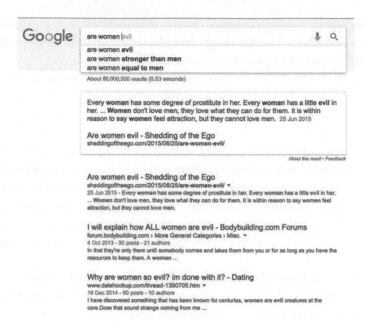

Stories about fake news on Facebook have dominated certain sections of the press for weeks following the American presidential election, but arguably this is even more powerful, more insidious. Frank Pasquale, professor of law at the University of Maryland, and one of the leading academic figures calling for tech companies to be more open and transparent, calls the results "very profound, very troubling."

He came across a similar instance in 2006 when, "If you typed 'Jew' in Google, the first result was jewwatch.org. It was 'look out for these awful Jews who are ruining your life.' And the Anti-Defamation League went after them and so they put an asterisk next to it which said: 'These search results may be disturbing but this is an automated process.' But what you're showing—and I'm very glad you are documenting it and screenshotting it—is that despite the fact they have vastly researched this problem, it has gotten vastly worse."

And ordering of search results does influence people, says Martin Moore, director of the Centre for the Study of Media, Communication and Power at King's College, London, who has written at length on the impact of the big tech companies on our civic and political spheres. "There's large-scale, statistically significant research into the impact of search results on political views. And the way in which you see the results and the types of results you see on the page necessarily has an impact on your perspective." Fake news, he says, has simply "revealed a much bigger problem. These companies are so powerful and so committed to disruption. They thought they were disrupting politics but in a positive way. They hadn't thought about the downsides. These tools offer remarkable empowerment, but there's a dark side to it. It enables people to do very cynical, damaging things."

Google is knowledge. It's where you go to find things out. And evil Jews are just the start of it. There are also evil women. I didn't go looking for them either. This is what I type: "a-r-e w-o-m-e-n." And Google offers me just two choices, the first of which is: "Are women evil?" I press return. Yes, they are. Every one of the 10 results "confirms" that they are, including the top one, from a site called sheddingoftheego.com, which is boxed out and highlighted: "Every woman has some degree of prostitute in her. Every woman has a little evil in her . . . Women don't love men, they love what they can do for them. It is within reason to say women feel attraction, but they cannot love men."

Next I type: "a-r-e m-u-s-l-i-m-s." And Google suggests I should ask: "Are Muslims bad?" And here's what I find out: yes, they are. That's what the top result says and six of the others. Without typing anything else, simply putting the cursor in the search box, Google offers me two new searches and I go for the first, "Islam is bad for society." In the next list of suggestions, I'm offered: "Islam must be destroyed."

Jews are evil. Muslims need to be eradicated. And Hitler? Do you want to know about Hitler? Let's Google it. "Was Hitler bad?" I type. And here's Google's top result: "10 Reasons Why Hitler Was One Of The

Good Guys." I click on the link: "He never wanted to kill any Jews"; "he cared about conditions for Jews in the work camps"; "he implemented social and cultural reform." Eight out of the other 10 search results agree: Hitler really wasn't that bad.

A few days later, I talk to Danny Sullivan, the founding editor of SearchEngineLand.com. He's been recommended to me by several academics as one of the most knowledgeable experts on search. Am I just being naive, I ask him? Should I have known this was out there? "No, you're not being naive," he says. "This is awful. It's horrible. It's the equivalent of going into a library and asking a librarian about Judaism and being handed 10 books of hate. Google is doing a horrible, horrible job of delivering answers here. It can and should do better."

He's surprised too. "I thought they stopped offering autocomplete suggestions for religions in 2011." And then he types "are women" into his own computer. "Good lord! That answer at the top. It's a featured result. It's called a 'direct answer.' This is supposed to be indisputable. It's Google's highest endorsement." That every woman has some degree of prostitute in her? "Yes. This is Google's algorithm going terribly wrong."

I contacted Google about its seemingly malfunctioning autocomplete 15 suggestions and received the following response: "Our search results are a reflection of the content across the web. This means that sometimes unpleasant portrayals of sensitive subject matter online can affect what search results appear for a given query. These results don't reflect Google's own opinions or beliefs—as a company, we strongly value a diversity of perspectives, ideas and cultures."

Google isn't just a search engine, of course. Search was the foundation of the company but that was just the beginning. Alphabet, Google's parent company, now has the greatest concentration of artificial intelligence experts in the world. It is expanding into healthcare, transportation, energy. It's able to attract the world's top computer scientists, physicists and engineers. It's bought hundreds of start-ups, including Calico, whose stated mission is to "cure death" and DeepMind, which aims to "solve intelligence."

Google cofounders Larry Page and Sergey Brin.

And 20 years ago it didn't even exist. When Tony Blair became prime minister, it wasn't possible to Google him: the search engine had yet to be invented. The company was only founded in 1998 and Facebook didn't appear until 2004. Google's founders Sergey Brin and Larry Page are still only 43. Mark Zuckerberg of Facebook is 32. Everything they've done, the world they've remade, has been done in the blink of an eye.

But it seems the implications about the power and reach of these companies are only now seeping into the public consciousness. I ask Rebecca MacKinnon, director of the Ranking Digital Rights project at the New America Foundation, whether it was the recent furor over fake news that woke people up to the danger of ceding our rights as citizens to corporations. "It's kind of weird right now," she says, "because people are finally saying, 'Gee, Facebook and Google really have a lot of power' like it's this big revelation. And it's like, 'D'oh.'"

MacKinnon has a particular expertise in how authoritarian governments adapt to the internet and bend it to their purposes. "China and

Russia are a cautionary tale for us. I think what happens is that it goes back and forth. So during the Arab spring, it seemed like the good guys were further ahead. And now it seems like the bad guys are. Pro-democracy activists are using the internet more than ever but at the same time, the adversary has gotten so much more skilled."

Last week Jonathan Albright, an assistant professor of communications 20 at Elon University in North Carolina, published the first detailed research on how right-wing websites had spread their message. "I took a list of these fake news sites that was circulating, I had an initial list of 306 of them and I used a tool—like the one Google uses—to scrape them for links and then I mapped them. So I looked at where the links went—into YouTube and Facebook, and between each other, millions of them . . . and I just couldn't believe what I was seeing.

"They have created a web that is bleeding through onto our web. This isn't a conspiracy. There isn't one person who's created this. It's a vast system of hundreds of different sites that are using all the same tricks that all websites use. They're sending out thousands of links to other sites and together this has created a vast satellite system of right-wing news and propaganda that has completely surrounded the mainstream media system."

He found 23,000 pages and 1.3 million hyperlinks. "And Facebook is just the amplification device. When you look at it in 3D, it actually looks like a virus. And Facebook was just one of the hosts for the virus that helps it spread faster. You can see the *New York Times* in there and the *Washington Post* and then you can see how there's a vast, vast network surrounding them. The best way of describing it is as an ecosystem. This really goes way beyond individual sites or individual stories. What this map shows is the distribution network and you can see that it's surrounding and actually choking the mainstream news ecosystem."

Like a cancer? "Like an organism that is growing and getting stronger all the time."

Charlie Beckett, a professor in the school of media and communications at LSE,* tells me: "We've been arguing for some time now that plurality of news media is good. Diversity is good. Critiquing the mainstream media is good. But now . . . it's gone wildly out of control. What Jonathan Albright's research has shown is that this isn't a byproduct of the internet. And it's not even being done for commercial reasons. It's motivated by ideology, by people who are quite deliberately trying to destabilize the internet."

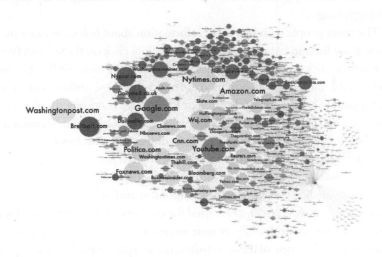

Jonathan Albright's map of the fake-news ecosystem.

Albright's map also provides a clue to understanding the Google search results I found. What these right-wing news sites have done, he explains, is what most commercial websites try to do. They try to find the tricks that will move them up Google's PageRank system. They try and "game" the algorithm. And what his map shows is how well they're doing that.

*LSE The London School of Economics

That's what my searches are showing too. That the right has colonized the digital space around these subjects—Muslims, women, Jews, the Holocaust, black people—far more effectively than the liberal left.

"It's an information war," says Albright. "That's what I keep coming back to."

But it's where it goes from here that's truly frightening. I ask him how it can be stopped. "I don't know. I'm not sure it can be. It's a network. It's far more powerful than any one actor."

So, it's almost got a life of its own? "Yes, and it's learning. Every day, it's getting stronger."

The more people who search for information about Jews, the more people will see links to hate sites, and the more they click on those links (very few people click on to the second page of results) the more traffic the sites will get, the more links they will accrue and the more authoritative they will appear. This is an entirely circular knowledge economy that has only one outcome: an amplification of the message. Jews are evil. Women are evil. Islam must be destroyed. Hitler was one of the good guys.

And the constellation of websites that Albright found—a sort of shadow internet—has another function. More than just spreading right-wing ideology, they are being used to track and monitor and influence anyone who comes across their content. "I scraped the trackers on these sites and I was absolutely dumbfounded. Every time someone likes one of these posts on Facebook or visits one of these websites, the scripts are then following you around the web. And this enables data-mining and influencing companies like Cambridge Analytica to precisely target individuals, to follow them around the web, and to send them highly personalized political messages. This is a propaganda machine. It's targeting people individually to recruit them to an idea. It's a level of social engineering that I've never seen before. They're capturing people and then keeping them on an emotional leash and never letting them go."

Cambridge Analytica, an American-owned company based in London, was employed by both the Vote Leave* campaign and the Trump campaign. Dominic Cummings, the campaign director of Vote Leave, has made few public announcements since the Brexit referendum but he did say this: "If you want to make big improvements in communication, my advice is—hire physicists."

Steve Bannon, founder of Breitbart News and the newly appointed chief strategist to Trump, is on Cambridge Analytica's board and it has emerged that the company is in talks to undertake political messaging work for the Trump administration. It claims to have built psychological profiles using 5,000 separate pieces of data on 220 million American voters. It knows their quirks and nuances and daily habits and can target them individually.

"They were using 40–50,000 different variants of ad every day that were continuously measuring responses and then adapting and evolving based on that response," says Martin Moore of Kings College. Because they have so much data on individuals and they use such phenomenally powerful distribution networks, they allow campaigns to bypass a lot of existing laws.

"It's all done completely opaquely and they can spend as much money 35 as they like on particular locations because you can focus on a five-mile radius or even a single demographic. Fake news is important but it's only one part of it. These companies have found a way of transgressing 150 years of legislation that we've developed to make elections fair and open."

Did such micro-targeted propaganda—currently legal—swing the Brexit vote? We have no way of knowing. Did the same methods used by Cambridge Analytica help Trump to victory? Again, we have no way of knowing. This is all happening in complete darkness. We have no way of knowing how our personal data is being mined and used to influence us. We don't realize that the Facebook page we are looking at, the Google

*Vote Leave An organization that campaigned for the United Kingdom to leave the European Union.

page, the ads that we are seeing, the search results we are using, are all being personalized to us. We don't see it because we have nothing to compare it to. And it is not being monitored or recorded. It is not being regulated. We are inside a machine and we simply have no way of seeing the controls. Most of the time, we don't even realise that there are controls.

Rebecca MacKinnon says that most of us consider the internet to be like "the air that we breathe and the water that we drink." It surrounds us. We use it. And we don't question it. "But this is not a natural landscape. Programmers and executives and editors and designers, they make this landscape. They are human beings and they all make choices."

But we don't know what choices they are making. Neither Google or Facebook make their algorithms public. Why did my Google search return nine out of 10 search results that claim Jews are evil? We don't know and we have no way of knowing. Their systems are what Frank Pasquale describes as "black boxes." He calls Google and Facebook "a terrifying duopoly of power" and has been leading a growing movement of academics who are calling for "algorithmic accountability." "We need to have regular audits of these systems," he says. "We need people in these companies to be accountable. In the US, under the Digital Millennium Copyright Act, every company has to have a spokesman you can reach. And this is what needs to happen. They need to respond to complaints about hate speech, about bias."

Is bias built into the system? Does it affect the kind of results that I was seeing? "There's all sorts of bias about what counts as a legitimate source of information and how that's weighted. There's enormous commercial bias. And when you look at the personnel, they are young, white and perhaps Asian, but not black or Hispanic and they are overwhelmingly men. The worldview of young wealthy white men informs all these judgments."

Later, I speak to Robert Epstein, a research psychologist at the American Institute for Behavioral Research and Technology, and the author of the study that Martin Moore told me about (and that Google has publicly criticized), showing how search-rank results affect voting patterns. On the other end of the phone, he repeats one of the searches I did. He types "do blacks . . ." into Google.

"Look at that. I haven't even hit a button and it's automatically populated the page with answers to the query: 'Do blacks commit more crimes?' And look, I could have been going to ask all sorts of questions. 'Do blacks excel at sports,' or anything. And it's only given me two choices and these aren't simply search-based or the most searched terms right now. Google used to use that but now they use an algorithm that looks at other things. Now, let me look at Bing and Yahoo. I'm on Yahoo and I have 10 suggestions, not one of which is 'Do black people commit more crime?'

"And people don't question this. Google isn't just offering a suggestion. This is a negative suggestion and we know that negative suggestions depending on lots of things can draw between five and 15 more clicks. And this is all programmed. And it could be programmed differently."

What Epstein's work has shown is that the contents of a page of search results can influence people's views and opinions. The type and order of search rankings was shown to influence voters in India in double-blind trials. There were similar results relating to the search suggestions you are offered.

"The general public are completely in the dark about very fundamental issues regarding online search and influence. We are talking about the most powerful mind-control machine ever invented in the history of the human race. And people don't even notice it."

Damien Tambini, an associate professor at the London School of Economics, who focuses on media regulation, says that we lack any sort of framework to deal with the potential impact of these companies on the democratic process. "We have structures that deal with powerful media corporations. We have competition laws. But these companies are not being held responsible. There are no powers to get Google or Facebook to disclose anything. There's an editorial function to Google and Facebook but it's being done by sophisticated algorithms. They say it's machines not editors. But that's simply a mechanized editorial function."

And the companies, says John Naughton, the *Observer* columnist and a senior research fellow at Cambridge University, are terrified of acquiring editorial responsibilities they don't want. "Though they can and regularly do tweak the results in all sorts of ways."

Certainly the results about Google on Google don't seem entirely neutral. Google "Is Google racist?" and the featured result—the Google answer boxed out at the top of the page—is quite clear: no. It is not.

But the enormity and complexity of having two global companies of a kind we have never seen before influencing so many areas of our lives is such, says Naughton, that "we don't even have the mental apparatus to even know what the problems are."

And this is especially true of the future. Google and Facebook are at the forefront of AI. They are going to own the future. And the rest of us can barely start to frame the sorts of questions we ought to be asking. "Politicians don't think long term. And corporations don't think long term because they're focused on the next quarterly results and that's what makes Google and Facebook interesting and different. They are absolutely thinking long term. They have the resources, the money, and the ambition to do whatever they want.

"They want to digitize every book in the world: they do it. They want 50
to build a self-driving car: they do it. The fact that people are reading about these fake news stories and realizing that this could have an effect on politics and elections, it's like, 'Which planet have you been living on?' For Christ's sake, this is obvious."

"The internet is among the few things that humans have built that they don't understand." It is "the largest experiment involving anarchy in history. Hundreds of millions of people are, each minute, creating and consuming an untold amount of digital content in an online world that is not truly bound by terrestrial laws." The internet as a lawless anarchic state? A massive human experiment with no checks and balances and untold potential consequences? What kind of digital doom-mongerer would say such a thing? Step forward, Eric Schmidt—Google's chairman. They are the first lines of the book, *The New Digital Age*, that he wrote with Jared Cohen.*

*Jared Cohen   Director of Jigsaw, formerly Google Ideas, a technology think tank.

We don't understand it. It is not bound by terrestrial laws. And it's in the hands of two massive, all-powerful corporations. It's their experiment, not ours. The technology that was supposed to set us free may well have helped Trump to power, or covertly helped swing votes for Brexit. It has created a vast network of propaganda that has encroached like a cancer across the entire internet. This is a technology that has enabled the likes of Cambridge Analytica to create political messages uniquely tailored to you. They understand your emotional responses and how to trigger them. They know your likes, dislikes, where you live, what you eat, what makes you laugh, what makes you cry.

And what next? Rebecca MacKinnon's research has shown how authoritarian regimes reshape the internet for their own purposes. Is that what's going to happen with Silicon Valley and Trump? As Martin Moore points out, the president-elect claimed that Apple chief executive Tim Cook called to congratulate him soon after his election victory. "And there will undoubtedly be pressure on them to collaborate," says Moore.

Journalism is failing in the face of such change and is only going to fail further. New platforms have put a bomb under the financial model—advertising—resources are shrinking, traffic is increasingly dependent on them, and publishers have no access, no insight at all, into what these platforms are doing in their headquarters, their labs. And now they are moving beyond the digital world into the physical. The next frontiers are healthcare, transportation, energy. And just as Google is a near-monopoly for search, its ambition to own and control the physical infrastructure of our lives is what's coming next. It already owns our data and with it our identity. What will it mean when it moves into all the other areas of our lives?

"At the moment, there's a distance when you Google 'Jews are' and get 'Jews are evil,'" says Julia Powles, a researcher at Cambridge on technology and law. "But when you move into the physical realm, and these concepts become part of the tools being deployed when you navigate around your city or influence how people are employed, I think that has really pernicious consequences."

Facebook founder Mark Zuckerberg.

Powles is shortly to publish a paper looking at DeepMind's relationship with the NHS.* "A year ago, 2 million Londoners' NHS health records were handed over to DeepMind. And there was complete silence from politicians, from regulators, from anyone in a position of power. This is a company without any healthcare experience being given unprecedented access into the NHS and it took seven months to even know that they had the data. And that took investigative journalism to find it out."

The headline was that DeepMind was going to work with the NHS to develop an app that would provide early warning for sufferers of kidney disease. And it is, but DeepMind's ambitions—"to solve intelligence"—goes way beyond that. The entire history of 2 million NHS patients is, for artificial intelligence researchers, a treasure trove. And, their entry into the NHS—providing useful services in exchange for our personal data—is another massive step in their power and influence in every part of our lives.

*NHS National Health Service, the name of the United Kingdom's public health care system.

[Because the stage beyond search is prediction.] Google wants to know what you want before you know yourself. "That's the next stage," says Martin Moore. "We talk about the omniscience of these tech giants, but that omniscience takes a huge step forward again if they are able to predict. And that's where they want to go. To predict diseases in health. It's really, really problematic."

For the nearly 20 years that Google has been in existence, our view of the company has been inflected by the youth and liberal outlook of its founders. Ditto Facebook, whose mission, Zuckerberg said, was not to be "a company. It was built to accomplish a social mission to make the world more open and connected."

It would be interesting to know how he thinks that's working out. Donald Trump is connecting through exactly the same technology.... And Facebook and Google are amplifying and spreading that message. And us too—the mainstream media. Our outrage is just another node on Jonathan Albright's data map.

"The more we argue with them, the more they know about us," he says. "It all feeds into a circular system. What we're seeing here is a new era of network propaganda."

We are all points on that map. And our complicity, our credulity, being consumers not concerned citizens, is an essential part of that process. And what happens next is down to us. "I would say that everybody has been really naive and we need to reset ourselves to a much more cynical place and proceed on that basis," is Rebecca MacKinnon's advice. "There is no doubt that where we are now is a very bad place. But it's we as a society who have jointly created this problem. And if we want to get to a better place, when it comes to having an information ecosystem that serves human rights and democracy instead of destroying it, we have to share responsibility for that."

Are Jews evil? How do you want that question answered? This is our internet. Not Google's. Not Facebook's. Not right-wing propagandists.' And we're the only ones who can reclaim it.

ANDREA LUNSFORD ⎰ *Our Semi-Literate Youth? Not*
⎱ *So Fast*

ANDREA LUNSFORD (b. 1942) is Professor Emerita of English at Stanford
University and is on the faculty at the Bread Loaf School of English. After
graduating from the University of Florida, Lunsford taught English at Colonial
High School in Orlando before earning a PhD in rhetoric from the Ohio State
University. "Our Semi-Literate Youth? Not So Fast" reports on research by
Lunsford and others about trends in undergraduate writing (and thinking) as a
result of increased use of digital technologies. Based on their findings, Lunsford
argues, writing and literacy should be redefined for the digital age—and teachers
of writing, she implies, should reconsider how they teach.

TWO STORIES ABOUT YOUNG PEOPLE, and especially college-age students, are circulating widely today. One script sees a generation of twit-
terers and texters, awash in self-indulgence and narcissistic twaddle,
most of it riddled with errors. The other script doesn't diminish the
effects of technology, but it presents young people as running a rat race
that is fueled by the internet and its toys, anxious kids who are inun-
dated with mountains of indigestible information yet obsessed with
making the grade, with success, with coming up with the "next big
thing," but who lack the writing and speaking skills they need to do so.

No doubt there's a grain of truth in both these depictions. But the
doomsayers who tell these stories are turning a blind eye on compelling
alternative narratives. As one who has spent the last 30-plus years studying the writing of college students, I see a different picture. For those who
think Google is making us stupid and Facebook is frying our brains, let me
sketch that picture in briefly.

"Our Semi-Literate Youth? Not So Fast," by Andrea Lunsford. Reprinted by permission of the
author.

In 2001, I and my colleagues began a longitudinal study of writing at Stanford, following a randomly selected group of 189 students from their first day on campus through one year beyond graduation; in fact, I am still in touch with a number of the students today. These students—about 12 percent of that year's class—submitted the writing they did for their classes and as much of their out-of-class writing as they wanted to an electronic database, along with their comments on those pieces of writing. Over the years, we collected nearly 15,000 pieces of student writing: lab reports, research essays, PowerPoint presentations, problem sets, honors theses, email and textings (in 11 languages), blogs and journals, poems, documentaries, even a full-length play entitled *Hip-Hopera*. While we are still coding these pieces of writing, several results emerged right away. First, these students were writing A LOT, both in class and out, though they were more interested in and committed to writing out of class, what we came to call "life writing," than they were in their school assignments. Second, they were increasingly aware of those to whom they were writing and adjusted their writing styles to suit the occasion and the audience. Third, they wanted their writing to count for something; as they said to us over and over, good writing to them was performative, the kind of writing that "made something happen in the world." Finally, they increasingly saw writing as collaborative, social, and participatory rather than solitary.

So yes, these students did plenty of emailing and texting; they were online a good part of every day; they joined social networking sites enthusiastically. But rather than leading to a new illiteracy, these activities seemed to help them develop a range or *repertoire* of writing styles, tones, and formats along with a range of abilities. Here's a student sending a text message to friends reporting on what she's doing on an internship in Bangladesh (she refers in the first few words to the fact that power has been going on and off ever since she arrived): "Next up: words stolen from before the power went out****~~~~~Whadda-ya-know, I am back in Dhaka from the villages of Mymensingh. I'm familiar enough with the villages now that

it's harder to find things that really surprise me, though I keep looking ☺."
In an informal message, this students feels free to use fragments ("Next
up"), slang ("whadda-ya-know"), asterisks and tildes for emphasis, and
a smiley.

Now look at a brief report she sends to the faculty adviser for her intern-   5
ship in Bangladesh: "In June of 2003, I traveled to Dhaka, Bangladesh for
9 weeks to intern for Grameen Bank. Grameen Bank is a micro-credit institution which seeks to alleviate poverty by providing access to financial
capital. Grameen Bank provides small loans to poor rural women, who
then use the capital to start small businesses and sustain income generating activities." Here the student is all business, using formal academic
style to begin her first report. No slang, no use of special-effects markings:
just the facts, ma'am.[1] In the thousands of pieces of student writing we
have examined, we see students moving with relative ease across levels of
style (from the most informal to the most formal): these young people are
for the most part aware of the context and audience for their writing—and
they make the adjustments necessary to address them effectively.

Ah, you say, but these are students at Stanford—the crème de la crème.
And I'll agree that these students were all very keen, very bright. But they
were not all strong writers or communicators (though our study shows that
they all improved significantly over the five years of the study) and they
did not all come from privilege—in fact, a good number far from it. Still,
they were part of what students on this campus call the "Stanford bubble."
So let's look beyond that bubble to another study I conducted with researcher Karen Lunsford. About 18 months ago, we gathered a sample
of first-year student writing from across all regions of the United States,
from two-year and four-year schools, big schools and small schools, private and public. Replicating a study I'd conducted twenty-five years ago,
we read a random sample of these student essays with a fine-tooth eye,

---

[1]Phrase made famous by the lead detective on *Dragnet*, a 1950s TV show in which Joe Friday, a
stern, no-nonsense cop, said the phrase often during witness interviews.

noting every formal error in every piece of writing. And what did we find? First, that the length of student writing has increased nearly three-fold in these 25 years, corroborating the fact that students today are writing more than ever before. Second, we found that while error patterns have changed in the last twenty-five years, the ratio of errors to number of words has remained stable not just for twenty-five years but for the last 100 years. In short, we found that students today certainly make errors—as all writers do—but that they are making no more errors than previous studies have documented. Different errors, yes—but more errors, no.

We found, for example, that spelling—the most prevalent error by over 300 percent some 25 years ago—now presents much less of a problem to writers. We can chalk up that change, of course, to spell-checkers, which do a good job overall—but still can't correct words that sound alike (to, too, two). But with technology, you win some and you lose some: the most frequent error in our recent study is "wrong word," and ironically a good number of these wrong words come from advice given by the sometimes-not-so-trusty spell-checkers. The student who seems from the context of the sentence to be trying to write "frantic," for example, apparently accepts the spell-checker's suggestion of "fanatic" instead. And finally, this recent study didn't turn up any significant interference from internet lingo—no IMHOs, no LOLs, no 2nites, no smileys. Apparently, by the time many, many students get to college, they have a pretty good sense of what's appropriate: at the very least, they know the difference between a Facebook friend and a college professor.

In short, the research my colleagues and I have been doing supports what other researchers are reporting about digital technologies and learning. First, a lot of that learning (perhaps most of it) is taking place outside of class, in the literate activities (musical compositions, videos, photo collages, digital stories, comics, documentaries) young people are pursuing on their own. This is what Mimi Ito[2] calls "kid-driven learning." Second,

---

[2]Cultural anthropologist (b. 1968) who studies learning and new media.

the participatory nature of digital media allows for more—not less—development of literacies, as Henry Jenkins[3] argues compellingly.

If we look beyond the hand-wringing about young people and literacy today, beyond the view that paints them as either brain-damaged by technology or as cogs in the latest race to the top, we will see that the changes brought about by the digital revolution are just that: changes. These changes alter the very grounds of literacy as the definition, nature, and scope of writing are all shifting away from the consumption of discourse to its production across a wide range of genres and media, away from individual "authors" to participatory and collaborative partners-in-production; away from a single static standard of correctness to a situated understanding of audience and context and purpose for writing. Luckily, young people are changing as well, moving swiftly to join in this expanded culture of writing. They face huge challenges, of course—challenges of access and of learning ever new ways with words (and images). What students need in facing these challenges is not derision or dismissal but solid and informed instruction. And that's where the real problem may lie—not with student semi-literacy but with that of their teachers.

WORKS CITED

Fishman, Jenn, et al. "Performing Writing, Performing Literacy." *College Composition and Communication*, vol. 57, no. 3, 2005, pp. 224–252.

Ito, Mizuko, et al. *Living and Learning with New Media: Summary of Findings from the Digital Youth Project*. MIT Press, 2009.

Ito, Mizuko, et al. *Hanging Out, Messing Around, and Geeking Out: Kids Living and Learning with New Media*. MIT Press, 2009.

Jenkins, Henry. *Confronting the Challenges of Participatory Culture: Media Education for the 21st Century*. MIT Press, 2009.

[3]Professor (b. 1958) and author of many books and articles about the role of media.

———. *Convergence Culture: When Old and New Media Collide.* NYU Press, 2008.

Lunsford, Andrea A., and Karen J. Lunsford. "'Mistakes are a Fact of Life': A National Comparative Study." *College Composition and Communication,* vol. 59, no. 4, 2008, pp. 781–807.

Rogers, Paul M. *The Development of Writers and Writing Abilities: A Longitudinal Study across and beyond the College-Span.* 2008. University of California, Santa Barbara, PhD dissertation.

MICHAELA CULLINGTON   {   *Does Texting Affect Writing?*

MICHAELA CULLINGTON was a student at Marywood University in Pennsylvania when she wrote this essay, which originally appeared in *Young Scholars in Writing*, an undergraduate journal of writing published by the University of Missouri–Kansas City. She received a masters degree in speech and language pathology from Marywood in 2014 and is a speech language pathologist in Delaware.

IT'S TAKING OVER OUR LIVES. We can do it almost anywhere—walking to class, waiting in line at the grocery store, or hanging out at home. It's quick, easy, and convenient. It has become a concern of doctors, parents, and teachers alike. What is it? It's texting!

Text messaging—or texting, as it's more commonly called—is the process of sending and receiving typed messages via a cellular phone. It is a common means of communication among teenagers and is even becoming popular in the business world because it allows quick messages to be sent without people having to commit to a telephone conversation. A person is able to say what is needed, and the other person will receive the information and respond when it's convenient to do so.

In order to more quickly type what they are trying to say, many people use abbreviations instead of words. The language created by these abbreviations is called textspeak. Some people believe that using these abbreviations is hindering the writing abilities of students, and others argue that texting is actually having a positive effect on writing. In fact, it seems likely that texting has no significant effect on student writing.

"Texting and Writing," by Michaela Cullington. Originally published in "Young Scholars in Writing: Undergraduate Research in Writing and Rhetoric," 2011. Reprinted by permission of the author.

CONCERNS ABOUT TEXTSPEAK

A September 2008 article in *USA Today* entitled "Texting, Testing Destroys Kids' Writing Style" summarizes many of the most common complaints about the effect of texting. It states that according to the National Center for Education Statistics, only 25% of high school seniors are "proficient" writers. The article quotes Jacquie Ream, a former teacher and author of *K.I.S.S.— Keep It Short and Simple*, a guide for writing more effectively. Ream states, "[W]e have a whole generation being raised without communication skills." She blames the use of acronyms and shorthand in text messages for students' inability to spell and ultimately to write well. Ream also points out that students struggle to convey emotion in their writing because, as she states, in text messages "emotions are always sideways smiley faces."

This debate became prominent after some teachers began to believe 5 they were seeing a decline in the writing abilities of their students. Many attributed this perceived decline to the increasing popularity of text messaging and its use of abbreviations. Naomi Baron, a linguistics professor at American University, blames texting for what she sees as the fact that "so much of American society has become sloppy and laissez faire about the mechanics of writing" ("Should We Worry or LOL?"). Teachers report finding "2" for "to," "gr8" for "great," "dat" for "that," and "wut" for "what," among other examples of textspeak, in their students' writing. A Minnesota teacher of the seventh and ninth grades says that she has to spend extra time in class editing papers and must "explicitly" remind her students that it is not acceptable to use text slang and abbreviations in writing (Walsh). Another English teacher believes that text language has become "second nature" to her students (Carey); they are so used to it that they do not even catch themselves doing it.

Many also complain that because texting does not stress the importance of punctuation, students are neglecting it in their formal writing. Teachers say that their students are forgetting commas, apostrophes, and even capital letters to begin sentences. Another complaint is that text messages lack emotion. Many argue that texts lack feeling because of their tendency to be short, brief, and to the point. Because students are not able to communicate emotion effectively through texts, some teachers worry, they may lose the ability to do so in writing.

To get a more personal perspective on the question of how teachers perceive texting to be influencing student writing, I interviewed two of my former high school teachers—my junior-year English teacher and my senior-year theology teacher. Both teachers stress the importance of writing in their courses. They maintain that they notice text abbreviations in their students' writing often. To correct this problem, they point it out when it occurs and take points off for its use. They also remind their students to use proper sentence structure and complete sentences. The English teacher says that she believes texting inhibits good writing—it reinforces simplistic writing that may be acceptable for conversation but is "not so good for critical thinking or analysis." She suggests that texting tends to generate topic sentences without emphasizing the following explanation. According to these teachers, then, texting is inhibiting good writing. However, their evidence is limited, based on just a few personal experiences rather than on a significant amount of research.

RESPONSES TO CONCERNS ABOUT TEXTSPEAK

In response to these complaints that texting is having a negative impact on student writing, others insist that texting should be viewed as beneficial because it provides students with motivation to write, practice in specific writing skills, and an opportunity to gain confidence in their writing. For example, Sternberg, Kaplan, and Borck argue that texting is a good way to motivate students: teens enjoy texting, and if they frequently write through texts, they will be more motivated to write formally. Texting also helps to spark students' creativity, these authors argue, because they are always coming up with new ways to express their ideas (417).

In addition, because they are engaging in written communication rather than oral speech, texting teens learn how to convey their message to a reader in as few words as possible. In his book *Txtng: The Gr8 Db8*, David Crystal discusses a study that concludes that texting actually helps foster "the ability to summarize and express oneself concisely" in writing (168). Furthermore, Crystal explains that texting actually helps people to "sharpen their diplomatic skills . . . [because] it allows more time to formulate their thoughts and express them carefully" (168). One language arts teacher from Minnesota believes that texting helps students develop their own "individual voice" (qtd. in Walsh). Perfecting such a voice allows the writer to offer personal insights and express feelings that will interest and engage readers.

Supporters of texting also argue that it not only teaches elements of 10 writing but provides extra practice to those who struggle with the conventions of writing. As Crystal points out, children who struggle with literacy will not choose to use a technology that requires them to do something that is difficult for them. However, if they do choose to text, the experience will help them "overcome their awkwardness and develop their social and communication skills" (*Txtng* 171). Shirley Holm, a junior high school teacher, describes texting as a "comfortable form of communication" (qtd. in Walsh). Teenagers are used to texting, enjoy doing so, and as a result are always writing. Through this experience of writing in ways they enjoy, they can learn to take pleasure in writing formally. If students are continually writing in some form, they will eventually develop better skills.

Furthermore, those who favor texting explain that with practice comes the confidence and courage to try new things, which some observers believe they are seeing happen with writing as a result of texting. Teenagers have, for example, created an entirely new language—one that uses abbreviations and symbols instead of words, does not require punctuation, and uses short, incomplete phrases throughout the entire conversation. It's a way of speaking that is a language in and of itself. Crystal, among others, sees this "language evolution" as a positive effect of texting; he seems, in fact, fascinated that teenagers are capable of creating such a phenomenon, which he describes as the "latest manifestation of the human ability" (*Txtng* 175). David Warlick, a teacher and author of books about technology in the classroom, would agree with Crystal. He believes students should be given credit for "inventing a new language ideal for communicating in a high-tech world" (qtd. in Carey).

METHODS

I decided to conduct my own research into this controversy. I wanted to get different, more personal, perspectives on the issue. First, I surveyed seven students on their opinions about the impact of texting on writing. Second, I questioned two high school teachers, as noted above. Finally, in an effort to compare what students are actually doing to people's perceptions of what they are doing, I analyzed student writing samples for instances of textspeak.[1]

To let students speak for themselves, I created a list of questions for seven high school and college students, some of my closest and most reliable friends. Although the number of respondents was small, I could trust my knowledge of them to help me interpret their responses. In addition, these students are very different from one another, and I believed their differences would allow for a wide array of thoughts and opinions on the issue. I was thus confident in the reliability and diversity of their answers but was cautious not to make too many assumptions because of the small sample size.

I asked the students how long they had been texting; how often they texted; what types of abbreviations they used most and how often they used them; and whether they noticed themselves using any type of textspeak in their formal writing. In analyzing their responses, I looked for commonalities to help me draw conclusions about the students' texting habits and if/how they believed their writing was affected.

I created a list of questions for teachers similar to the one for the stu-   15
dents and asked two of my high school teachers to provide their input. I
asked if they had noticed their students using textspeak in their writing
assignments and, if so, how they dealt with it. I also asked if they believed
texting had a positive or negative effect on writing. Next, I asked if they
were texters themselves. And, finally, I solicited their opinions on what
they believed should be done to prevent teens from using text abbreviations and other textspeak in their writing.

I was surprised at how different the students' replies and opinions were
from the teachers'. I decided to find out for myself whose impressions
were more accurate by comparing some students' actual writing with students' and teachers' perceptions of that writing. To do this I looked at
twenty samples of student writing—end-of-semester research arguments
written in two first-year college writing courses with different instructors.
The topics varied from increased airport security after September 11 to
the weapons of the Vietnam War to autism, and lengths ranged from eight
to ten pages. To analyze the papers for the presence of textspeak, I looked
closely for use of abbreviations and other common slang terms, especially
those usages which the students had stated in their surveys were most
common. These included "hbu" ("How about you?"); "gtg" ("Got to
go"); and "cuz" ("because"). I also looked for the numbers 2 and 4 used
instead of the words "to" and "for."

DISCUSSION OF FINDINGS

My research suggests that texting actually has a minimal effect on student writing. It showed that students do not believe textspeak is appropriate in formal writing assignments. They recognize the difference
between texting friends and writing formally and know what is appropriate in each situation. This was proven true in the student samples, in
which no examples of textspeak were used. Many experts would agree

that there is no harm in textspeak, as long as students continue to be taught and reminded that occasions where formal language is expected are not the place for it. As Crystal explains, the purpose of the abbreviations used in text messages is not to replace language but rather to make quick communications shorter and easier, since in a standard text message, the texter is allowed only 160 characters for a communication ("Texting" 81).

Dennis Baron, an English and linguistics professor at the University of Illinois, has done much research on the effect of technology on writing, and his findings are aligned with those of my own study. In his book *A Better Pencil: Readers, Writers, and the Digital Revolution,* he concludes that students do not use textspeak in their writing. In fact, he suggests students do not even use abbreviations in their text messages very often. Baron says that college students have "put away such childish things, and many of them had already abandoned such signs of middle-school immaturity in high school" (qtd. in Golden).

In surveying the high school and college students, I found that most have been texting for a few years, usually starting around ninth grade. The students said they generally text between thirty and a hundred messages every day but use abbreviations only occasionally, with the most common being "lol" ("Laugh out loud"), "gtg" ("Got to go"), "hbu" ("How about you?"), "cuz" ("because"), and "jk" ("Just kidding"). None of them believed texting abbreviations were acceptable in formal writing. In fact, research has found that most students report that they do not use textspeak in formal writing. As one Minnesota high school student says, "[T]here is a time and a place for everything," and formal writing is not the place for communicating the way she would if she were texting her friends (qtd. in Walsh). Another student admits that in writing for school she sometimes finds herself using these abbreviations. However, she notices and corrects them before handing in her final paper (Carey). One teacher reports that, despite texting, her students' "formal writing remains solid." She occasionally sees an abbreviation; however, it is in informal, "warm-up" writing. She believes that what students choose to use in everyday types of writing is up to them as long as they use standard English in formal writing (qtd. in Walsh).

Also supporting my own research findings are those from a study 20 which took place at a midwestern research university. This study involved eighty-six students who were taking an Introduction to Education course at the university. The participants were asked to complete a questionnaire that included questions about their texting habits, the spelling instruction they had received, and their proficiency at spelling. They also took a standardized spelling test. Before starting the study, the researchers had hypothesized that texting and the use of abbreviations would have a negative impact on the spelling abilities of the students. However, they found that the results did not support their hypothesis. The researchers did note that text messaging is continuing to increase in popularity; therefore, this issue should continue to be examined (Shaw et al.).

I myself am a frequent texter. I chat with my friends from home every day through texting. I also use texting to communicate with my school friends, perhaps to discuss what time we are going to meet for dinner or to ask quick questions about homework. According to my cell phone bill, I send and receive around 6,400 texts a month. In the messages I send, I rarely notice myself using abbreviations. The only time I use them is if I do not have time to write out the complete phrase. However, sometimes I find it more time-consuming to try to figure out how to abbreviate something so that my message will still be comprehensible.

Since I rarely use abbreviations in my texting, I never use them in my formal writing. I know that they are unacceptable and that it would make me look unintelligent if I included acronyms and symbols instead of proper and formal language. I also have not noticed an effect on my spelling as a result of texting. I am confident in my spelling abilities, and even when I use an abbreviation, I know how to spell the word(s) it stands for.

On the basis of my own research, expert research, and personal observations, I can confidently state that texting is not interfering with students' use of standard written English and has no effect on their writing abilities in general. It is interesting to look at the dynamics of the arguments over these issues. Teachers and parents who claim that they are seeing a decline in the writing abilities of their students and children mainly support the negative-impact argument. Other teachers and researchers suggest that texting provides a way for teens to practice writing in a casual setting and thus helps prepare them to write formally. Experts and students themselves, however, report that they see no effect, positive or negative. Anecdotal experiences should not overshadow the actual evidence.

NOTE

1. All participants in the study have given permission for their responses to be published.

WORKS CITED

Baron, Dennis. *A Better Pencil: Readers, Writers, and the Digital Revolution.* Oxford UP, 2009.

Carey, Bridget. "The Rise of Text, Instant Messaging Vernacular Slips into Schoolwork." *Miami Herald*, 6 Mar. 2007. *Academic Search Elite*, www .ebscohost.com/academic/academic-search-elite. Accessed 27 Oct. 2009.

Crystal, David. "Texting." *ELT Journal*, vol. 62, no. 1, Jan. 2008, pp. 77–83. *WilsonWeb*, doi:10.1093/elt/ccm080. Accessed 8 Nov. 2009.

———. *Txtng: The Gr8 Db8*. Oxford UP, 2008.

Golden, Serena. Review of *A Better Pencil*, by Dennis Baron. *Inside Higher Ed*, 18 Sept. 2009, www.insidehighered.com/news/2009/09/18/barron. Accessed 9 Nov. 2009.

Shaw, Donita M., et al. "An Exploratory Investigation into the Relationship between Text Messaging and Spelling." *New England Reading Association Journal*, vol. 43, no. 1, June 2007, pp. 57–62. *Ebscohost*, connection.ebscohost.com/c/articles/25648081/exploratory-investigation-relationship-between-text-messaging-spelling. Accessed 8 Nov. 2009.

"Should We Worry or LOL?" *NEA Today*, vol. 22, no. 6, Mar. 2004, p. 12. *Ebscohost*, connection.ebscohost.com/c/articles/12405267/should-we-worry-lol. Accessed 27 Oct. 2009.

Sternberg, Betty, et al. "Enhancing Adolescent Literacy Achievement through Integration of Technology in the Classroom." *Reading Research Quarterly*, vol. 42, no. 3, July–Sept. 2007, pp. 416–20. *ERIC*, eric.ed.gov/?id=EJ767777. Accessed 8 Nov. 2009.

"Texting, Testing Destroys Kids' Writing Style." *USA Today*, vol. 137, no. 2760, Sept. 2008, p. 8. *Ebscohost*, connection.ebscohost.com/c/articles/34214935/texting-testing-destroys-kids-writing-style. Accessed 9 Nov. 2009.

Walsh, James. "Txt Msgs Creep in2 class—Some Say That's gr8." *Star Tribune*, 23 Oct. 2007. *Academic Search Elite*, www.ebscohost.com/academic/academic-search-elite. Accessed 27 Oct. 2009.

STEPHANIE OWEN AND
ISABEL SAWHILL

{

Should Everyone Go to College?

STEPHANIE OWEN AND ISABEL SAWHILL are the authors of *Should Everyone Go to College?*, a report published in 2013 by the Brookings Institution, a centrist think tank in Washington, D.C. Owen was a senior research assistant at Brookings' Center on Children and Families at the time of the report's publication and is currently a Phd student in public policy and economics at the University of Michigan. Sawhill is a senior fellow in economic studies at Brookings and the author of *Generation Unbound: Drifting into Sex and Parenthood without Marriage* (2014).

SUMMARY

FOR THE PAST FEW DECADES, it has been widely argued that a college degree is a prerequisite to entering the middle class in the United States. Study after study reminds us that higher education is one of the best investments we can make, and President Obama has called it "an economic imperative." We all know that, on average, college graduates make significantly more money over their lifetimes than those with only a high school education. What gets less attention is the fact that not all college degrees or college graduates are equal. There is enormous variation in the so-called return to education depending on factors such as institution attended, field of study, whether a student graduates, and post-graduation occupation. While the average return to obtaining a college degree is clearly positive, we emphasize that it is not universally so. For certain schools, majors, occupations, and individuals, college may not

"Should Everyone Go to College?" From the Center on Children at Brookings Institute, CCF Brief # 50, May 2013. Used by permission of Brookings Institution Press.

be a smart investment. By telling all young people that they should go to college no matter what, we are actually doing some of them a disservice.

THE RATE OF RETURN ON EDUCATION

One way to estimate the value of education is to look at the increase in earnings associated with an additional year of schooling. However, correlation is not causation, and getting at the true causal effect of education on earnings is not so easy. The main problem is one of selection: if the smartest, most motivated people are both more likely to go to college and more likely to be financially successful, then the observed difference in earnings by years of education doesn't measure the true effect of college.

Researchers have attempted to get around this problem of causality by employing a number of clever techniques, including, for example, comparing identical twins with different levels of education. The best studies suggest that the return to an additional year of school is around 10 percent. If we apply this 10 percent rate to the median earnings of about $30,000 for a 25- to 34-year-old high school graduate working full time in 2010, this implies that a year of college increases earnings by $3,000, and four years increases them by $12,000. Notice that this amount is less than the raw differences in earnings between high school graduates and bachelor's degree holders of $15,000, but it is in the same ballpark. Similarly, the raw difference between high school graduates and associate's degree holders is about $7,000, but a return of 10% would predict the causal effect of those additional two years to be $6,000.

There are other factors to consider. The cost of college matters as well: the more someone has to pay to attend, the lower the net benefit of attending. Furthermore, we have to factor in the opportunity cost of college, measured as the foregone earnings a student gives up when he or she leaves or delays entering the workforce in order to attend school. Using average earnings for 18- and 19-year-olds and 20- and 21-year-olds with high school degrees (including those working part-time or not at all),

Michael Greenstone and Adam Looney of Brookings' Hamilton Project calculate an opportunity cost of $54,000 for a four-year degree.

In this brief, we take a rather narrow view of the value of a college degree, focusing on the earnings premium. However, there are many nonmonetary benefits of schooling which are harder to measure but no less important. Research suggests that additional education improves overall wellbeing by affecting things like job satisfaction, health, marriage, parenting, trust, and social interaction. Additionally, there are social benefits to education, such as reduced crime rates and higher political participation. We also do not want to dismiss personal preferences, and we acknowledge that many people derive value from their careers in ways that have nothing to do with money. While beyond the scope of this piece, we do want to point out that these noneconomic factors can change the cost-benefit calculus.

As noted above, the gap in annual earnings between young high school graduates and bachelor's degree holders working full time is $15,000. What's more, the earnings premium associated with a college degree grows over a lifetime. Hamilton Project research shows that 23- to 25-year-olds with bachelor's degrees make $12,000 more than high school graduates but by age 50, the gap has grown to $46,500 (Figure 1). When we look at lifetime earnings—the sum of earnings over a career—the total premium is $570,000 for a bachelor's degree and $170,000 for an associate's degree. Compared to the average up-front cost of four years of college (tuition plus opportunity cost) of $102,000, the Hamilton Project is not alone in arguing that investing in college provides "a tremendous return."

It is always possible to quibble over specific calculations, but it is hard to deny that, on average, the benefits of a college degree far outweigh the costs. The key phrase here is "on average." The purpose of this brief is to highlight the reasons why, for a given individual, the benefits may not outweigh the costs. We emphasize that a 17- or 18-year-old deciding whether and where to go to college should carefully consider his or her own likely path of education and career before committing a considerable amount

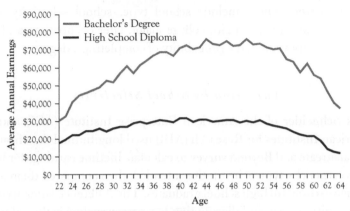

FIGURE 1. EARNING TRAJECTORIES
BY EDUCATIONAL ATTAINMENT

Source: Greenstone and Looney (2011).

Note: Sample includes all civilian U.S. citizens, excluding those in school. Annual earnings are averaged over the entire sample, including those without work. Source: March CPS 2007–2010.

of time and money to that degree. With tuitions rising faster than family incomes, the typical college student is now more dependent than in the past on loans, creating serious risks for the individual student and perhaps for the system as a whole, should widespread defaults occur in the future. Federal student loans now total close to $1 trillion, larger than credit card debt or auto loans and second only to mortgage debt on household balance sheets.

VARIATION IN THE RETURN TO EDUCATION

It is easy to imagine hundreds of dimensions on which college degrees and their payoffs could differ. Ideally, we'd like to be able to look into a crystal ball and know which individual school will give the highest net benefit for a given student with her unique strengths, weaknesses, and interests. Of course, we are not able to do this. What we can do is lay out several key dimensions that seem to significantly affect the return to a college degree. These include school type, school selectivity level, school cost and financial aid, college major, later occupation, and perhaps most importantly, the probability of completing a degree.

Variation by School Selectivity

Mark Schneider of the American Enterprise Institute (AEI) and the American Institutes for Research (AIR) used longitudinal data from the Baccalaureate and Beyond survey to calculate lifetime earnings for bachelor's earners by type of institution attended, then compared them to the lifetime earnings of high school graduates. The difference (after accounting for tuition costs and discounting to a present value) is the value of a bachelor's degree. For every type of school (categorized by whether the school was a public institution or a nonprofit private institution and by its selectivity) this value is positive, but it varies widely. People who attended the most selective private schools have a lifetime earnings premium of over $620,000 (in 2012 dollars). For those who attended a minimally selective or open admission private school, the premium is only a third of that. Schneider performed a similar exercise with campus-level data on college graduates (compiled by the online salary information company PayScale), calculating the return on investment (ROI) of a bachelor's degree (Figure 2). These calculations suggest that public schools tend to have higher ROIs than private schools, and more selective schools offer higher returns than less selective ones. Even within a school type and selectivity category, the variation is striking. For example, the average ROI for a competitive public school in 2010 is 9 percent, but the highest rate within this category is 12 percent while the lowest is 6 percent.

Another important element in estimating the ROI on a college educa- 10 tion is financial aid, which can change the expected return dramatically.

FIGURE 2. RETURN ON INVESTMENT OF A BACHELOR'S
DEGREE BY INSTITUTION TYPE

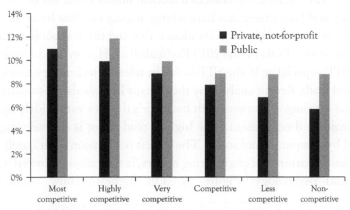

Source: Schneider (2010).
Note: Data uses PayScale return on investment data and Barron's index of school selectivity.

For example, Vassar College is one of the most expensive schools on the 2012 list and has a relatively low annual ROI of 6%. But when you factor in its generous aid packages (nearly 60% of students receive aid, and the average amount is over $30,000), Vassar's annual ROI increases 50%, to a return of 9% (data available at http://www.payscale.com/college-education-value-2012).

One of the most important takeaways from the PayScale data is that not every bachelor's degree is a smart investment. After attempting to account for in-state vs. out-of-state tuition, financial aid, graduation rates, years taken to graduate, wage inflation, and selection, nearly two hundred schools on the 2012 list have negative ROIs. Students may want to think twice about attending the Savannah College of Art and Design in Georgia or Jackson State University in Mississippi. The problem is compounded if the students most likely to attend these less selective schools come from disadvantaged families.

Variation by Field of Study and Career

Even within a school, the choices a student makes about his or her field of study and later career can have a large impact on what he or she gets out of her degree. It is no coincidence that the three schools with the highest 30-year ROIs on the 2012 PayScale list—Harvey Mudd, Caltech, and MIT—specialize in the STEM fields: science, technology, engineering, and math. Recent analysis by the Census Bureau also shows that the lifetime earnings of workers with bachelor's degrees vary widely by college major and occupation. The highest paid major is engineering, followed by computers and math. The lowest paid major, with barely half the lifetime earnings of engineering majors, is education, followed by the arts and psychology (Figure 3). The highest-earning occupation

FIGURE 3. WORK-LIFE EARNINGS OF BACHELOR'S DEGREE
HOLDERS BY COLLEGE MAJOR

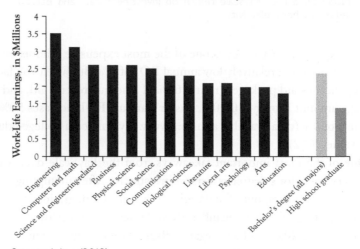

Source: Julian (2012).

Note: Synthetic work-life earnings estimates are calculated by finding median earnings for each 5-year age group between 25 and 64 (25–29, 30–34, etc.). Earnings for each group is multiplied by 5 to get total earnings for that period, then aggregated to get total lifetime earnings. This is done for high school graduates, bachelor's degree holders, and bachelor's degree holders by major.

category is architecture and engineering, with computers, math, and management in second place. The lowest-earning occupation for college graduates is service (Figure 4). According to Census's calculations, the lifetime earnings of an education or arts major working in the service sector are actually lower than the average lifetime earnings of a high school graduate.

When we dig even deeper, we see that just as not all college degrees are equal, neither are all high school diplomas. Anthony Carnevale and his colleagues at the Georgetown Center on Education and the Workforce use similar methodology to the Census calculations but disaggregate even

FIGURE 4. WORK-LIFE EARNINGS OF BACHELOR'S DEGREE
HOLDERS BY OCCUPATION

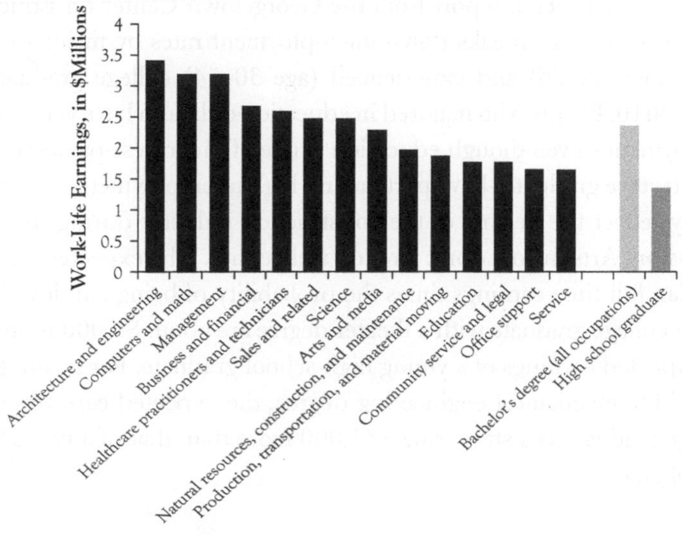

Source: Julian (2012).

Note: Synthetic work-life earnings estimates are calculated by finding median earnings for each 5-year age group between 25 and 64 (25–29, 30–34, etc.). Earnings for each group is multiplied by 5 to get total earnings for that period, then aggregated to get total lifetime earnings. This is done for high school graduates, bachelor's degree holders, and bachelor's degree holders by occupation.

further, estimating median lifetime earnings for all education levels by occupation. They find that 14 percent of people with a high school diploma
make at least as much as those with a bachelor's degree, and 17 percent of
people with a bachelor's degree make more than those with a professional
degree. The authors argue that much of this finding is explained by occupation. In every occupation category, more educated workers earn more.

But, for example, someone working in a STEM job with only a high
school diploma can expect to make more over a lifetime than someone
with a bachelor's degree working in education, community service and
arts, sales and office work, health support, blue collar jobs, or personal
services.

The numbers above are for full-time workers in a given field. In fact, 15
choice of major can also affect whether a college graduate can find a job
at all. Another recent report from the Georgetown Center on Education
and the Workforce breaks down unemployment rates by major for both
recent (age 22–26) and experienced (age 30–54) college graduates in
2009–2010. People who majored in education or health have very low unemployment—even though education is one of the lowest-paying majors.
Architecture graduates have particularly high unemployment, which may
simply reflect the decline of the construction industry during the Great
Recession. Arts majors don't fare too well, either. The expected earnings
(median full-time earnings times the probability of being employed) of a
young college graduate with a theater degree are about $6,000 more than
the expected earnings of a young high school graduate. For a young person with a mechanical engineering degree, the expected earnings of the
college graduate is a staggering $35,000 more than that of a typical high
school graduate.

Variation in Graduation Rates

Comparisons of the return to college by highest degree attained include
only people who actually complete college. Students who fail to obtain a

degree incur some or all of the costs of a bachelor's degree without the ultimate payoff. This has major implications for inequalities of income and wealth, as the students least likely to graduate—lower-income students—are also the most likely to take on debt to finance their education.

Fewer than 60 percent of students who enter four-year schools finish within six years, and for low-income students it's even worse. Again, the variation in this measure is huge. Just within Washington, D.C., for example, six-year graduation rates range from a near-universal 93 percent at Georgetown University to a dismal 19 percent at the University of D.C. Of course, these are very different institutions, and we might expect high-achieving students at an elite school like Georgetown to have higher completion rates than at a less competitive school like UDC. In fact, Frederick Hess and his colleagues at AEI have documented that the relationship between selectivity and completion is positive, echoing other work that suggests that students are more likely to succeed in and graduate from college when they attend more selective schools (Figure 5). At the

FIGURE 5. AVERAGE SIX-YEAR GRADUATION RATES
BY SCHOOL SELECTIVITY

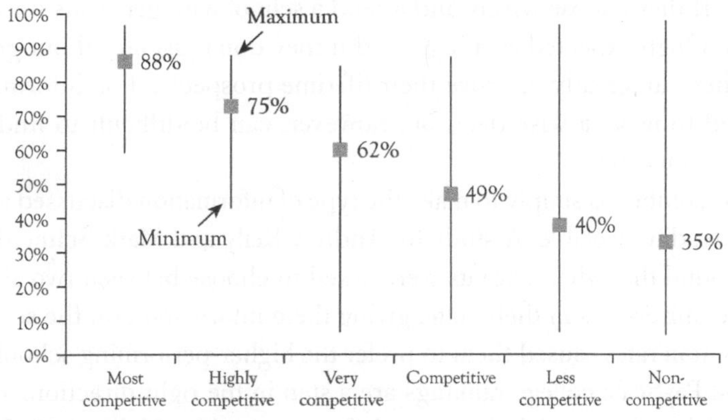

Source: Hess et al. (2009).

most selective schools, 88 percent of students graduate within six years; at non-competitive schools, only 35 percent do. Furthermore, the range of completion rates is negatively correlated with school ranking, meaning the least selective schools have the widest range. For example, one non-competitive school, Arkansas Baptist College, graduates 100 percent of its students, while only 8 percent of students at Southern University at New Orleans finish. Not every student can get into Harvard, where the likelihood of graduating is 97 percent, but students can choose to attend a school with a better track record within their ability level.

Unfortunately, recent evidence by Caroline Hoxby of Stanford and Christopher Avery of Harvard shows that most high-achieving low-income students never even apply to the selective schools that they are qualified to attend—and at which they would be eligible for generous financial aid. There is clearly room for policies that do a better job of matching students to schools.

POLICY IMPLICATIONS

All of this suggests that it is a mistake to unilaterally tell young Americans that going to college—any college—is the best decision they can make. If they choose wisely and attend a school with generous financial aid and high expected earnings, and if they don't just enroll but graduate, they can greatly improve their lifetime prospects. The information needed to make a wise decision, however, can be difficult to find and hard to interpret.

One solution is simply to make the type of information discussed above [20] more readily available. A study by Andrew Kelly and Mark Schneider of AEI found that when parents were asked to choose between two similar public universities in their state, giving them information on the schools' graduation rates caused them to prefer the higher-performing school.

The PayScale college rankings are a step in the right direction, giving potential students and their parents information with which to make better decisions. Similarly, the Obama Administration's new College Scorecard is being developed to increase transparency in the college application process. As it operates now, a prospective student can type in a college's name and learn its average net price, graduation rate, loan default rate, and median borrowed amount. The Department of Education is working to add information about the earnings of a given school's graduates. There is also a multi-dimensional search feature that allows users to find schools by location, size, and degrees and majors offered. The Student Right to Know Before You Go Act, sponsored by Senators Ron Wyden (D-OR) and Marco Rubio (R-FL), also aims to expand the data available on the costs and benefits of individual schools, as well as programs and majors within schools.

The College Scorecard is an admirable effort to help students and parents navigate the complicated process of choosing a college. However, it may not go far enough in improving transparency and helping students make the best possible decisions. A recent report by the Center for American Progress (CAP) showed a draft of the Scorecard to a focus group of college-bound high school students and found, among other things, that they are frequently confused about the term "net price" and give little weight to six-year graduation rates because they expect to graduate in four. It appears that the White House has responded to some of these critiques, for example showing median amount borrowed and default rates rather than the confusing "student loan repayment." Nevertheless, more information for students and their parents is needed.

There is also room for improvement in the financial aid system, which can seem overwhelmingly complex for families not familiar with the process. Studies have shown that students frequently underestimate how much aid they are eligible for, and don't claim the tax incentives that would save them money. Since 2009, the Administration has worked to simplify the FAFSA, the form that families must fill out to receive federal aid—but more could be done to guide low-income families through the process.

In the longer run, colleges need to do more to ensure that their students graduate, particularly the lower-income students who struggle most with persistence and completion. Research suggests that grants and loans increase enrollment but that aid must be tied to performance in order to affect persistence. Currently, we spend over $100 billion on Pell Grants and federal loans, despite a complete lack of evidence that this money leads to higher graduation rates. Good research on programs like Georgia's HOPE scholarships or West Virginia's PROMISE scholarships suggest that attaching strings to grant aid can improve college persistence and completion.

Finally, we want to emphasize that the personal characteristics and 25 skills of each individual are equally important. It may be that for a student with poor grades who is on the fence about enrolling in a four-year program, the most bang for the buck will come from a vocationally oriented associate's degree or career-specific technical training. Indeed, there are many well-paid job openings going unfilled because employers can't find workers with the right skills—skills that young potential workers could learn from training programs, apprenticeships, a vocational certificate, or an associate's degree. Policymakers should encourage these alternatives at the high school as well as the postsecondary level, with a focus on high-demand occupations and high-growth sectors. There has long been resistance to vocational education in American high schools, for fear that "tracking" students reinforces socioeconomic (and racial) stratification and impedes mobility. But if the default for many lower-achieving students was a career-focused training path rather than a path that involves dropping out of traditional college, their job prospects would probably improve. For example, Career Academies are high schools organized around an occupational or industry focus, and have partnerships with local employers and colleges. They have been shown by gold standard research to increase men's wages, hours worked, and employment stability after high school, particularly for those at high risk of dropping out.

CONCLUSIONS

In this brief, we have corralled existing research to make the point that while on average the return to college is highly positive, there is a considerable spread in the value of going to college. A bachelor's degree is not a smart investment for every student in every circumstance. We have outlined three important steps policymakers can take to make sure every person does make a smart investment in their choice of postsecondary education. First, we must provide more information in a comprehensible manner. Second, the federal government should lead the way on performance-based scholarships to incentivize college attendance and persistence. Finally, there should be more good alternatives to a traditional academic path, including career and technical education and apprenticeships.

ADDITIONAL READING

Anthony P. Carnevale, Ban Cheah, and Jeff Strohl, "Hard Times: College Majors, Unemployment, and Earnings: Not All College Degrees Are Created Equal" (Washington, D.C.: The Georgetown University Center on Education and the Workforce, January 2012).

Anthony P. Carnevale, Stephen J. Rose, and Ban Cheah, "The College Payoff: Education, Occupations, Lifetime Earnings" (Washington, D.C.: The Georgetown University Center on Education and the Workforce, August 2011).

Michael Greenstone and Adam Looney, "Where Is the Best Place to Invest $102,000—In Stocks, Bonds, or a College Degree?" (Washington, D.C.: The Brookings Institution, June 2011).

Frederick M. Hess, Mark Schneider, Kevin Carey, and Andrew P. Kelly, "Diplomas and Dropouts: Which Colleges Actually Graduate Their Students (and Which Don't)" (Washington, D.C.: American Enterprise Institute for Public Policy Research, June 2009).

Harry J. Holzer and Robert I. Lerman, "The Future of Middle-Skill Jobs," (Washington, D.C.: The Brookings Institution, February 2009).

Caroline M. Hoxby and Christopher Avery, "The Missing 'One-Offs': The Hidden Supply of High-Achieving, Low Income Students" (Cambridge, MA, Working Paper, National Bureau of Economic Research, 2012).

Tiffany Julian, "Work-Life Earnings by Field of Degree and Occupation for People With a Bachelor's Degree: 2011" (Washington, D.C.: U.S. Census Bureau, October 2012).

Andrew P. Kelly and Mark Schneider, "Filling In the Blanks: How Information Can Affect Choice in Higher Education" (Washington, D.C.: American Enterprise Institute for Public Policy Research, January 2011).

Julie Margetta Morgan and Gadi Dechter, "Improving the College Scorecard: Using Student Feedback to Create an Effective Disclosure" (Washington, D.C.: Center for American Progress, November 2012).

Mark Schneider, "How Much Is That Bachelor's Degree Really Worth? The Million Dollar Misunderstanding" (Washington, D.C.: American Enterprise Institute for Public Policy Research, May 2009).

Mark Schneider, "Is College Worth the Investment?" (Washington, D.C.: American Enterprise Institute for Public Policy Research, October 2010).

MICHELLE ALEXANDER   { *The New Jim Crow*

MICHELLE ALEXANDER is a lawyer and scholar known for her work to protect civil rights. She has taught at Stanford Law School and has a joint appointment at Ohio State University's law school and its institute for the study of race and ethnicity. She has written opinion pieces for the *New York Times, Huffington Post, The Nation, Washington Post, and Los Angeles Times,* among other publications. She is the author of *The New Jim Crow: Mass Incarceration in the Age of Colorblindness* (2010); this selection is from the book's introduction.

JARVIOUS COTTON CANNOT VOTE. Like his father, grandfather, great-grandfather, and great-great-grandfather, he has been denied the right to participate in our electoral democracy. Cotton's family tree tells the story of several generations of black men who were born in the United States but who were denied the most basic freedom that democracy promises— the freedom to vote for those who will make the rules and laws that govern one's life. Cotton's great-great-grandfather could not vote as a slave. His great-grandfather was beaten to death by the Ku Klux Klan for attempting to vote. His grandfather was prevented from voting by Klan intimidation. His father was barred from voting by poll taxes and literacy tests. Today, Jarvious Cotton cannot vote because he, like many black men in the United States, has been labeled a felon and is currently on parole.[1]

Cotton's story illustrates, in many respects, the old adage "The more things change, the more they remain the same." In each generation, new tactics have been used for achieving the same goals—goals shared by the

Excerpt from *The New Jim Crow*. Copyright © 2010, 2012 by Michelle Alexander. Reprinted by permission of The New Press. www.thenewpress.com

Founding Fathers. Denying African Americans citizenship was deemed essential to the formation of the original union. Hundreds of years later, America is still not an egalitarian democracy. The arguments and rationalizations that have been trotted out in support of racial exclusion and discrimination in its various forms have changed and evolved, but the outcome has remained largely the same. An extraordinary percentage of black men in the United States are legally barred from voting today, just as they have been throughout most of American history. They are also subject to legalized discrimination in employment, housing, education, public benefits, and jury service, just as their parents, grandparents, and great-grandparents once were.

What has changed since the collapse of Jim Crow has less to do with the basic structure of our society than with the language we use to justify it. In the era of colorblindness, it is no longer socially permissible to use race, explicitly, as a justification for discrimination, exclusion, and social contempt. So we don't. Rather than rely on race, we use our criminal justice system to label people of color "criminals" and then engage in all the practices we supposedly left behind. Today it is perfectly legal to discriminate against criminals in nearly all the ways that it was once legal to discriminate against African Americans. Once you're labeled a felon, the old forms of discrimination—employment discrimination, housing discrimination, denial of the right to vote, denial of educational opportunity, denial of food stamps and other public benefits, and exclusion from jury service—are suddenly legal. As a criminal, you have scarcely more rights, and arguably less respect, than a black man living in Alabama at the height of Jim Crow. We have not ended racial caste in America; we have merely redesigned it.

I have reached these conclusions reluctantly. Ten years ago, I would have argued strenuously against the central claim made here—namely, that something akin to a racial caste system currently exists in the United States. Indeed, if Barack Obama had been elected president back then, I would have argued that his election marked the nation's triumph over racial caste—the final nail in the coffin of Jim Crow. My elation would have been tempered by the distance yet to be traveled to reach the promised land of racial justice in America, but my conviction that nothing remotely similar to Jim Crow exists in this country would have been steadfast.

Today my elation over Obama's election is tempered by a far more 5 sobering awareness. As an African American woman, with three young children who will never know a world in which a black man could not be president of the United States, I was beyond thrilled on election night. Yet when I walked out of the election night party, full of hope and enthusiasm, I was immediately reminded of the harsh realities of the New Jim Crow. A black man was on his knees in the gutter, hands cuffed behind his back, as several police officers stood around him talking, joking, and ignoring his human existence. People poured out of the building; many stared for a moment at the black man cowering in the street, and then averted their gaze. What did the election of Barack Obama mean for him?

Like many civil rights lawyers, I was inspired to attend law school by the civil rights victories of the 1950s and 1960s. Even in the face of growing social and political opposition to remedial policies such as affirmative action, I clung to the notion that the evils of Jim Crow are behind us and that, while we have a long way to go to fulfill the dream of an egalitarian, multiracial democracy, we have made real progress and are now struggling to hold on to the gains of the past. I thought my job as a civil rights lawyer was to join with the allies of racial progress to resist attacks on affirmative action and to eliminate the vestiges of Jim Crow segregation, including our still separate and unequal system of education. I understood the problems plaguing poor communities of color, including problems associated with crime and rising incarceration rates, to be a function of poverty and lack of access to quality education—the continuing legacy of slavery and Jim Crow. Never did I seriously consider the possibility that a new racial caste system was operating in this country. The new system had been developed and implemented swiftly, and it was largely invisible, even to people, like me, who spent most of their waking hours fighting for justice.

I first encountered the idea of a new racial caste system more than a decade ago, when a bright orange poster caught my eye. I was rushing to catch the bus, and I noticed a sign stapled to a telephone pole that screamed in large bold print: The Drug War Is the New Jim Crow. I paused for a moment and skimmed the text of the flyer. Some radical group was holding a community meeting about police brutality, the new three-strikes law in California, and the expansion of America's prison system. The meeting was being held at a small community church a few blocks away; it had seating capacity for no more than fifty people. I sighed, and muttered to myself something like, "Yeah, the criminal justice system is racist in many ways, but it really doesn't help to make such an absurd comparison. People will just think you're crazy." I then crossed the street and hopped on the bus. I was headed to my new job, director of the Racial Justice Project of the American Civil Liberties Union (ACLU) in Northern California.

When I began my work at the ACLU, I assumed that the criminal justice system had problems of racial bias, much in the same way that all

Michelle Alexander speaks about her book *The New Jim Crow.*

major institutions in our society are plagued with problems associated with conscious and unconscious bias. As a lawyer who had litigated numerous class-action employment-discrimination cases, I understood well the many ways in which racial stereotyping can permeate subjective decision-making processes at all levels of an organization, with devastating consequences. I was familiar with the challenges associated with reforming institutions in which racial stratification is thought to be normal—the natural consequence of differences in education, culture, motivation, and, some still believe, innate ability. While at the ACLU, I shifted my focus from employment discrimination to criminal justice reform and dedicated myself to the task of working with others to identify and eliminate racial bias whenever and wherever it reared its ugly head.

By the time I left the ACLU, I had come to suspect that I was wrong about the criminal justice system. It was not just another institution infected with racial bias but rather a different beast entirely. The activists who posted the sign on the telephone pole were not crazy; nor were the smattering of lawyers and advocates around the country who were beginning to connect the dots between our current system of mass incarceration and earlier forms of social control. Quite belatedly, I came to see that mass incarceration in the United States had, in fact, emerged as a stunningly comprehensive and well-disguised system of racialized social control that functions in a manner strikingly similar to Jim Crow.

In my experience, people who have been incarcerated rarely have difficulty identifying the parallels between these systems of social control. Once they are released, they are often denied the right to vote, excluded from juries, and relegated to a racially segregated and subordinated existence. Through a web of laws, regulations, and informal rules, all of which are powerfully reinforced by social stigma, they are confined to the margins of mainstream society and denied access to the mainstream economy. They are legally denied the ability to obtain employment, housing, and public benefits—much as African Americans were once forced into a segregated, second-class citizenship in the Jim Crow era. 10

Those of us who have viewed that world from a comfortable distance—yet sympathize with the plight of the so-called underclass—tend to interpret the experience of those caught up in the criminal justice system primarily through the lens of popularized social science, attributing the staggering increase in incarceration rates in communities of color to the predictable, though unfortunate, consequences of poverty, racial segregation, unequal educational opportunities, and the presumed realities of the drug market, including the mistaken belief that most drug dealers are black or brown. Occasionally, in the course of my work, someone would make a remark suggesting that perhaps the War on Drugs is a racist conspiracy to put blacks back in their place. This type of remark was invariably accompanied by nervous laughter, intended to convey the impression that although the idea had crossed their minds, it was not an idea a reasonable person would take seriously.

Most people assume the War on Drugs was launched in response to the crisis caused by crack cocaine in inner-city neighborhoods. This view holds that the racial disparities in drug convictions and sentences, as well as the rapid explosion of the prison population, reflect nothing more than the government's zealous—but benign—efforts to address rampant drug crime in poor, minority neighborhoods. This view, while understandable, given the sensational media coverage of crack in the 1980s and 1990s, is simply wrong.

While it is true that the publicity surrounding crack cocaine led to a dramatic increase in funding for the drug war (as well as to sentencing policies that greatly exacerbated racial disparities in incarceration rates), there is no truth to the notion that the War on Drugs was launched in response to crack cocaine. President Ronald Reagan officially announced the current drug war in 1982, before crack became an issue in the media or a crisis in poor black neighborhoods. A few years after the drug war was declared, crack began to spread rapidly in the poor black neighborhoods of Los Angeles and later emerged in cities across the country.[2] The Reagan administration hired staff to publicize the emergence of crack cocaine

Then-President Ronald Reagan and his wife Nancy Reagan prepare for
their joint address, calling for a national campaign against drug abuse.

in 1985 as part of a strategic effort to build public and legislative support
for the war. The media campaign was an extraordinary success. Almost
overnight, the media was saturated with images of black "crack whores,"
"crack dealers," and "crack babies"—images that seemed to confirm the
worst negative racial stereotypes about impoverished inner-city residents.
The media bonanza surrounding the "new demon drug" helped to cata-
pult the War on Drugs from an ambitious federal policy to an actual war.

The timing of the crack crisis helped to fuel conspiracy theories and
general speculation in poor black communities that the War on Drugs
was part of a genocidal plan by the government to destroy black people

in the United States. From the outset, stories circulated on the street that crack and other drugs were being brought into black neighborhoods by the CIA. Eventually, even the Urban League came to take the claims of genocide seriously. In its 1990 report "The State of Black America," it stated: "There is at least one concept that must be recognized if one is to see the pervasive and insidious nature of the drug problem for the African American community. Though difficult to accept, that is the concept of genocide."[3] While the conspiracy theories were initially dismissed as far-fetched, if not downright loony, the word on the street turned out to be right, at least to a point. The CIA admitted in 1998 that guerrilla armies it actively supported in Nicaragua were smuggling illegal drugs into the United States—drugs that were making their way onto the streets of inner-city black neighborhoods in the form of crack cocaine. The CIA also admitted that, in the midst of the War on Drugs, it blocked law enforcement efforts to investigate illegal drug networks that were helping to fund its covert war in Nicaragua.[4]*

It bears emphasis that the CIA never admitted (nor has any evidence   15 been revealed to support the claim) that it intentionally sought the destruction of the black community by allowing illegal drugs to be smuggled into the United States. Nonetheless, conspiracy theorists surely must be forgiven for their bold accusation of genocide, in light of the devastation wrought by crack cocaine and the drug war, and the odd coincidence that an illegal drug crisis suddenly appeared in the black community after—not before—a drug war had been declared. In fact, the War on Drugs began at a time when illegal drug use was on the decline.[5] During this same time period, however, a war was declared, causing arrests and convictions for drug offenses to skyrocket, especially among people of color.

*Covert war in Nicaragua   In December 1981, then-President Ronald Reagan authorized the CIA to support the Contras, an opposition group that fought the Sandinistas, a revolutionary socialist group that the United States opposed in its fight against communism during the Cold War.

The impact of the drug war has been astounding. In less than thirty years, the U.S penal population exploded from around 300,000 to more than 2 million, with drug convictions accounting for the majority of the increase.[6] The United States now has the highest rate of incarceration in the world, dwarfing the rates of nearly every developed country, even surpassing those in highly repressive regimes like Russia, China, and Iran. In Germany, 93 people are in prison for every 100,000 adults and children. In the United States, the rate is roughly eight times that, or 750 per 100,000.[7]

The racial dimension of mass incarceration is its most striking feature. No other country in the world imprisons so many of its racial or ethnic minorities. The United States imprisons a larger percentage of its black population than South Africa did at the height of apartheid. In Washington, D.C., our nation's capitol, it is estimated that three out of four young black men (and nearly all those in the poorest neighborhoods) can expect to serve time in prison.[8] Similar rates of incarceration can be found in black communities across America.

These stark racial disparities cannot be explained by rates of drug crime. Studies show that people of all colors *use and sell* illegal drugs at remarkably similar rates.[9] If there are significant differences in the surveys to be found, they frequently suggest that whites, particularly white youth, are more likely to engage in drug crime than people of color.[10] That is not what one would guess, however, when entering our nation's prisons and jails, which are overflowing with black and brown drug offenders. In some states, black men have been admitted to prison on drug charges at rates twenty to fifty times greater than those of white men.[11] And in major cities wracked by the drug war, as many as 80 percent of young African American men now have criminal records and are thus subject to legalized discrimination for the rest of their lives.[12] These young men are part of a growing undercaste, permanently locked up and locked out of mainstream society.

It may be surprising to some that drug crime was declining, not rising, when a drug war was declared. From a historical perspective, however, the lack of correlation between crime and punishment is nothing new. Sociologists have frequently observed that governments use punishment primarily as a tool of social control, and thus the extent or severity of punishment is often unrelated to actual crime patterns. Michael Tonry explains in *Thinking About Crime*: "Governments decide how much punishment they want, and these decisions are in no simple way related to crime rates."[13] This fact, he points out, can be seen most clearly by putting crime and punishment in comparative perspective. Although crime rates in the United States have not been markedly higher than those of other Western countries, the rate of incarceration has soared in the United States while it has remained stable or declined in other countries. Between 1960 and 1990, for example, official crime rates in Finland, Germany, and the United States were close to identical. Yet the U.S. incarceration rate quadrupled, the Finnish rate fell by 60 percent, and the German rate was stable in that period.[14] Despite similar crime rates, each government chose to impose different levels of punishment.

Today, due to recent declines, U.S. crime rates have dipped below the international norm. Nevertheless, the United States now boasts an incarceration rate that is six to ten times greater than that of other industrialized nations[15]—a development directly traceable to the drug war. The only country in the world that even comes close to the American rate of incarceration is Russia, and no other country in the world incarcerates such an astonishing percentage of its racial or ethnic minorities.

The stark and sobering reality is that, for reasons largely unrelated to actual crime trends, the American penal system has emerged as a system of social control unparalleled in world history. And while the size of the system alone might suggest that it would touch the lives of most Americans, the primary targets of its control can be defined largely by race. This is an astonishing development, especially given that as recently as the mid-1970s, the most well-respected criminologists were predicting that the prison system would soon fade away. Prison did not deter crime significantly, many experts concluded. Those who had meaningful economic

20

and social opportunities were unlikely to commit crimes regardless of the penalty, while those who went to prison were far more likely to commit crimes again in the future. The growing consensus among experts was perhaps best reflected by the National Advisory Commission on Criminal Justice Standards and Goals, which issued a recommendation in 1973 that "no new institutions for adults should be built and existing institutions for juveniles should be closed."[16] This recommendation was based on their finding that "the prison, the reformatory and the jail have achieved only a shocking record of failure. There is overwhelming evidence that these institutions create crime rather than prevent it."[17]

These days, activists who advocate "a world without prisons" are often dismissed as quacks, but only a few decades ago, the notion that our society would be much better off without prisons—and that the end of prisons was more or less inevitable—not only dominated mainstream academic discourse in the field of criminology but also inspired a national campaign by reformers demanding a moratorium on prison construction. Marc Mauer, the executive director of the Sentencing Project, notes that what is most remarkable about the moratorium campaign in retrospect is the context of imprisonment at the time. In 1972, fewer than 350,000 people were being held in prisons and jails nationwide, compared with more than 2 million people today. The rate of incarceration in 1972 was at a level so low that it no longer seems in the realm of possibility, but for moratorium supporters, that magnitude of imprisonment was egregiously high. "Supporters of the moratorium effort can be forgiven for being so naïve," Mauer suggests, "since the prison expansion that was about to take place was unprecedented in human history."[18] No one imagined that the prison population would more than quintuple in their lifetime. It seemed far more likely that prisons would fade away.

Far from fading away, it appears that prisons are here to stay. And despite the unprecedented levels of incarceration in the African American community, the civil rights community is oddly quiet. One in three young African American men will serve time in prison if current trends continue, and in some cities more than half of all young adult black men are currently under correctional control—in prison or jail, on probation or parole.[19] Yet mass incarceration tends to be categorized as a criminal justice issue as opposed to a racial justice or civil rights issue (or crisis).

The attention of civil rights advocates has been largely devoted to other issues, such as affirmative action. During the past twenty years, virtually every progressive, national civil rights organization in the country has mobilized and rallied in defense of affirmative action. The struggle to preserve affirmative action in higher education, and thus maintain diversity in the nation's most elite colleges and universities, has consumed much of the attention and resources of the civil rights community and dominated racial justice discourse in the mainstream media, leading the general public to believe that affirmative action is the main battlefront in U.S. race relations—even as our prisons fill with black and brown men. . . .

This is not to say that important criminal justice reform work has not 25 been done. Civil rights advocates have organized vigorous challenges to specific aspects of the new caste system. One notable example is the successful challenge led by the NAACP Legal Defense Fund to a racist drug sting operation in Tulia, Texas. The 1999 drug bust incarcerated almost 15 percent of the black population of the town, based on the uncorroborated false testimony of a single informant hired by the sheriff of Tulia. More recently, civil rights groups around the country have helped to launch legal attacks and vibrant grassroots campaigns against felon disenfranchisement laws and have strenuously opposed discriminatory crack sentencing laws and guidelines, as well as "zero tolerance" policies that effectively funnel youth of color from schools to jails. The national ACLU recently developed a racial justice program that includes criminal justice issues among its core priorities and has created a promising Drug Law Reform Project. And thanks to the aggressive advocacy of the ACLU, NAACP, and other civil rights organizations around the country, racial profiling is widely condemned, even by members of law enforcement who once openly embraced the practice.

Still, despite these significant developments, there seems to be a lack of appreciation for the enormity of the crisis at hand. There is no broad-based movement brewing to end mass incarceration and no advocacy effort that approaches in scale the fight to preserve affirmative action. There also remains a persistent tendency in the civil rights community to treat the criminal justice system as just another institution infected with lingering racial bias. The NAACP's Web site offers one example. As recently as May 2008, one could find a brief introduction to the organization's criminal justice work in the section entitled Legal Department. The introduction explained that "despite the civil rights victories of our past, racial prejudice still pervades the criminal justice system." Visitors to the Web site were urged to join the NAACP in order to "protect the hard-earned civil rights gains of the past three decades." No one visiting the Web site would learn that the mass incarceration of African Americans had already eviscerated many of the hard-earned gains it urged its members to protect.

Imagine if civil rights organizations and African American leaders in the 1940s had not placed Jim Crow segregation at the forefront of their racial justice agenda. It would have seemed absurd, given that racial segregation was the primary vehicle of racialized social control in the United States during that period. Mass incarceration is, metaphorically, the New Jim Crow and all those who care about social justice should fully commit themselves to dismantling this new racial caste system. Mass incarceration—not attacks on affirmative action or lax civil rights enforcement—is the most damaging manifestation of the backlash against the Civil Rights Movement. The popular narrative that emphasizes the death of slavery and Jim Crow and celebrates the nation's "triumph over race" with the election of Barack Obama, is dangerously misguided. The colorblind public consensus that prevails in America today—i.e., the widespread belief that race no longer matters—has blinded us to the realities of race in our society and facilitated the emergence of a new caste system.

The language of caste may well seem foreign or unfamiliar to some. Public discussions about racial caste in America are relatively rare. We avoid talking about caste in our society because we are ashamed of our racial history. We also avoid talking about race. We even avoid talking about class. Conversations about class are resisted in part because there is a tendency to imagine that one's class reflects upon one's character. What is key to America's understanding of class is the persistent belief—despite all evidence to the contrary—that anyone, with the proper discipline and drive, can move from a lower class to a higher class. We recognize that mobility may be difficult, but the key to our collective self-image is the assumption that mobility is always possible, so failure to move up reflects on one's character. By extension, the failure of a race or ethnic group to move up reflects very poorly on the group as a whole.

What is completely missed in the rare public debates today about the plight of African Americans is that a huge percentage of them are not free to move up at all. It is not just that they lack opportunity, attend poor schools, or are plagued by poverty. They are barred by law from doing so. And the major institutions with which they come into contact are designed to prevent their mobility. To put the matter starkly: The current system of control permanently locks a huge percentage of the African American community out of the mainstream society and economy. The system operates through our criminal justice institutions, but it functions more like a caste system than a system of crime control. Viewed from this perspective, the so- called underclass is better understood as an *undercaste*—a lower caste of individuals who are permanently barred by law and custom from mainstream society. Although this new system of racialized social control purports to be colorblind, it creates and maintains racial hierarchy much as earlier systems of control did. Like Jim Crow (and slavery), mass incarceration operates as a tightly networked system of laws, policies, customs, and institutions that operate collectively to ensure the subordinate status of a group defined largely by race. . . .

Skepticism about the claims made here is warranted. There are important differences, to be sure, among mass incarceration, Jim Crow, and slavery—the three major racialized systems of control adopted in the United States to date. Failure to acknowledge the relevant differences, as   30 well as their implications, would be a disservice to racial justice discourse. Many of the differences are not as dramatic as they initially appear, however; others serve to illustrate the ways in which systems of racialized social control have managed to morph, evolve, and adapt to changes in the political, social, and legal context over time. Ultimately, I believe that the similarities between these systems of control overwhelm the differences and that mass incarceration, like its predecessors, has been largely immunized from legal challenge. If this claim is substantially correct, the implications for racial justice advocacy are profound.

With the benefit of hindsight, surely we can see that piecemeal policy reform or litigation alone would have been a futile approach to dismantling Jim Crow segregation. While those strategies certainly had their place, the Civil Rights Act of 1964 and the concomitant cultural shift would never have occurred without the cultivation of a critical political consciousness in the African American community and the widespread, strategic activism that flowed from it. Likewise, the notion that the *New* Jim Crow can ever be dismantled through traditional litigation and policy-reform strategies that are wholly disconnected from a major social movement seems fundamentally misguided.

Such a movement is impossible, though, if those most committed to abolishing racial hierarchy continue to talk and behave as if a state-sponsored racial caste system no longer exists. If we continue to tell ourselves the popular myths about racial progress or, worse yet, if we say to ourselves that the problem of mass incarceration is just too big, too daunting for us to do anything about and that we should instead direct our energies to battles that might be more easily won, history will judge us harshly. A human rights nightmare is occurring on our watch.

A new social consensus must be forged about race and the role of race in defining the basic structure of our society, if we hope ever to abolish the New Jim Crow. This new consensus must begin with dialogue, a conversation that fosters a critical consciousness, a key prerequisite to effective social action. My writing is an attempt to ensure that the conversation does not end with nervous laughter.

NOTES

1. Jarvious Cotton was a plaintiff in *Cotton v. Fordice*, 157 F.3d 388 (5th Cir. 1998), which held that Mississippi's felon disenfranchisement provision had lost its racially discriminatory taint. The information regarding Cotton's family tree was obtained by Emily Bolton on March 29, 1999, when she interviewed Cotton at Mississippi State Prison. Jarvious Cotton was released on parole in Mississippi, a state that denies voting rights to parolees.

2. The *New York Times* made the national media's first specific reference to crack in a story published in late 1985. Crack became known in a few impoverished neighborhoods in Los Angeles, New York, and Miami in early 1986. See Craig Reinarman and Harry Levine, "The Crack Attack: America's Latest Drug Scare, 1986–1992," in *Images of Issues: Typifying Contemporary Social Problems* (New York: Aldine De Gruyter, 1995), 152.

3. Clarence Page, "'The Plan': A Paranoid View of Black Problems," *Dover* (Delaware) *Herald*, Feb. 23, 1990. See also Manning Marable, *Race, Reform, and Rebellion: The Second Reconstruction in Black America, 1945–1990* (Jackson: University Press of Mississippi, 1991), 212–13.

4. See Alexander Cockburn and Jeffrey St. Clair, *Whiteout: The CIA, Drugs, and the Press* (New York: Verso, 1999). See also Nick Shou, "The Truth in 'Dark Alliance,'" *Los Angeles Times*, Aug. 18, 2006; Peter Kornbluh, "CIA's Challenge in South Central." *Los Angeles Times* (Washington edition), Nov. 15, 1996; and Alexander Cockburn, "Why They Hated Gary Webb," *The Nation*, Dec. 16, 2004.

5. Katherine Beckett and Theodore Sasson, *The Politics oj Injustice: Crime and Punishment in America* (Thousand Oaks, CA: Sage Publications, 2004), 163.

6. Marc Mauer, *Race to Incarcerate*, rev. ed. (New York: The New Press, 2006), 33.

7. PEW Center on the States, *One in 100: Behind Bars in America 2008* (Washington, DC: PEW Charitable Trusts, 2008), 5.

8. Donald Braman, *Doing Time on the Outside: Incarceration and Family Life in Urban America* (Ann Arbor: University of Michigan Press, 2004), 3, citing D.C. Department of Corrections data for 2000.

9. See, e.g., U.S. Department of Health and Human Services, Substance Abuse and Mental Health Services Administration, *Summary of Findings from the 2000 National Household Survey on Drug Abuse*, NHSDA series H-13, DHHS pub. no. SMA 01-3549 (Rockville, MD: 2001), reporting that 6.4 percent of whites, 6.4 percent of blacks, and 5.3 percent of Hispanics were current users of illegal drugs in 2000; *Results from the 2002 National Survey on Drug Use and Health: National Findings*, NHSDA series H-22, DHHS pub. no. SMA 03-3836 (2003), revealing nearly identical rates of illegal drug use among whites and blacks, only a single percentage point between them; and *Results from the 2007 National Survey on Drug Use and Health: National Findings*, NSDUH series H-34, DHHS pub. no. SMA 08-4343 (2007), showing essentially the same finding. See also Marc Mauer and Ryan S. King, *A 25-Year Quagmire: The "War on Drugs" and Its Impact on American Society* (Washington, DC: Sentencing Project, 2007), 19, citing a study suggesting that African Americans have slightly higher rates of illegal drug use than whites.

10. See, e.g., Howard N. Snyder and Melissa Sickman, *Juvenile Offenders and Victims: 2006 National Report*, U.S. Department of Justice, Office of Justice Programs, Office of Juvenile Justice and Delinquency Prevention (Washington, DC: U.S. Department of Justice,

2006), reporting that white youth are more likely than black youth to engage in illegal drug sales. See also Lloyd D. Johnson, Patrick M. O'Malley, Jerald G. Bachman, and John E. Schulunberg, *Monitoring the Future, National Survey Results on Drug Use, 1975–2006*, vol. 1, *Secondary School Students*, U.S. Department of Health and Human Services, National Institute on Drug Abuse, NIH pub. no. 07-6205 (Bethesda, MD: 2007), 32, "African American 12th graders have consistently shown lower usage rates than White 12th graders for most drugs, both licit and illicit"; and Lloyd D. Johnston, Patrick M. O'Malley, and Jerald G. Bachman, *Monitoring the Future: National Results on Adolescent Drug Use: Overview of Key Findings 2002*, U.S. Department of Health and Human Services, National Institute on Drug Abuse, NIH pub. no. 03-5374 (Bethesda, MD: 2003), presenting data showing that African American adolescents have slightly lower rates of illicit drug use than their white counterparts.

11. Human Rights Watch, *Punishment and Prejudice: Racial Disparities in the War on Drugs*, HRW Reports, vol. 12, no. 2 (New York, 2000).

12. See, e.g., Paul Street, *The Vicious Circle: Race, Prison, Jobs, and Community in Chicago, Illinois, and the Nation* (Chicago: Chicago Urban League, Department of Research and Planning, 2002).

13. Michael Tonry, *Thinking About Crime: Sense and Sensibility in American Penal Culture* (New York: Oxford University Press, 2004), 14.

14. Ibid.

15. Ibid., 20.

16. National Advisory Commission on Criminal Justice Standards and Goals, *Task Force Report on Corrections* (Washington, DC: Government Printing Office, 1973), 358.

17. Ibid., 597.

18. Mauer, *Race to Incarcerate*, 17–18.

19. The estimate that one in three black men will go to prison during their lifetime is drawn from Thomas P. Boncszar, "Prevalence of Imprisonment in the U.S. Population, 1974–2001," U.S. Department of Justice, Bureau of Justice Statistics, August 2003. In Baltimore, like many large urban areas, the majority of young African American men are currently under correctional supervision. See Eric Lotke and Jason Ziedenberg, "Tipping Point: Maryland's Overuse of Incarceration and the Impact on Community Safety," Justice Policy Institute, March 2005, 3.

GABRIELA MORO ⎰ *Minority Student Clubs:*
⎱ *Segregation or Integration?*

GABRIELA MORO wrote this essay in her first-year composition class at the University of Notre Dame in South Bend, Indiana. It was published in 2015 in the university's journal *Fresh Writing*, "an interactive archive of exemplary first-year writing projects." A neuroscience and behavior pre-health major, Moro plans to pursue a career in medicine.

MINORITY REPRESENTATION on US college campuses has increased significantly in recent years, and many schools have made it a priority to increase diversity on their campuses in order to prepare students for a culturally diverse US democratic society (Hurtado and Ruiz 3–4). To complement this increase, many schools have implemented minority student clubs to provide safe and comfortable environments where minority students can thrive academically and socially with peers from similar backgrounds. However, do these minority groups amplify students' tendency to interact only with those who are similar to themselves? Put another way, do these groups inhibit students from engaging in diverse relationships?

Many view such programs to be positive and integral to minority students' college experience; some, however, feel that these clubs are not productive for promoting cross-cultural interaction. While minority clubs have proven to be beneficial to minority students in some cases, particularly on campuses that are not very diverse, my research suggests that colleges would enrich the educational experience for all students by introducing multicultural clubs as well.

"Minority Students Clubs: Segregation or Integration?" Originally published in *Fresh Writing: An Interactive Archive of Exemplary First-Year Writing Projects*, Vol. 16. Reprinted by permission of the University of Notre Dame College of Arts and Letters.

To frame my discussion, I will use an article from *College Student Journal* that distinguishes between two types of students: one who believes minority clubs are essential for helping minority students stay connected with their cultures, and another who believes these clubs isolate minorities and work against diverse interaction among students. To pursue the question of whether or not such groups segregate minorities from the rest of the student body and even discourage cultural awareness, I will use perspectives from minority students to show that these programs are especially helpful for first-year students. I will also use other student testimonials to show that when taken too far, minority groups can lead to self-segregation and defy what most universities claim to be their diversity goals. Findings from research will contribute to a better understanding of the role minority clubs play on college campuses and offer a complete answer to my question about the importance of minority programs.

Before I go further, I would like to differentiate among three kinds of diversity that Gurin et al. identify in their article "Diversity and Higher Education: Theory and Impact on Educational Outcomes." The first type is *structural diversity*, "the numerical representation of diverse [racial and ethnic] groups." The existence of structural diversity alone does not assure that students will develop valuable intergroup relationships. *Classroom diversity*, the second type, involves gaining "content knowledge" or a better understanding about diverse peers and their backgrounds by doing so in the classroom. The third type of diversity, *informal interactional diversity*, refers to "both the frequency and the quality of intergroup interaction as keys to meaningful diversity experiences during college." Students often encounter this kind of diversity in social settings outside the classroom (Gurin 332–33). Informal interactional diversity is the focus of my research, since it is the concept that leads colleges to establish social events and organizations that allow all students to experience and appreciate the variety of cultures present in a student body.

In a study published in *College Student Journal*, three administrators 5
at Pennsylvania State University explored how biracial students interact

with others on a college campus. The authors concluded that views of minority clubs and related programs, which the authors call race-oriented student services (ROSS), tend to fall into two groups: "Although some argue that these race-oriented student services (ROSS) are divisive and damage white-minority relations (Stern & Gaiter, 1994), others support these services as providing a safe place and meeting the needs of minority students to develop a sense of racial pride, community and importance (Patton, 2006)" (Ingram 298). I will start by examining the point of view of those who associate minority clubs with positive outcomes.

A study by Samuel D. Museus in the *Journal of College Student Development* found that minority student programs help students to stay connected with their culture in college and help ease first-year minority students' transition into the college environment. The study also shows that ethnic student organizations help students adjust and find their place at universities that have a predominantly white student body (584). Museus concluded that universities should stress the importance of racial and ethnic groups and develop more opportunities for minority students to make connections with them. This way, students can find support from their minority peers as they work together to face academic and social challenges. Museus's findings suggest that minority student groups are essential for allowing these students to preserve and foster connections to their own cultures.

In another study, Hall et al. evaluated how minority and non-minority students differed in their inclinations to take part in diversity activities and to communicate with racially and ethnically diverse peers at a predominantly white university. These scholars concluded that "engagement [with diverse peers] is learned" (434). Students who engaged with diverse students before going to college were more likely to interact with diverse peers by the end of their sophomore year. Minority students were more predisposed than their white peers to interact with diverse peers during their freshman year (435). These findings indicate that minority student clubs can be helpful for first-year minority students who have not previously engaged with other minority students, especially if the university has a predominantly white student body.

Professors and scholars are not the only ones who strongly support minority clubs. For example, three students at Harvard College—Andrea Delgado, Denzel (no last name given), and Kimi Fafowora—give their perspective on student life and multicultural identity on campus to incoming students via *YouTube*. The students explain how minority programs on campus have helped them adjust to a new college environment as first-year students. As Delgado put it, "I thought [cultural clubs were] something I maybe didn't need, but come November, I missed speaking Spanish and I missed having tacos, and other things like that. That's the reason why I started attending meetings more regularly. Latinas Unidas has been a great intersection of my cultural background and my political views." The experiences these minority students shared support the scholarly evidence that minority clubs help incoming students transition into a new and often intimidating environment.

While the benefits of these clubs are quite evident, several problems can also arise from them. The most widely recognized is self-segregation. Self-segregating tendencies are not exclusive to minority students: college students in general tend to self-segregate as they enter an unfamiliar environment. As a study by Martin et al. finds, "Today, the student bodies of our leading colleges and universities are more diverse than ever. However, college students are increasingly self-segregating by race or ethnicity" (720). Several studies as well as interviews with students suggest that minority clubs exacerbate students' inclination to self-segregate. And as students become comfortable with their minority peers, they may no longer desire or feel the need to branch out of their comfort zone.

In another study, Julie J. Park, a professor at the University of Mary- 10
land, examined the relationship between participation in college student organizations and the development of interracial friendships. Park suggests, "if students spend the majority of time in such groups [Greek, ethnic, and religious student organizations], participation may affect student

involvement in the broader diversity of the institution" (642). In other words, if minority students form all of their social and academic ties within their minority group, the desired cultural exchange among the study body could suffer.

So what can be done? In the Penn State study mentioned earlier, in which data were collected by an online survey, participants were asked to respond to an open-ended question about what they think universities should do to create a more inviting environment for biracial students (Ingram et al. 303). On one hand, multiple students responded with opinions opposing the formation of both biracial and multiracial clubs: "I feel instead of having biracial and multiracial clubs the colleges should have diversity clubs and just allow everyone to get together. All these 'separate' categorizing of clubs, isn't that just separation of groups?" "Having a ton of clubs that are for specific races is counterproductive. It creates segregation and lack of communication across cultures" (304–305).

On the other hand, students offered suggestions for the formation of multicultural activities: "Encourage more racial integration to show students races aren't so different from each other and to lessen stereotypes." "Hold cultural events that allow students of different races to express/ share their heritage." Ingram et al. concluded that, while biracial and multiracial student organizations are helpful in establishing an inviting college environment for minority students,

> creating a truly inclusive environment...requires additional efforts: these include multicultural awareness training for faculty, staff, and students, and incorporation of multicultural issues into the curriculum (White, 2006; Gasser, 2002). In addition to the creation of biracial/multiracial clubs and organization, the students in this study want to increase awareness of the mixed heritage population among others on college campuses. (308)

The two very different opinions reported in this study point to the challenges minority student programs can create, but also suggest ways to resolve these challenges. Now that evidence from both research studies and student perspectives confirm that these clubs, while beneficial to minority students' experiences, can inhibit cultural immersion, I will continue with my original argument that the entire student body would benefit if campuses also implemented multicultural advocacy clubs, rather than just selective minority clubs. Gurin et al., the researchers who identified the three types of diversity in higher education, contend that even with the presence of diverse racial and ethnic groups and regular communication among students formally and informally, a greater push from educators is needed:

> In order to foster citizenship for a diverse democracy, educators must intentionally structure opportunities for students to leave the comfort of their homogenous peer group and build relationships across racially/ethnically diverse student communities on campus. (363)

This suggestion implies that participation from students and faculty is needed to foster cultural immersion in higher education.

Another way to improve cross-cultural exchange is by developing a diverse curriculum. An article on multiculturalism in higher education by Alma Clayton-Pedersen and Caryn McTighe Musil in the *Encyclopedia of Education* reviewed the ways in which universities have incorporated diversity studies into their core curriculum over the last several decades. They found that the numbers of courses that seek to prepare students for a democratic society rich in diversity have increased (1711, 1714). However, they recommend that institutions need to take a more holistic approach to their academic curricula in order to pursue higher education programs that prepare students to face "complex and demanding questions" and to "use their new knowledge and civic, intercultural capacities to address real-world problems" (1714). My research supports that a more holistic approach to the importance of diversity studies in the college curriculum, as well as multicultural advocacy clubs, are necessary in order to prepare *all* students, not just minority students, for the diverse world and society ahead of them.

Thus, even though minority student clubs can lead to self-segregation among students and result in less cross-cultural interaction, their benefits to minority students suggest that a balance needs to be found between providing support for minorities and avoiding segregation of these groups from the rest of the student body. Besides sponsoring minority student programs, colleges and universities can implement multicultural events and activities for all students to participate in, especially during the freshman year. An initiative like this would enhance the diverse interactions that occur on campuses, promote cultural immersion, and garner support for minority student clubs.

Beyond the reach of this evaluation, further research should be conducted, specifically on the types of cultural events that are most effective in promoting cultural awareness and meaningful diverse interactions among the student body. By examining different multicultural organizations from both public and private institutions, and comparing student experiences and participation in those programs, researchers can suggest an ideal multicultural program to provide an optimal student experience. 15

WORKS CITED

Clayton-Pedersen, Alma R., and Caryn McTighe Musil. "Multiculturalism in Higher Education." *Encyclopedia of Education*, edited by James W. Guthrie, 2nd ed., vol. 5, Macmillan, 2002, pp. 1709–1716. *Gale Virtual Reference Library*. Accessed 26 Feb. 2015.

Gurin, Patricia, Eric L. Dey, Sylvia Hurtado, and Gerald Gurin. "Diversity and Higher Education: Theory and Impact on Educational Outcomes." *Harvard Educational Review*, vol. 72, no. 3, 2002, pp. 330–36. *ResearchGate*, doi:10.17763/haer.72.3.01151786u134n051. Accessed 28 Mar. 2015.

Hall, Wendell, Alberto Cabrera, and Jeffrey Milem. "A Tale of Two Groups: Differences Between Minority Students and Non-Minority Students in

Their Predispositions to and Engagement with Diverse Peers at a Predominantly White Institution." *Research in Higher Education*, vol. 52, no. 4, 2011, pp. 420–439. *Academic Search Premier*, doi: 10.1007/s11162 -010-9201-4. Accessed 10 Mar. 2015.

Harvard College Admissions & Financial Aid. "Student Voices: Multicultural Perspectives." *YouTube*, 7 Aug. 2014, https://www.youtube.com/ watch?v=djIWQgDx-Jc. Accessed 12 Mar. 2015.

Hurtado, Sylvia, and Adriana Ruiz. "The Climate for Underrepresented Groups and Diversity on Campus." Higher Education Research Institute at UCLA (HERI) and Cooperative Institutional Research Program (CIRP), 2012, heri.ucla.edu/briefs/urmbrief.php. Accessed 26 Feb. 2015.

Ingram, Patreese, Anil Kumar Chaudhary, and Walter Terrell Jones. "How Do Biracial Students Interact with Others on the College Campus?" *College Student Journal*, vol. 48, no. 2, 2014, pp. 297–311. Questia, www.questia. com/library/journal/1G1-377286773/how-do-biracial-students-interact-with-others-on-the. Accessed 28 July 2017.

Martin, Nathan D., William Tobin, and Kenneth I. Spenner. "Interracial Friendships Across the College Years: Evidence from a Longitudinal Case Study." *Journal of College Student Development*, vol. 55, no. 7, 2014, pp. 720–725. *Academic Search Premier*, doi: 10.1353/csd.2014.0075. Accessed 16 Mar. 2015.

Museus, Samuel D. "The Role of Ethnic Student Organizations in Fostering African American and Asian American Students' Cultural Adjustment and Membership at Predominantly White Institutions." *Journal of College Student Development*, vol. 49, no. 6, 2008, pp. 568–86. *Project MUSE*, doi:10.1353/csd.0.0039. Accessed 26 Feb. 2015.

Park, Julie J. "Clubs and the Campus Racial Climate: Student Organizations and Interracial Friendship in College." *Journal of College Student Development*, vol. 55, no. 7, 2014, pp. 641–660. *Academic Search Premier*, doi:10.1353/csd.2014.0076. Accessed 16 March. 2015.

TIME

JOHN MCWHORTER { *Why "Redskins" Is a Bad Word*

JOHN MCWHORTER (b. 1965) is an associate professor of English and comparative literature at Columbia University, specializing in creole languages as well as the philosophy and sociology of language. A Philadelphia native, McWhorter holds degrees from Simon's Rock College, Rutgers University, New York University, and Stanford University. In addition to his teaching and appearances as a commentator on radio and television programs, he is a prolific writer, with many essays and books on linguistics and race relations, among them *Losing the Race: Self-Sabotage in Black America* (2000). In 2015, McWhorter wrote the essay "Why 'Redskins' Is a Bad Word" for *Time* magazine. Discussing the controversy surrounding this common name for athletic teams, McWhorter argues that the connotations of the word make it inherently insulting to Native Americans. "As always," he writes, "life is more than the literal."

CALIFORNIA'S BAN OF THE USE OF THE NAME "REDSKINS" by schools is likely the beginning of a trend. Native Americans have been decrying the term "Redskin" as a slur for a good while now, and Washington Redskins owner Dan Snyder's refusal to change the name of the team is looking increasingly callous and antique. Many will celebrate that "Redskin" is likely starting to go the way of "Oriental" and—well, you know.

Yet some may quietly be harboring another question: What's so terrible about referring to the fact that many Native Americans have a reddish skin tone compared to other people? It's not as if having "red" skin is a negative or even humorous trait. It isn't illogical to wonder, deep down, whether Native Americans are fashioning a controversy.

"Why "Redskins" Is a Bad Word" by John McWhorter from Time, October 12, 2015. Copyright © 2015 Time Inc. All rights reserved. Reprinted and published with the permission of Time Inc. Reproduction in any manner in any language in whole or in part without written permission is prohibited.

They aren't, though, because words can come to have meanings quite different from their literal ones, and when it comes to matters of insult and dignity, meaning counts.

For example, the term "Oriental" for Asians became impolite 25 years ago. Yet it's true that Asian heritage, for Chinese, Japanese and Korean people, is in "the Orient," traditionally a Western word for Asia. One now and then hears someone, usually of a certain age, grousing that "Well, now they want to be called Asians" with an air of dismissal, as if people go around willfully creating confusion and feigning hurt.

But actually, "Oriental" came to be associated with stereotypes of the 5 people in question, such that it was felt that a new term was necessary. Long ago, the same thing happened to "Chinaman." What's wrong with calling a man from China a "Chinaman"? Nothing, in the literal sense— but as always, life is more than the literal. "Chinaman" signifies the subservient, exotified "Ah, sohhh!" figure from Charlie Chan[1] movies; out it went and few miss it. "Oriental" was next.

These things can be subtle. I once had to inform a foreign student that in class discussion it was unseemly to refer to another person directly as "a Jew," rather than as "a Jewish person." To be American is to internalize that "a Jew" has an air of accusation and diminishment (ironically the student was from Israel!). That makes no literal sense, but it is a reality, as it is that to many, "blacks" sounds abrupt and hostile compared to "black people."

We are faced with something analogous to what Steven Pinker has artfully called the "euphemism treadmill." When something has negative associations, the word referring to it gradually takes on implied meanings connected with that contempt. This happens under the radar, but after about a generation, the reality becomes impossible to ignore.

[1] A fictional detective of mystery novels in the 1920s and, later, of more than fifty films. Chan was presented as a positive, sympathetic character, but also displayed stereotypical qualities and was the object of light mockery.

A detail view of a Washington Redskins helmet. California Governor Jerry Brown signed a bill into law banning public schools from using the term "Redskins" as a team name or mascot.

What was once called "home relief" became more politely called "welfare" after a while, for example. But it's easy to forget what a positive and even warm word "welfare" is, given the associations it had amassed by the 1970s. Today one increasingly speaks of "cash assistance," and that term will surely have the same bad odor about it among many sooner rather than later. Yet all of these terms mean the same thing literally. The literal is but one part of language as we actually live it.

"Crippled," for example, is in itself a neutral, descriptive term—taken literally, it even harbors an element of sympathy. However, the realities of discrimination meant that "crippled" had a less neutral connotation after a while, upon which "handicapped" was a fine substitute. But after a while, we needed "disabled," and of course now there is "differently abled," and indeed there will likely be something else before long.

This, then, is why "Redskins" qualifies as a slur despite not being a 10 literal insult. Words have not only core meanings, but resonances of the kind that may not make it into the dictionary but are deeply felt by all of us. Sometimes we need to get back down to cases[2] with a new word.

It may not be mean to tell someone their skin happens to be reddish. But it's mean to call someone a Redskin. There's a difference.

[2]"Back down to cases": expression meaning to discuss closely.

DIANE GUERRERO { *My Parents Were Deported*

DIANE GUERRERO (b. 1986) is an actress best known for her roles in the television series *Orange Is the New Black* and *Jane the Virgin*. Born in New Jersey and raised in Boston, her parents and older brother are from Colombia and came to the United States before she was born. They immigrated without documentation, and though they made every effort to legalize their status, they were then deported back to Colombia. In her memoir *In the Country We Love: My Family Divided* (2016), Guerrero writes about her and her family's experience of being undocumented immigrants in the United States. In "My Parents Were Deported," which appeared in the *Los Angeles Times* (2014), Guerrero uses her family's story to argue for more justice and compassion in the immigration system.

IN ORANGE IS THE NEW BLACK, I play Maritza Ramos, a tough Latina from the 'hood. In *Jane the Virgin*, I play Lina, Jane's best friend and a funny know-it-all who is quick to offer advice.

I love both parts, but they're fiction. My real story is this: I am the citizen daughter of immigrant parents who were deported when I was 14. My older brother was also deported.

My parents came here from Colombia during a time of great instability there. Escaping a dire economic situation at home, they moved to New Jersey, where they had friends and family, seeking a better life, and then moved to Boston after I was born.

Throughout my childhood I watched my parents try to become legal but to no avail. They lost their money to people they believed to be attorneys, but who ultimately never helped. That meant my childhood was

"Orange Is the New Black Actress: My Parents Were Deported," by Diane Guerrero. Originally printed in the *Los Angeles Times*, November 15, 2014. Reprinted by permission of Abrams Artists.

haunted by the fear that they would be deported. If I didn't see anyone when I walked in the door after school, I panicked.

And then one day, my fears were realized. I came home from school 5 to an empty house. Lights were on and dinner had been started, but my family wasn't there. Neighbors broke the news that my parents had been taken away by immigration officers, and just like that, my stable family life was over.

Not a single person at any level of government took any note of me. No one checked to see if I had a place to live or food to eat, and at 14, I found myself basically on my own.

While awaiting deportation proceedings, my parents remained in detention near Boston, so I could visit them. They would have liked to fight deportation, but without a lawyer and an immigration system that rarely gives judges the discretion to allow families to stay together, they never had a chance. Finally, they agreed for me to continue my education at Boston Arts Academy, a performing arts high school, and the parents of friends graciously took me in.

I was lucky to have good friends, but I had a rocky existence. I was always insecure about being a nuisance and losing my invitation to stay. I worked a variety of jobs in retail and at coffee shops all through high school. And, though I was surrounded by people who cared about me, part of me ached with every accomplishment because my parents weren't there to share my joy.

My family and I worked hard to keep our relationships strong, but too-short phone calls and the annual summer visits I made to Colombia didn't suffice. They missed many important events in my life, including my singing recitals—they watched my senior recital on a tape I sent them instead of from the audience. And they missed my prom, my college application process, and my graduations from high school and college.

My story is all too common. Every day, children who are U.S. citizens 10 are separated from their families as a result of immigration policies that need fixing.

I consider myself lucky because things turned out better for me than for most, including some of my own family members. When my brother was deported, his daughter was just a toddler. She still had her mother, but in a single-parent household, she faced a lot of challenges. My niece made the wrong friends and bad choices. Today, she is serving time in jail, living the reality that I act out on screen. I don't believe her life would have turned out this way if her father and my parents had been here to guide and support her.

I realize the issues are complicated. But it's not just in the interest of immigrants to fix the system: It's in the interest of all Americans. Children who grow up separated from their families often end up in foster care, or worse, in the juvenile justice system despite having parents who love them and would like to be able to care for them.

I don't believe it reflects our values as a country to separate children and parents in this way. Nor does it reflect our values to hold people in detention without access to good legal representation or a fair shot in a court of law. President Obama has promised to act on providing deportation relief for families across the country, and I would urge him to do so quickly. Keeping families together is a core American value.

Congress needs to provide a permanent, fair legislative solution, but in the meantime families are being destroyed every day, and the president should do everything in his power to provide the broadest relief possible now. Not one more family should be separated by deportation.

TEXT CREDITS

James Fallows: "Throwing Like a Girl," *The Atlantic Monthly*, August 1996. Copyright (c) 1996 The Atlantic Media Co., as first published in The Atlantic Magazine. All Rights Reserved. Distributed by Tribune Content Agency, LLC. Reprinted with permission.

Nicholas Kristof: "Our Blind Spot about Guns" from the *New York Times*, July 30, 2014. (c) 2014 The New York Times. All rights reserved. Used by permission and protected by Copyright Laws of the United States. The printing, copying, redistribution, or retransmission of the Material without express written permission is prohibited.

Andrew Leonard: "Black Friday: Consumerism Minus Civilization" from Salon.com, November 25, 2011. This article first appeared in Salon.com, at http://www.Salon.com. An online version remains in the Salon archives. Reprinted with permission.

Michael J. Sandel: Excerpt from "What Wounds Deserve the Purple Heart?" by Michael J. Sandel, in "Doing the Right Thing" from *Justice: What's the Right Thing to Do?* Copyright (c) 2009 by Michael J. Sandel. Repritned by permission of Farrar, Straus, and Giroux, LLC.

ILLUSTRATION CREDITS

Chapter 4: 43 www.ted com; 47 Andy Mead/Icon SMI/ Newscom. **Chapter 5:** 52 top U.S. Commission on Civil Rights; center Wikipedia; 54 © 1993 Peter Steiner, The New Yorker Collection, Cartoonbank. All Rights Reserved; 55 courtesy Google; 59 courtesy of SugarScience.org. **Chapter 6:** 62 Alastair Grant/AP/Corbis; 65 courtesy Adam Westbook; 66 Gary Markstein. **Chapter 7:** 69 Carin Berger; 72 Library of Congress, Prints and Photographs Division; 82 erlucho/iStockphoto. **Chapter 9:** 95 Courtesy of Jessica Ann Olson.

Chapter 10: 123 © Reagan Louie; 124 RecycleManiacs.org. **Chapter 11:** 136 Evan Agostini/Invision/AP Photo; 138 © Corbis; 139 Courtesy of Andrew Leonard; 140 YouTube; 141 YouTube; 142 YouTube. **Chapter 12:** 161 Jim Mone/AP. **Chapter 17:** MLA Style: 211 Jessamyn Neuhaus, "Marge Simpson, Blue-Haired Housewife Defining Domesticity on The Simpsons," Journal of Popular Culture 43.4 (2010): 761-81. © 2010 Wiley Periodicals, Inc.; 213 Michael Segal, "The Hit Book That Came from Mars," Nautilus-Think. 8 January 2015. Web. 10 October 2016.

Permission by Nautilus; 214 © 2015 Ebsco Industries, Inc. All rights reserved; 219 left and right from PINK SARI REVOLUTION: A TALE OF WOMEN AND POWER IN INDIA by Amana Fontanella-Khan. Copyright © 2013 by Amana Fontanella-Khan. Used by permission of W. W. Norton & Company, Inc.; 224 McIlwain, John, Molly Simpson, and Sara Hammerschmidt, Housing in America: Integrating Housing, Health, and Resilience in a Changing Environment, Urban Land Institute, 2014. Web. 17 Sept. 2016. © 2015 Urban Land Institute. All rights reserved; 241 United Artists/The Kobal Collection; 249 Paramount/Rafran/ The Kobal Collection. **Chapter 18:** 264 from THE GREAT DIVIDE: UNEQUAL SOCIETIES AND WHAT WE CAN DO ABOUT THEM by Joseph E. Stiglitz. Copyright © 2015 by Joseph E. Stiglitz. Used by permission of W. W. Norton & Company, Inc.; 271 M. P. Lazette (2015, February 25), A hurricane's hit to households. © 2015 Federal Reserve Bank of Cleveland; 273 Smart Technology and the Moral Life by C. F. Guthrie. Copyright 2013. Reproduced by permission of Taylor & Francis LLC (www.tandfonline.com); 274 © 2015 Ebsco Industries, Inc. All rights reserved.